OXFORD MONOGRAPHS ON MUSIC

Naples and
Neapolitan Opera

Naples and Neapolitan Opera

MICHAEL F. ROBINSON

Clarendon Press · Oxford
1972

Oxford University Press, Ely House, London W.1

GLASGOW NEW YORK TORONTO MELBOURNE WELLINGTON
CAPE TOWN DELHI IBADAN NAIROBI DAR ES SALAAM LUSAKA ADDIS ABABA
BOMBAY CALCUTTA MADRAS KARACHI LAHORE DACCA
KUALA LUMPUR SINGAPORE HONG KONG TOKYO

PRINTED IN GREAT BRITAIN BY
WILLIAM CLOWES & SONS LIMITED
LONDON, COLCHESTER AND BECCLES

Preface

It is usual at the start of a book to state what its aims are. But in this case a gentle warning should also be issued about what it is not. The first problem confronting anyone beginning a study of Naples and eighteenth-century music is to define the term 'Neapolitan'. This is because 'Neapolitan' is one of those words in the musicologist's vocabulary whose meaning shifts with context. A phrase commonly found in late eighteenth- and nineteenth-century literature is 'Neapolitan school', which has usually meant the chain of teacher-composers of vocal music and opera that stretches back to some teacher or training institute in seventeenth- or eighteenth-century Naples. Certain twentieth-century authors have also used the phrase 'Neapolitan style'. This has generally denoted the homophonic, galant style developed in Italy and elsewhere in the first decades of the 1700s. Finally, there is 'Neapolitan opera', another phrase coined this century, which normally denotes a type of Italian opera prevalent in the eighteenth century and distinguishable by its pronounced recitative-aria subdivisions. This particular phrase therefore denotes not just a style of operatic music but a dramaturgical method as well. Part of the confusion arises from the fact that many eighteenth-century operas of the so-called 'Neapolitan' type, perhaps with 'Neapolitan-style' music, were written by composers with no very obvious connections with the 'Neapolitan school'. The fact, furthermore, that several commentators now reckon they know little about how operatic artists and composers in Naples affected 'Neapolitan opera' as a whole has led to denigration of the phrase and advocacy that it be discarded. Let it be admitted that this book alone will not resolve the issue of whether the phrase is a good one. Little attempt has been made to find out the extent to which Neapolitans determined universal taste in the eighteenth century. The real purpose has been to review the basic facts, and add some new ones here and there, about opera in eighteenth-century Naples. Because opera at Naples was not opera in isolation, it had many features in common with opera else-where. For this reason we have felt free to utilize non-Neapolitan source material if it has relevance to the local product. Indeed it may be argued that without such material a discussion of the local product is incomplete. The study has limits, nevertheless, and this means that other researchers still have to determine what universals apply both in local Neapolitan opera and in so-called 'Neapolitan opera' anywhere else. It is to be hoped that some such line of enquiry will soon be contemplated.

It is a pleasure to thank Anna Mondolfi Bossarelli and Francesco Bossarelli of the Conservatory S. Pietro a Maiella, Naples; Emilia Zanetti of the S. Cecilia Academy in Rome; the authorities of the Marciana Library, Venice; the British Museum; the Fitzwilliam Museum, Cambridge; and other institutions, for help in finding source material for this book. The late Ulisse Prota-Giurleo of Ponticelli, Naples, kindly gave some valuable information he had collected in the pre-war period from a section of the Neapolitan state archives that was destroyed in 1943. Kathleen Toomey collected material for the author's researches at the faculty of music library, McGill University, Montreal. Professor Daniel Heartz of Berkeley, California, and Professor Marvin Duchow of Montreal deserve special mention for agreeing to read the manuscript and make comments upon it. Professor Sir Jack Westrup, Egon Wellesz, and Frederick Sternfeld gave valuable assistance to the author at the time he was beginning his studies into Neapolitan Opera while a student at Oxford University. Professor Hanns-Bertold Dietz of Austin, Texas, and Professor Claudio Sartori of Milan also gave useful information and advice. Professor Antonio Gismondi of Pisa assisted with the translation of certain difficult passages of Neapolitan dialect. Finally, it is necessary to record the financial assistance given by McGill University, Montreal, and by the Canada Council of Ottawa toward the cost and completion of this project.

Contents

Abbreviations

AM	*Archiv für Musikwissenschaft*
CSIM	*Cronache e documenti per la storia dell' Italia meridionale dei secoli xvi e xvii*
DM	*Documenta musicologica*
GMN	*Gazzetta musicale di Napoli*
IMS	*Proceedings of the International Musicological Society*
JAMS	*Journal of the American Musicological Society*
JMP	*Jahrbuch der Musikbibliothek Peters*
M&L	*Music and Letters*
MM	*Monatshefte für Musikgeschichte*
MQ	*Musical Quarterly*
RCRMA	*Research Chronicle of the Royal Musical Association*
RIM	*Rivista italiana di musicologia*
RMA	*Proceedings of the Royal Musical Association*
RMI	*Rivista musicale italiana*
SIM	*Sammelbände der internazionalen Musikgesellschaft*
SM	*Studien zur Musikwissenschaft*
VM	*Vierteljahrschrift für Musikwissenschaft*

The Neapolitan Environment

CHARLES DE BROSSES wrote of Naples in 1739 that it was 'the capital of the world's music'.[1] Statement and date are significant since they usher in a period when Naples was generally recognized as first in a hierarchy of Italian musical cities. It is difficult to find pre-1739 statements praising the music of Naples especially, but it is easy to find ones made thereafter. Lady Mary Wortley Montagu, for example, wrote from there in the autumn of 1740 to the Countess of Pomfret that she was 'last night at the opera, which is far the finest in Italy'.[2] P. J. Grosley, a visitor in 1758, thought that Italian music improved as one travelled southward down the peninsula toward the city. 'As one advances into Italy', he wrote, 'this disposition [for music] is found to grow stronger, so that with regard to this taste, and the perfection which proportionally follows it, Italy may be compared to a diapason and Naples the octave.'[3] And G. F. Coyer, a later visitor, declared: 'All knowledgeable travellers agree that [music] gets better and better from Turin to Naples; Naples is its summit.'[4]

Although de Brosses called Naples the 'capital of the world's music', he did not mean that Neapolitans were supreme executants and composers in every branch of the art. He had nothing to say about instrumental music there; in his view the centre for this type of music was the province of Lombardy in North Italy.[5] The composers he mentioned in connection with Naples—Alessandro Scarlatti, Leo, Vinci, Latilla, Porpora, Domenico Sarri, Porta, Pergolesi[6]—were all in fact much better known for their vocal and operatic compositions than for their instrumental. This does not mean of course that they could not, and did not, produce good instrumental music. But it does mean that Neapolitan training, taste, even intellectual theory, tended to encourage the composition of vocal music. Most

[1] *Lettres familiéres écrites d'Italie en 1739 et 1740*, 2nd edn., Paris, 1858, i. 386.
[2] Lady Mary Montagu, *The letters and works*, ed. Wharncliffe, London, 1893, ii. 82.
[3] *New observations on Italy*, London, 1769, i, 60–1.
[4] *Voyages d'Italie et de Hollande*, Paris, 1775, i. 244.
[5] *Lettres familières*, ii. 387.
[6] He also mentioned 'Les Zinaldo' [*sic*] which is probably a misprint for 'Les Rinaldo' and may refer to Rinaldo da Capua among others.

Neapolitan composers were thus in a different category from that of the Venetian, Antonio Vivaldi, who wrote large numbers of both instrumental concertos and operas, and excelled especially in the first of these two genres. Other eighteenth-century Italian composers who, like Vivaldi, were top-ranking virtuosi on the violin—Tartini, Geminiani, Veracini, Locatelli, Pugnani, Somis, and Nardini—were none of them Neapolitan. Naples was able to gain its position of supremacy in the mid-century nonetheless because of the comparative importance at that time of certain types of music associated with it. Opera was first among them. Here was a field offering very considerable renown and financial reward to the successful composer or executant. Performances of opera in Italian were major artistic and social events in many European countries. Naples gained its fame, basically, because its operatic artists were then good enough to be able to capitalize on this international interest in opera. The first question to be answered is: why were they good at this particular art-form?

Part of the answer lies in the Neapolitan cultural environment and in the encouragement given to the local institutions that nurtured opera. Two sets of institutions stand out at once as having played a major role: the theatres and the music conservatories. The first were the focal point of interest to opera lovers among residents and visitors; the second provided much of the talent on which the first depended. Behind both sets stood the court, which interfered or did not interfere according to its policy of the moment. An examination of both types of institution, their connections with the court, and the composers emerging from the conservatories, seems the logical first step in our enquiry.

The first operatic performances at Naples occurred long before de Brosses's visit of 1739. The story begins in either 1651 or 1652 when the Spanish viceroy of Naples, Count Ognatte, encouraged an operatic troupe by the name of 'Febi Armonici' to move to Naples from Rome. Toward the end of last century Benedetto Croce discovered a libretto published in Naples in 1651 of Busenello's *L'incoronazione di Poppea*, first set to music by Monteverdi and performed in Venice in 1642. He believed this libretto was for some Neapolitan performance presumably in 1651. Recently, the notion of a Neapolitan production of *Poppea* has been called in question.[7] This could mean that what was thought the second opera at Naples— *L'Amazzone d'Aragona*, produced at the Royal Palace in December,

---

[7] A. Mondolfi Bossarelli argues against the chances of a performance in 'Ancora intorno al codice napoletano della "Incoronazione di Poppea"', *RIM*, 1967, ii. 294 ff.

1652[8]—was in fact the very first. This work was almost certainly a variant of Cavalli's *Veremonda, l'Amazzone d'Aragona* performed in Venice the previous January. The circumstances of the Neapolitan *Amazzone* prove that the Febi in 1652 were working in some official capacity under the viceroy. The opera was staged during a court festival celebrating the recent capture of Barcelona by the Spaniards. Whether the group also performed in Neapolitan public theatres in these first years is an interesting question. Ulisse Prota-Giurleo pleads the case that they remained a private company under Ognatte till his departure from Naples in November, 1653, and that they started to run commercial productions at the S. Bartolomeo theatre not before 1654.[9] Much depends on evidence he has unearthed about the S. Bartolomeo. In 1652 this theatre was apparently sublet by three new lessees to a company of actors under Captain Giovanni Abreu.[10] In April 1654 the same three renegotiated their lease and decided to reserve the theatre for their own use.[11] The interesting thing is that one of the three lessees was Antonio Generoli, manager of the Febi. Did he or did he not use influence to bring the company on to the stage of the S. Bartolomeo between 1652 and '54?

Whatever the answer[12] it is clear that by the mid 1650s, at the latest, the Febi Armonici were associated with the S. Bartolomeo and operated commercially there. Successive opera companies acted on its stage till 1737, the year it was pulled down. Though their base was not now the court, their relationships with the viceroys remained generally good, and several viceroys gave them a so-called *aiuto di costa* or subsidy. One common sign of viceregal approval was an invitation to the company to give a palace performance of a new work before or during its commercial run. According to Prota-Giurleo this practice was begun at least as early as 1662.[13] The viceroys also had the option of visiting the theatre, an uncommon event, this, at first, since there was no tradition at Naples of royalty or their deputies going to public theatres, and since players could as easily be brought to them. But such a tradition did grow. An initial precedent for a Neapolitan viceroy to visit a public theatre had been set

[8] I. Fuidoro, 'Successi del governo del Conte d'Onatte, mdcxlviii–mdcliii', *CSIM*, Naples, 1932, iii. 189.

[9] *Breve storia del teatro di corte e della musica a Napoli nei secoli xvii–xviii*, Naples, 1952, pp. 21 ff.

[10] *I teatri di Napoli nel'600, la commedia e le maschere*, Naples, 1962, p. 138.

[11] *Breve storia*, p. 23; and *I teatri*, p. 142.

[12] Further facts relating to this question are in W. P. Stalnaker, Jnr., 'The beginnings of Opera in Naples', unpubl. doctoral diss., Princeton, 1968.

[13] *Breve storia*, p. 26.

by Count Monterey when he saw a play at the S. Bartolomeo in the 1630s.[14] A later viceroy, Marquis Astorga, witnessed an opera there on the night of 22 November 1673.[15] Thereafter viceregal visits to the public opera gradually became more frequent. The Duke of Medinaceli, in particular, passed several evenings at the S. Bartolomeo. It was he who, on his arrival as viceroy in 1696, inspected the theatre and, finding it too small for his liking, arranged with its owners to have it reconstructed on 'a larger and more magnificent scale, comparable with other theatres in other cities'.[16] The theatre had already been reconstructed following a fire in 1681 but clearly not in a good enough manner for him. The official Neapolitan gazette, the *Gazzetta* (or *Avvisi*) *di Napoli* for 20 November 1696 reported on the new reopening of the theatre in this way:

On the 18th of the current month in the S. Bartolomeo theatre, the drama entitled Commodo Antonino, adapted and embellished with beautiful arias written by Signor Abbate Francesco Paglia and set to music by the master of the royal chapel Signor Alessandro Scarlatti, was presented by the finest singers in Italy, brought here with enormous stipends generously paid by His Excellency. The drama gave the utmost delight, being watched by His Excellency with the Signora his consort, and by a larger crowd than ever.

The 'enormous stipends' required to engage the singers also drew comment from the chronicler Confuorto in his diary for 18 November. 'The performers are the best to be found in Italy', he wrote, adding that the viceroy was responsible for their engagement.[17] Other talented artists Medinaceli brought to Naples that year included Silvio Stampiglia, the poet and librettist. The noted architect and stage designer, Ferdinando Galli called Bibbiena, arrived to help the stage productions in 1698. Such was Medinaceli's interest that he took personal responsibility for the operas produced at the S. Bartolomeo during the 1698–9 season. In other words the theatre became temporarily a kind of extension of the royal palace run to please himself. All in all this interest was a mixed blessing. The productions themselves were probably as fine as any the Neapolitans had yet seen at home and equal to any in Italy at that time. But E. J. Dent has complained that A. Scarlatti's operas written for Naples at this very period contained music below his best—the viceroy's taste, Dent thought, was

---

[14] B. Croce, 'I teatri di Napoli', *Archivio storico per le province napoletane*, Naples, 1889, xiv. 134.
[15] I. Fuidoro, 'Giornali di Napoli dal mdclx al mdclxxx', *CSIM*, 1939, vii, 134.
[16] Croce, 'I teatri di Napoli', 1890, xv. 251.
[17] D. Confuorto, 'Giornali di Napoli dal mdclxxix al mdcic', *CSIM*, 1930, ii. 250.

probably responsible.[18] The costs incurred through raising the quality of production were enormous; and because of them Medinaceli contracted large debts which he left unhonoured on his departure for Madrid in 1702.[19]

Mention of singers brought to Naples, of Ferdinando Galli and Scarlatti, brings to the fore another aspect of support for the S. Bartolomeo company, namely, court patronage for its individual members. There is no need here to delve into the relationships of certain persons at court and actresses of the company, since others have studied this already.[20] Suffice it to say that the theatrical world of the time was cavalier by necessity and that certain illicit affairs occurred that may have contributed to opera's support. A related case should be mentioned however because of its connection with A. Scarlatti. The by now well-known extract from Confuorto's diary for November 1684 states that the viceroy, the Marquis del Carpio, dismissed two court officials and a page for 'holding close and illicit intercourse with certain actresses, one of whom was called the Scarlati, whose brother was by this viceroy made maestro di cappella of the palace'.[21] Since Confuorto goes on to say that these officials and friends worked behind the viceroy's back to influence palace appointments, historians have assumed that Scarlatti owed his appointment as *maestro* in February 1684 partly to the qualities of his sister, Melchiorra. It has yet to be explained whether del Carpio chose Scarlatti personally or merely accepted the nomination put forward by Scarlatti's group of supporters.[22] But he cannot have been ignorant of the appointment and must have approved of it, at least partly, on musical grounds.[23]

The appointment is even more interesting, though, because Scarlatti was at the time, and had been since his arrival in Naples in 1683, music director of the S. Bartolomeo company. It may therefore be interpreted as a sign of viceregal interest in opera since it brought a prominent opera

---

[18] *Alessandro Scarlatti: his life and works*, new impression, London, 1960, p. 65.

[19] Croce, 'I teatri', 1890, xv. 271.

[20] See especially essays on Giulia di Caro and Giulia Francesca Zuffi in Prota-Giurleo, *I teatri di Napoli nel'600*, pp. 293 ff. and 307 ff.

[21] Quoted in Dent, *Alessandro Scarlatti*, p. 35.

[22] Prota-Giurleo implies that Scarlatti's patron, the Duke of Maddaloni, was somehow involved in his selection, see *I teatri di Napoli nel'600*, p. 311, and *Breve storia*, p. 38.

[23] There is the interesting point that Ognatte, del Carpio, and Medinaceli were all in turn Spanish ambassadors to the Holy See before becoming Neapolitan viceroys. Each had thus a good chance to observe the operatic scene in Rome and understand what some of the major developments in opera were.

composer within the Neapolitan chapel royal. Chapel members them-
selves seem to have shown little interest in opera before 1675. In that year
Giulia di Caro, manageress of the S. Bartolomeo, suggested to the viceroy
Los Velez that it might be a good idea for the chapel and her company to
produce a joint venture in honour of the coronation of Charles II of Spain.
This suggestion was not welcomed by the royal musicians, who considered
themselves a cut above 'public' actors; but a palace performance of Cesti's
La Dori was nonetheless given by the two groups. The event seems to have
had the unexpected result of inspiring the chapel to create their own
operas. Headed by their *maestro*, Filippo Coppola, they gave several of
these in the palace with either Italian or Spanish text. Their aloofness to the
public company could not be sustained after the viceroys decided to
change the membership of the chapel by appointing to the post of court
maestro di cappella composers already noted in Naples and elsewhere for
their operas. When Coppola died in 1680 the post went to the Venetian
opera composer Pietro A. Ziani, whose work had been heard at the S.
Bartolomeo theatre and who was then in the city. When Ziani died in
1684, the post went once again to a non-Neapolitan, the twenty-three-year-
old Scarlatti. The doyen of Neapolitan operatic composers, Francesco
Provenzale, who was *maestro onorario* of the chapel and expected to follow
Ziani, resigned on discovering he had been bypassed.[24] Six of the royal
singers left, after protesting too violently against the viceroy's wish to hear
certain opera singers in the chapel in Holy Week of 1684. Their departure
gave Scarlatti the chance to fill their places with appointees to his liking and
most of these had associations with the public theatre.[25]

A link was now forged between the city's opera and the chapel royal
that remained unbroken for a long time to come. Several prominent
Neapolitan composers of opera, including Sarri, Mancini, Vinci, Leo,
Pergolesi, G. Francesco di Maio, and Cimarosa, were later appointed to
the chapel in paid or supernumerary positions.[26] So the indirect support
for opera the rulers gave by installing its major artists within their chapel
became part of the tradition, and no subsequent political change altered

[24] Prota-Giurleo, *Breve storia*, p. 40. F. Walker, in his additional notes to Dent, *Alessandro Scarlatti*,
1960, p. 240, declares that Provenzale resigned the day Scarlatti was appointed.

[25] The names of these appointees are in Prota-Giurleo, *Breve storia*, p. 40.

[26] Some of these obtained the top post of *maestro di cappella* to the Neapolitan court. The *maestri*
were in turn: Alessandro Scarlatti 1684–1703, Gaetano Veneziano 1704–7, Francesco Mancini 1707–8,
Alessandro Scarlatti 1708–25, Francesco Mancini 1725–37, Domenico Sarri 1737–44, Leonardo Leo
1744, Giuseppe di Maio 1745–71, Pasquale Cafaro 1771–87, Vincenzo Orgitano 1787–99.

that support in principle. This could be one of the reasons why the history of opera at Naples has continuity in spite of the dynastic squabbles and wars the state was involved in. The first major political change came during the War of Spanish Succession when Spain was occupied by two warring dynasties, Philip V in Madrid representing the Bourbon interests and Charles, later the Emperor Charles VI of Austria, in Barcelona representing the Hapsburgs. In 1707 Marshall Daun seized Naples on behalf of Charles, and Austrian viceroys planted their standard over the Neapolitan royal palace. By the Treaty of Utrecht Austrian suzerainty over Naples was confirmed, while all Spain reverted to Philip V. The Spanish party later had its revenge when, in 1734, Charles Bourbon, son of Philip V and at that moment Prince of Parma, marched down on Naples and captured it from the Hapsburgs. Charles now became King Charles III of the Two Sicilies, and Naples therefore an independent monarchy for the first time since the sixteenth century.

We should pay some attention to the reign of Charles (1734–59) not just because it was an unusually prosperous period of Neapolitan history but also because it was now that foreigners began to single out the city's opera for special comment. Charles was not devoid of cultural interests: he brought the Farnese collection of paintings to Naples from Parma, founded a porcelain factory at Capodimonte, and concerned himself with the excavations at Herculaneum. But no one has attempted to credit him with love of music. It would be wrong, therefore, to place him in the same category as Frederick the Great of Prussia or Duke Charles Eugene of Württemberg, two operatic enthusiasts of the period whose personal dynamism was responsible for the high-quality opera productions in their respective capitals. It is true that Charles's wife, Maria Amalia, appreciated music, for she was daughter of Augustus II of Saxony, a noted music patron. But Charles's personal interest in it was purely political. It was a fact of life that opera had become the European court entertainment *par excellence*, a recognized means of propaganda and prestige, and a delight for most of the courts' supporters into the bargain. In a newly independent kingdom like Naples where there were excellent artistic traditions, opera was too much of an asset to be relinquished. So Charles was prepared to look upon opera with favour and support it in a practical way. His first major step was to order the construction of a new, 'Royal' theatre, the S. Carlo, in 1737. This state theatre was designed to gather unto itself the high-class audience of the privately-owned S. Bartolomeo and the privileges that had accrued to that older house over the years. The S. Bartolomeo was by agreement pulled down the same year. As there are no known architectural plans of the S. Bartolomeo, it is difficult to tell just how superior the S. Carlo was to it. One extant print of the inside of the S. Bartolomeo before its reconstruction of 1696 suggests the building was then of the old-fashioned kind with a rectangular stalls area, with two rows of boxes and an open top gallery.[27] In 1696 five rows of boxes were created.[28] By comparison the S. Carlo had a horseshoe-shaped auditorium and six rows of boxes. The new theatre was a large one. Diderot included plans of this and three other Italian theatres, the Royal Theatre at Turin and the Argentina and Tordinone theatres at Rome, in volume 10 of his *Encyclopédie, Recueil de Planches*.[29] These plans show that the S. Carlo was significantly larger than the two Roman theatres and had a larger auditorium and wider stage than the one at Turin. Not only size but also position made the S. Carlo a symbol of the new state. Whereas the S. Bartolomeo had been situated a little way away from the palace, the S. Carlo was built next to it. The location ideally suited the monarch since he no longer needed to go outside to witness a public performance. His attendance on gala nights seems to have been fairly regular, though something of his attitude toward them may be judged from the record of de Brosses who, on his visit to Naples in 1739, saw the king chattering through one half of Sarri's opera *Partenope* and sleeping through the other.[30]

The privileged status and size of the S. Carlo made it the centre of attention of all visitors to Naples who were interested in opera. Several made flattering remarks on the interior of the building.[31] Like other theatres in Italy, the S. Carlo was not well lit on nights of ordinary performances, and the Englishman Samuel Sharp wrote that it was quite impossible on such occasions 'to distinguish a feature a-cross the house'.[32] On gala nights, however, extra candles and torches reflected their light in

[27] Plate in Prota-Giurleo, *I teatri di Napoli nel'600*, opposite p. 128, and in F. Mancini, *Scenografia napoletana dell'età barocca*, Naples, 1965, opposite p. 16.

[28] Croce, 'I teatri di Napoli', 1890, xv. 254–5.

[29] Paris, chez Briasson, 1772. Sizes of various Italian theatres can also be compared from data in F. Milizia, *Del teatro*, Venice, Pasquale, pp. 72 ff.

[30] *Lettres familières*, i. 383.

[31] P. J. Grosley, *New observations*, ii. 232–3; J. de Lalande, *Voyage d'un françois en Italie, fait dans les années 1765 & 1766*, Venice, 1769, vi. 350; Sara Goudar, *Relation historique des divertissements du carnaval de Naples*, Lucca, 1774, p. 8; *et passim*.

[32] *Letters from Italy, describing the customs and manners of that country in the years 1765 & 1766*, London, 1766, pp. 84–5.

mirrors all over the building, and visitors were then able to see the full magnificence of the interior. They also reported enthusiastically on the extravagant stage productions: the appearance of ballet troupes, for example, or of teams of soldiers and fencers for realistic battle scenes, or of the king's cavalry.[33] So much of the visitor's descriptions centred on these aspects of the theatre that it is plain some of them were more fascinated by the visual sights on and off stage than by anything else. Only the most musically minded commented on the aural side of opera, and it was they who complained that the theatre had acoustical defects. De Brosses declared that in one part of the auditorium 'one hardly sees a thing and in the other one hears nothing at all'.[34] Charles Burney, on his visit of 1770, wrote that 'not one of the present voices is sufficiently powerful for such a theatre, when so crowded and so noisy'.[35]

Reports of chatter and noise are not peculiar to the Neapolitan S. Carlo, and it is clear that audiences in most fashionable opera houses in eighteenth-century Italy made the most of a performance to see their friends and talk about what they wished. Sharp reported that the Neapolitan aristocracy preferred to meet each other in their boxes at the S. Carlo than at home. For this reason they rarely missed a performance, 'though the Opera be played three nights successively, and it be the same Opera, without any change, during ten or twelve weeks'.[36] Such customs tended to encourage a certain blasé attitude toward the show itself, but they also encouraged patronage of the theatre without which the show would not have existed. Financial responsibility for the theatre lay with the artistic managers— either an impresario or a directorate of royal nominees, dependent upon governmental policy of the moment. These relied mainly on seasonal rentals of boxes and of seats at the front of the stalls;[37] to a much lesser extent on receipts from occasional visitors. The prominent Neapolitan families who had bought the right to a box at the time the S. Carlo was built continued to pay rent year by year, and Charles made sure they did so by ordering that no box owner in the first to fourth rows could relinquish his box without royal approval.[38] It should be added that rarely was the

[33] C. de Brosses, *Lettres familières*, i. 385–6; Grosley, *New observations*, ii. 233 *et passim*.

[34] *Lettres familières*, i. 383.

[35] *The present state of music in France and Italy*, London, 1771, p. 340.

[36] *Letters from Italy*, p. 82.

[37] Sharp, *Letters from Italy*, pp. 84–5, states that whoever rented a seat in the first rows had a key to lock and unlock it so that he could come and go as he pleased.

[38] Croce, 'I teatri di Napoli', 1890, xv. 493. See also Lalande, *Voyage*, vi. 350.

S. Carlo made to pay by these means, and Charles came to contribute an annual subsidy from the exchequer to help offset the deficit.

The fact that neither Charles nor his son Ferdinand IV of Naples (1759–1825) was enthusiastic about the music of the opera at the S. Carlo may have had something to do with the way neither insisted upon relative silence throughout. When Burney on his visit of 1770 noted the singers could not be heard, he added somewhat significantly that 'on account of the King and the Queen being present, the people were much less noisy than on common nights.'[39] But if rules were lax over certain aspects of behaviour, they were not over others. Croce mentions several decreed at the time the S. Carlo was first opened. For example, no person other than the king or his official deputy, the Auditor of the Army (*Uditore dell'esercito*), could order an encore. There was to be no clapping of hands to show approval of a singer. Servants in livery could not enter the stalls area. It was forbidden to tamper with the illuminations.[40] In the king's absence discipline was maintained by the Auditor, a man whose predecessors in the job had gradually acquired jurisdiction over protocol within the S. Bartolomeo and who was now given responsibility of keeping order in the S. Carlo. The following anecdote told by Lalande demonstrates the power he wielded. The trouble began when the impresario, hoping to save money in a lean 1766 season, cut down on the number of torches during a gala performance, though illuminations had been advertised:

The public being impatient, the Duchess of Potenza took a light from one of the chandeliers in her box and lit the torchstick that was nearest. Everyone followed her example, and the entire auditorium was in course of being illuminated when the Marquis Pirelli, Auditor of the Army who maintains order in the house, had the big lamps before the stage extinguished, and forbade the performance. No tickets or money were refunded. Meanwhile everyone withdrew; and although they were furious, the nobility behaved with the prudence and respect demanded within the king's theatre.[41]

The élite status of the S. Carlo during Charles's reign was underlined by his failure to attend opera at the other Neapolitan public theatres like the Fiorentini. Croce states that some operas had been staged at this theatre back in 1681–2 while the S. Bartolomeo was being restored following a fire.[42] The Fiorentini properly enters our story in 1706, when the manage-

---

[39] *The present state*, p. 339.
[40] 'I teatri di Napoli', 1890, xv. 493.
[41] *Voyage*, vi. 322–3.
[42] 'I teatri di Napoli', 1890, xv. 235.

ment decided to give up presenting regular seasons of spoken drama and start opera in competition with the S. Bartolomeo. The venture drew the initial support of a certain number of aristocracy. The type of opera that both the Fiorentini and S. Bartolomeo produced between 1706 and 1709 was the fashionable one of the time, with heroic, or tragic, subject matter. In October of the latter year a new artistic management at the Fiorentini announced the production of a comic opera in Neapolitan dialect, *Patrò Calienno de la Costa*, the music being by A. Orefice and libretto by someone with the pseudonym of Agasippo Mercotellis.[43] Nothing like it had previously been seen on the Neapolitan public stage.[44] Causes of this second change of policy at the Fiorentini have not properly been explained, though both Croce and Prota-Giurleo hint at some kind of financial trouble. Because of the success of *Patrò*, the management largely abandoned the production of heroic opera and concentrated on comic opera instead.[45]

It is difficult to know how different the Fiorentini and S. Bartolomeo audiences were from now on. The *Gazzetta di Napoli* reported that the Austrian viceroy visited the Fiorentini on 31 October 1719, so clearly this theatre retained some admirers among the upper class. We must add, however, that successive Austrian viceroys made several visits to the S. Bartolomeo. Charles was not interested in the Fiorentini. It is a fair assumption that his visits exclusively to the S. Carlo after 1737 (where under normal circumstances heroic opera was performed) helped concentrate other high-class attention on the same theatre and genre. This did not mean an end to comic opera. So popular were comic plays and operas with the early eighteenth-century Neapolitan public that two additional theatres, neither of great size, were built in order that there could be more of them. These theatres were the Della Pace and the Nuovo, both inaugurated in 1724.[46] The first was never of much importance, and ceased to be a locale for comic opera after *c.* 1751.[47] The Nuovo on the other hand became a strong rival of the Fiorentini. Much later, in 1779, another theatre was opened for comic operas and plays—the Del Fondo.

[43] It is now generally agreed the author was Nicolò Corvo, see p. 189 below.

[44] Though a similar opera, *La Cilla*, had previously been seen in Neapolitan private circles, see especially C. Sartori, 'Gli Scarlatti a Napoli', *R MI*, 1942, xlvi. 380-3.

[45] Lists of operas performed at the Fiorentini in F. Florimo, *La Scuola musicale di Napoli*, Naples, 1881, iv. 34 ff., suggest that between 1709 and the late 1790s the management promoted heroic opera only in 1713-14.

[46] Croce, 'I teatri di Napoli', 1890, xv. 303-4, 307.

[47] In Florimo's lists of operas at the Della Pace, there is mention of one opera after 1751. This came in 1767. See *La scuola musicale di Napoli*, iv. 30-1.

Few foreigners made favourable comments on the entertainment at the Fiorentini and other small theatres; and one good reason may have been that since part of the opera was usually in Neapolitan dialect, they probably did not understand all that was going on. There were other reasons for their lack of enthusiasm. The singing was variable and the stage productions were often very dowdy indeed. Many visitors failed to mention comic opera altogether. Sharp did refer to the opera at the Fiorentini and Nuovo, but consigned it all to oblivion: 'The two burletta Opera Houses are not in much request, except when they happen to procure some favourite composition . . . I shall not enter into any detail of the two houses; but their dresses, their scenery, and their actors, are much more despicable than one could possibly imagine.'[48] But this only represents one viewpoint. The phrase 'not in much request' is obviously to be interpreted 'not in much request among those interested only in superb production', and the whole paragraph ignores the musical quality of comic opera which a few less prejudiced foreigners were able to perceive. Charles de Brosses went as often as possible to the Nuovo to see Leo's *Amor vuol sofferenza*, otherwise known as *La finta Frascatana*, in 1739 because he liked it so.[49] Charles Burney in 1770 found the operas at the Fiorentini and Nuovo so entertaining that he went no fewer than five times to one or other. [50] He thought the singing and the text of the operas bad, but enjoyed the acting and the music especially. He reported that people in these theatres talked and played cards among themselves,[51] as they did at the S. Carlo. Nevertheless the popular nature of the shows must have won a large measure of attention from the public—witness Burney's remark about how the Neapolitan comic singer (Antonio?) Casaccia was able to make the Fiorentini audience roar with laughter.[52]

The final point to be made in this brief survey of the Neapolitan theatres is that Ferdinand, unlike Charles, saw comic operas at the Fiorentini and Nuovo. His first visit was to Paisiello's *Dal finto il vero* at the Nuovo in 1776.[53] His decision to go there followed a period during which he had become familiar with comic opera by watching royal command performances by the public companies in the palace. The first such

---

[48] *Letters from Italy*, p. 92.
[49] *Lettres familières*, i. 386.
[50] *The present state*, pp. 292–3, 305–6, 309–10, 314–15, and 320–1.
[51] ibid., p. 315.
[52] ibid., pp. 292–3.
[53] Prota-Giurleo, *Breve storia*, p. 138.

performance was of Paisiello's *L'idolo cinese*, brought from the Nuovo in 1767.[54] By going to a public performance Ferdinand contributed further to the social acceptability of comic opera and also increased the prestige of the theatres where it was staged.

What has been written so far indicates that opera, originally introduced by the Spanish viceroy Ognatte, became an established and popular art-form in Naples. But this is not sufficient to explain the extraordinary fame gained by the city in the operatic field. When declaring that Naples was 'capital of the world's music', de Brosses also stressed the importance of its teaching establishments, or conservatories. 'The best schools of music . . . are at Naples', he wrote.[55] Josse de Villeneuve was of the same opinion. In his *Lettre sur le méchanisme de l'opéra italien* of 1756 we find several remarks on music education in Italy. In large families of the artisan class, he declared, one son was normally destined to become a priest, another an instrumental player, another perhaps a singer. Pupils were sometimes sent to music masters upon the following terms: 'In every town there are teachers who instruct without charge but who legally bind their pupils to pay them a share of whatever profits they may obtain from their art, once they have reached a certain age, and for a number of years following.'[56] In Naples, on the other hand, there were excellent schools of music, each having 'two music masters, the senior being selected from among the most celebrated composers and giving three lessons a week'.[57]

The conservatories S. Maria di Loreto, S. Maria della Pietà dei Turchini, Poveri di Gesù Cristo, and S. Onofrio a Capuana, were founded at various times in the sixteenth century with the object of giving free board and education to orphans of the city. Three came to be run by layman boards of governors ultimately responsible to the viceroy. The fourth, the Gesù Cristo, put itself under the patronage of the Archbishop of Naples who appointed two clerical governors to it.[58] The resident masters of academic subjects, rectors, bursars, etc., were priests in most instances. The earliest music masters of whom there is record were priests also. Music was

---

[54] Prota-Giurleo, op. cit., p. 97, says Vinci's *Silla dittatore*, 1723, was the last opera heard at the palace in viceregal times. If we exclude certain short intermezzos performed at the palace in Charles's reign, *L'idolo cinese* seems to be the first palace opera for over forty years.

[55] *Lettres familières*, ii. 386.

[56] *Lettre sur le méchanisme*, Naples, 1756, p. 105.

[57] Ibid., p. 106. Other evidence suggests that most senior and junior masters came to their conservatory each working day, *i.e.* more than three times weekly.

[58] For more on the foundation of the conservatories, see S. di Giacomo, *I quattro antichi conservatorii musicali di Napoli*, 2 vols., Palermo, 1924–8.

introduced into the curriculum for the reason that churches were attached to the foundations and the boys provided the church music. The students of the Gesù Cristo, furthermore, used to collect alms walking through the streets singing litanies.[59] While music was not at first the most important subject, more and more it became so. This meant each conservatory acquired the dual character of orphanage and music school. The change is apparent in the new types of music teacher and student entering c. 1630 and after. As the demand for good music teaching grew, so the institutes began to elect as teachers highly professional musicians, many of them laymen, who were active in other posts in the city. The dangers of this system may be guessed at from a glance at the minute for 24 February, 1669, of the governors of the Loreto, stipulating that the *maestro di cappella*, Francesco Provenzale, and the violin teacher were to be reported when they failed to appear for lessons.[60] Teachers' contracts at the Loreto commonly contained a clause about deductions from their salary for non-attendance. The policy of employing the best teacher talent was advantageous even if teachers occasionally did not turn up. It encouraged talented music students, many of them not orphans, to apply to enter; and it enabled the conservatories to earn extra money by accepting some of them as paying boarders. This meant that each conservatory came to educate two main types of student.[61] Among the paying students more and more came from outside the Neapolitan area. By the early eighteenth century some were coming from as far afield as Spain and Germany.

Financial reasons lay behind the enormous growth in the conservatories' music that occurred in the seventeenth century. Civic, ecclesiastical, and private societies all wanted to engage the boys for functions requiring music. The conservatories acted to meet the demand. The following describes students contributing to the traditional Carnival parade in 1681:

By order of the People's Nominee the butchers made a float covered with meat, with wholesome thighs of beef, halves of pork . . . flanks of pork and similar things. And on top there was the usual music by the boys of the Loreto, among whom were two, one dressed as Coviello and the other as Pulcinella, singing in praise of the viceroy. The float travelled the entire length of the Toledo street as far as the palace

---

[59] S. di Giacomo, op. cit., ii. 36.

[60] *Conservatory S. M. di Loreto, Conclusioni dal 1664 al 1699*, vol. 166 (MS. now in the Conservatory S. Pietro a Maiella, Naples).

[61] M. F. Robinson discusses the different status of orphan and fee-paying groups at the Loreto in a forthcoming publication: 'The governors' minutes of the Conservatory S. Maria di Loreto, Naples', *RCRMA*, 1972, x.

where, when it had reached a point below the viceroy's balcony, a construction upon it shaped like a cloud opened up to let out a boy in fancy dress. By means of a screw and windlass the boy was transported through the air up to the balcony where the viceroy stood. He then presented a document [*cartello*] to the viceroy, after which he descended to the float by the same device. The viceroy was extremely pleased and wished him to return once again by the same means; and when he arrived, gave him twelve golden doubloons in a bag. When this was over, the float was with much jostling and confusion sacked by the mob.[62]

The social and economic advantages of making the pupils perform in various parts of the city and outside it were well summed up by de Villeneuve in the mid-eighteenth century:

Whenever a church or society wishes to promote some music (as happens very frequently in Italy), a letter is sent to the director requesting the services of twenty, thirty, or more of these children for a small, recognized price. This benefits the institution, contributes to its upkeep, and multiplies the number of musical performances.[63]

This practice suited the music students, since it added variety to their routine and extra relevance to the skills they were taught in class. It also gave the seniors among them increased independence and authority, since teachers could not always lead the students in person and the seniors then took charge. These seniors did much of the teaching in the school itself, and the teacher depended heavily upon them to relay his lessons to the juniors. In fact both musicians and administration benefited from the system; and there were great advantages to be found in it so long as the income derived from music was sufficient to help the conservatory pay its way and continue its other, charitable work, and so long as all-powerful authorities like the court did not step in with demands that overstrained the conservatory's musical resources.

The first sacred music-drama known to have been performed by a conservatory occurred in 1656, a few years after the introduction of opera to the city. This work was *Il fido campione ovvero il B. Gaetano*, a so-called *opera drammatica in musica* with text by Giovan Francesco del Gesù, performed at the Loreto.[64] From the 1660s other sacred dramas were performed by the conservatories and were the means whereby music students learnt the techniques of modern stage production. The works were 'sacred' in the sense that the characters and plot were drawn from

[62] D. Confuorto, 'Giornali', *CSIM* 1930, i. 60.
[63] *Lettre sur le méchanisme*, p. 108.
[64] Croce, *I teatri di Napoli*, 4th revised edn., Bari, 1947, p. 86.

stories of the saints or other religious sources. The treatment of the subject however was often similar to that of 'secular' opera of the period. Anyone reading, for example, the libretto of *Il ritorno d'Onofrio in padria*, performed by the S. Onofrio in 1671,[65] will see that its structure is reminiscent of secular opera then playing in Venice, Naples, and elsewhere. As in secular opera the plot contains a confused mass of personal and political intrigues. Onofrio, son of the King of Persia, and other nobles are surrounded, as in opera, by their political and military advisers and by their servants who provide the comedy. The supernatural events caused by angelic and satanic powers are similar to those caused by operatic gods and goddesses. The major difference is the didactic and moralizing bias of part of *Il ritorno's* dialogue, largely absent in Venetian works though present in earlier Roman operas with a religious content like Landi's *S. Alessio* (1632).

In the eighteenth century it was conservatory policy to let students compose either the whole or sections of an opera themselves. Some conservatories also permitted the production of stage works without a religious or didactic content. In 1712 the libretto of a comic opera, *Lo Masillo*, was printed with a dedication by the S. Onofrio to one Mattia di Franco. The music to Act II, the libretto states, was by a student of the conservatory, Michele Falco.[66] The inference to be drawn here is that the S. Onofrio was involved in the performance and keeping abreast of recent developments by aping the new type of opera at the Fiorentini. There are several later examples of student operas of this type. Take, for instance, the libretto with the following on its title page:

Il Medico / comedia per musica / di / Liviano Lantino / da rap-
presentarsi nel Real Conser– / vatorio di S. Onofrio a Capuana /
dagl'Alunni dello stesso / Conservatorio . . . in Napoli
MDCCLXVII.[67]

(Il Medico, comedy in music by Liviano Lantino to be performed

[65] Libretto in the Biblioteca Nazionale, Naples. The work is mentioned by S. di Giacomo, *I quattro antichi conservatorii*, i. 66–8.

[66] See libretto and also di Giacomo, op. cit. i. 80–1. This composer is presumably the same Michele Falco who composed the comic opera *Lollo pisciaportelle* performed at the house of one 'Barone Paternò' and perhaps also at the Fiorentini in 1709, see C. Sartori, 'Gli Scarlatti a Napoli', *RMI*, 1942, xlvi. 384–5. This would suggest that Falco was in a fairly senior 'student' position three years later.

[67] Libretto in the National Library, Naples, and in the library of the Conservatory S. Pietro a Maiella, Naples.

in the Royal Conservatory S. Onofrio a Capuana by the pupils of the same Conservatory . . . in Naples 1767)

The music throughout, the libretto informs us, was by a student of the S. Onofrio, Andrea Festa. The policy of making senior composition pupils like Festa take a hand in the creation of operas—some pupils seem to have composed sacred or comic operas as a type of graduation exercise—meant that many left their conservatories ready to write for the professional stage right away.

In the early eighteenth century a stream of well-qualified opera composers began to emerge from the conservatories. It would be impossible to give a full list of them, both because of their number and because of lack of complete documentation. The following were among the opera composers who received the whole or part of their education at a conservatory.[68]

F. Mancini	(1672–1737)
D. Sarri	(1679–1744)
G. Porsile	(1680–1750)
N. Porpora	(1686–1768)
L. Vinci	(1690/6(?)–1730)
F. Feo	(1691–1761)
L. Leo	(1694–1744)
G. di Maio	(1697–1771)
P. Auletta	(1698–1771)
N. Logroscino	(1698– ?)
R. Broschi	(1698–1756)
P. Cafaro	(1706–87)
E. Duni	(1709–75)
G. B. Pergolesi	(1710–36)
D. Perez	(1711–78)
G. Latilla	(1711–88)
D. Terradellas	(1713–51)
N. Jommelli	(1714–74)
G. Manna	(1715–79)
G. Abos	(1715–60)

[68] The dates of composers on the list are taken from the *Enciclopedia della musica*, Ricordi, Milan, 1963–4. Not on the list is the name of Nicolò Piccinni (1728–1800). Dictionaries have long declared Piccinni was a conservatory pupil, but U. Prota-Giurleo, 'La biografia di Nicola Piccinni alla luce di nuovi documenti', *Il Fuidoro*, 1954, i. 27–8, has found no direct evidence of this. According to Prota-Giurleo, Piccinni lived in Bari till the middle of 1753 and could, at best, have been a senior student at a Neapolitan conservatory from late 1753 to 1755.

I. Fiorillo	(1715–87)
N. Conforto	(1718– ?)
D. Fischietti	(c.1720–c.1810)
T. Traetta	(1727–79)
P. Anfossi	(1727–97)
P. A. Guglielmi	(1728–1804)
G. Insanguine	(1728–95)
A. Sacchini	(1730–86)
G. Tritto	(1733–1824)
G. Paisiello	(1740–1816)
G. Gazzaniga	(1743–1818)
G. Giordani	(1743–98)
D. Cimarosa	(1749–1801)
N. Zingarelli	(1752–1837)
L. Caruso	(1754–1822)
S. Palma	(1754–1834)
G. Andreozzi	(1755–1826)
A. Tarchi	(c.1759–1814)
S. Storace	(1763–96)
G. Spontini	(1774–1851)

Two of the above-mentioned came from outside Italy—Terradellas from Spain and Storace from Britain.

The quality of education and high standards of these institutes were not kept up indefinitely. The first conservatory to give up was the Gesù Cristo, suppressed in 1743 when its building was required as a seminary for priests. Published statements to the effect that all was not well with the other three first appeared in Burney's *The present state of music in France and Italy* of 1771. His report on the S. Onofrio has already been quoted so often that there is no need to quote it here. Finding so much overcrowding that students were forced to practise different instruments and carry on other activities in one and the same room, he concluded that the young musicians were being given no chance to acquire finesse in their work.[69] He had previously attended religious functions with music by different conservatories and liked each performance they gave less and less.[70] He severely criticized the students in general for the 'slovenly coarseness' of their playing and singing and for their 'total want of taste, neatness, and expression'. Their poor showing was a major factor in his conclusion that music in Naples was not all it had been built up to be.

[69] pp. 324–6.
[70] pp. 293–7, 304–5, 307–9.

Burney's account of conditions within the conservatories was cor-
roborated by Michael Kelly, the Irish tenor famous for being among the
original cast of Mozart's *Nozze di Figaro*. In 1779, at the age of sixteen,
Kelly went to Naples for music lessons and there presented himself to
Fedele Fenaroli, first music master of the Loreto:

Finerolli [*sic*] was a light, sprightly, animated little man, about fifty: he heard me
sing, and was pleased to say, I evinced promising abilities; he took me to see his
Conservatorio, in which there were between three and four hundred boys;[71] they
studied composition, singing, and to play on all instruments. There were several
rooms, but in the great schoolroom into which I was introduced, there were some
singing, others playing upon the violin, hautboy, clarionet, horn, trumpet, &. &.
each different music, and in different keys. The noise was horrible; and in the midst
of this terrific Babel, the boy who studied composition was expected to perform
his task, and harmonize a composition given him by his master. I left the place in
disgust, and swore to myself never to become an inmate of it.[72]

However Fenaroli overcame his objections by offering him accommoda-
tion in his own house. Kelly then entered the conservatory for certain
lessons, and so obtained benefit from the establishment without belonging
to either the paying or non-paying group of student boarders. The
arrangement was ideal for a pupil with means of his own, and may have
been entered upon in a few other cases between young musicians and
conservatory teachers.[73]

Communal practising cannot have been the prime reason for the
decline of musical standards that is supposed to have set in at the three
conservatories in the last decades of the eighteenth century, since the same
conditions of practising had been in operation before, in the conservatories'
heyday. The evidence suggesting a decline of musical standards gives no
firm reason. The symptoms of a decline are clear enough, and include
Burney's reports of unsatisfactory performances by the boys, a gradual
reduction in the numbers of famous pupils emerging from the conservatories, and occasional suggestions by Neapolitans for reforms of the
conservatories' musical activities. These proposals for reform were really
designed to direct the student's attention to the best of old music so as to
broaden his taste and improve his technique. Michele Afeltro in the early

---

[71] In fact the student total at the Loreto in 1779 was well below 200.

[72] *Reminiscences of Michael Kelly of the King's Theatre, and Theatre Royal, Drury Lane*, London,
1826, i. 43.

[73] Note the statement by Valentino Fioravanti (1770?–1837) that during his two-year stay in
Naples he visited several conservatories and there met and learnt from the best teachers, see A. della
Corte, *L'opera comica italiana nel'700*, Bari, 1923, ii. 177.

1770s suggested the founding of an academy to promote productions of the best operas, old and new, by the students in a theatre hired every so often for the purpose.[74] Saverio Mattei, the poet and scholar appointed in 1791 to head the Turchini, suggested in a 1795 memorandum to the court that students should become familiar with, among other things, the technique of cantus fermus, with duets by Steffani, the Marcello psalms, music by Scarlatti, Leo, and Durante, and with the best music treatises from Zarlino onwards.[75] With royal approval he promoted a large music collection so that students could always have access to the best source material. Posterity should thank him for this, for his collection forms the basis of the library of the present Naples' conservatory of music. It was during Mattei's time at the Turchini that there appeared the largest and most handsome book on music theory by an eighteenth-century Neapolitan teacher. This was the *Regole del contrappunto pratico* (1794) by Nicola Sala, then first *maestro di cappella* of the Turchini. The book demonstrated all manner of contrapuntal writing from simple, two-part exercises in first species to elaborate, eight-part fugues. Its reformist spirit shines in the following passage from the dedication to the king, Ferdinand IV: 'The philosophers themselves advise us that the most effective way to halt the decline [of the arts] is to return to ancient and first principles by rigid observation of those artistic fundamentals without which talent is undisciplined and unchecked liberty degenerates into confusion.' No one should get the impression that pupils had previously been deprived of training in the severer forms of counterpoint and in the so-called *stile antico*. Religious choral music by older graduates like Feo and Leo contains plenty of evidence of old-fashioned contrapuntal skill. Nevertheless the conservatories had thrived as a result of what we might call a pragmatic rather than doctrinaire approach to teaching and had kept themselves abreast of new fashions favouring the *stile moderno*. Now there seems to have been a deliberate attempt to reinstate 'old' music in the curriculum as though there was danger it would otherwise be lost sight of entirely.

The fall of the conservatories' financial fortunes is related to this artistic decline. In the last decades of the eighteenth century prices rose in Naples, and conservatory administrations found they had to make economies to close the gap between income and expenditure. One method to cut expenditure was to cut the number of students, and total numbers of

---

[74] Di Giacomo, *I quattro antichi conservatorii*, i. 246–54.
[75] Ibid. i. 262–4.

students at all three conservatories came down. The problem was to reduce size in such a way as to stabilize the economy without reducing the efficiency. For various reasons, including, it seems, a fall in the income from music, administrations were unable to do this. Consequently more reductions were planned and the whole scale of the conservatories' operations had to be contracted.

The court could have done much to remedy the situation if it had had a mind to do so. Evidence suggests that the seventeenth- and eighteenth-century viceroys interfered little in the affairs of the institutes but that Charles and Ferdinand (and/or their advisors) interfered more often. This interference produced little material benefit. Between 1748 and 1750 the Loreto was under threat of closure by Charles who wanted its site for a new institution to shelter the poor and destitute. In 1751 he founded a class in sciences there,[76] paying for its teacher but not for its students whom the conservatory had to support. In the 1760s and early '70s Bernardo Tanucci, then the most powerful minister at court, placed some of his own recommended students in the Turchini and Loreto. The court now found that it was being asked by various parents and students to settle their grudges against conservatory administrations. And it also had to answer complaints from the governors of the Turchini and S. Onofrio that the management of the S. Carlo theatre was commandeering their pupils to fill up the ranks of the opera chorus. The governors of the Turchini protested in 1759 that their students were returning late at night from the theatre, frequenting bad company there, and being too tired to work the next morning.[77] The governors of the S. Onofrio complained in 1774. The court's reply to the delegate, or head, of the S. Onofrio has recently come to light and is worth quoting because it shows the comparative indifference of government to the boys' welfare.

The King has understood the reasons behind the representations of your Excellency and the governors of the Conservatory S. Onofrio caused by your dislike of sending the boys to sing the choruses in the S. Carlo theatre at the bidding of the impresario D. Gaetano Santoro. He has commanded me to write back, as I am doing, [and say] that it is necessary to reach agreed terms with the impresario and that, if terms cannot be reached, you are to refer back. Please be informed that these orders have also been sent to the Delegate of the Pietà de'Torchini [sic], so that the two conservatories may share the duty. The Palace, May 14, 1774.[78]

[76] Celano, *Notizie*, 4th edn., Naples, 1792, iv. 317.
[77] Di Giacomo, op. cit., i. 237–43.
[78] MS. in the Conservatory S. Pietro a Maiella, Naples. A catalogue number has yet to be assigned.

The unsettled political situation in Europe at the end of the eighteenth century and beginning of the nineteenth crushed any remaining hope that the conservatories might stage a recovery. In 1797 the Loreto's buildings were required for a military hospital, and its students passed into the S. Onofrio.[79] Many students in the two remaining institutions joined the republicans during the short-lived Parthenopaean Republic of 1799 and were either apprehended or had to flee their conservatory when the Republic fell and the Bourbons returned to power.[80] In 1806 Joseph Bonaparte occupied Naples and initiated a series of reforms including the setting up of a state-owned conservatory of music to replace the old ones. All students were collected together inside the Turchini at the end of that year. On 1 January 1807 this institute was turned into a college for music students only and renamed the Collegio Reale di Musica.[81] A further change occurred the next year when the college was transferred to different buildings and became known as the Collegio S. Sebastiano. It is unnecessary to pursue the subsequent history of music education at Naples, as it lies outside our period. The only point that should be raised is that changes of institute and management in 1807 did not mean an end to traditional methods of music teaching. The music in the Collegio was placed under a triumvirate of Paisiello, Fenaroli, and Tritto, representing respectively the old S. Onofrio, Loreto, and Turchini. Later, in 1813, Nicola Zingarelli became artistic director. All these men had been trained at one or other of the old conservatories and carried the fruits of their eighteenth-century experience into nineteenth-century practice.[82]

The problem is now to try and gather the threads of information on the theatres and conservatories and see whether they offer any explanation for the reputation that Naples enjoyed internationally from c. 1740. The first and obvious point is that the S. Carlo, a much more impressive theatre than any Naples had had previously, was erected in 1737. A second point relates to the quantitative build-up of composers emerging from the conservatories in the first decades of the eighteenth century. This build-up can be checked by a glance at the list of composers on pp. 17–18 above and

---

[79] Di Giacomo, op. cit., i. 120 ff. From 1797 the Conservatory S. Onofrio took the Loreto's name as well as its own.

[80] Di Giacomo, op. cit., i. 281–3.

[81] Ibid., i. 292.

[82] Not always apparently with the best results. Note the criticism of Zingarelli's directorship by the violinist and composer Ludwig Spohr who visited Naples in 1817, see Spohr's *Autobiography*, English edn., London, 1865, ii. 16–17.

at their dates which will give some idea of when they began to write in earnest. The list of course is not comprehensive even of major composers of opera who were then associated with Naples. It does not include A. Scarlatti, for example, who came to reside there after his studentship was over, or Rinaldo da Capua, about whose life little is known, or G. Francesco di Maio (1732–70). It does not mention Johann Hasse (1699–1783), the famous German composer, who came to Naples in 1722 for private tuition and stayed till sometime between 1727 and 1730. All the facts point to the presence in Naples of an increasing amount of good talent. The trouble was that the conservatories' output of musicians in the early eighteenth century outstripped the home demand for them. The result was that more and more musicians sought work elsewhere. Emigrating, forming small Neapolitan groups in various European cities or travelling between them, these men did much to bring Naples to the attention of the international public.

It would be wrong to suggest that Naples became entirely self-sufficient musically in the early eighteenth century, but it is true to say that whereas much of its opera was originally imported, it relied more and more for its operatic entertainment on the work of its own composers and became an exporter. Various exceptions to this statement will become clear later. For the moment it is instructive to examine in more detail when composers resident and/or trained in Naples began to dominate the scene locally and then internationally, and what factors other than those already mentioned in the sections on the theatres and conservatories helped the trend. If we turn back once more to the seventeenth-century situation in Naples and examine lists of early Neapolitan opera productions, we soon find that a large proportion of these were Venetian works altered slightly to suit local conditions. Of only a small minority of operas before Scarlatti's arrival in Naples in 1683 can it be said that the scores were all-Neapolitan creations. Much of Scarlatti's importance for Neapolitans lies in the fact that during his long residence in the city he was able to persuade the impresarios of the S. Bartolomeo to commission and stage many works from him.[83] Though not Neapolitan by origin, he became so by association, and did much to help the process whereby the city switched from being an importer to a source of its own opera. Romain Rolland in his *Histoire de l'opéra en Europe avant Lully et Scarlatti* (1895) was the first to point out the good quality of

---

[83] Many of these Scarlatti operas were first performed at the Royal Palace before passing on to the stage of the S. Bartolomeo.

two operas, *Lo schiavo di sua moglie* (1671) and *Stellidaura vendicata* (1674), by the much older Neapolitan composer Francesco Provenzale.[84] His discovery of these two works did more than convince him of the merits of this long forgotten composer. The new evidence suggested that opera in Naples developed distinctive features before Scarlatti and that it rapidly became 'superior to that of all other cities in Italy, Venice excepted'.[85] His remarks also brought into doubt the previously-held view that Scarlatti was the 'founder' or father of the long line of Neapolitan opera composers stretching right through the eighteenth century. With our extra knowledge we can confirm that Scarlatti's arrival in 1683 was the result of the growing operatic movement in the city rather than the cause of it. Nevertheless Scarlatti is a much more important historical figure than Provenzale. We have already hinted at one reason, namely Scarlatti's ability to remain in favour with the management of the S. Bartolomeo in a way unknown to Provenzale or other Neapolitans of Provenzale's generation. Another point was that Scarlatti had, and preserved, contacts with various parts of Italy that no native Neapolitan opera composer as yet made.

Scarlatti came to Naples from Rome with a reputation already established. Partly by maintaining contact with his Roman friends and patrons—and his Roman visits and commissions of the 1680s and '90s prove the closeness of that contact—he never committed himself to being a Neapolitan composer only. His major operas of those years were taken up by impresarios in some of the other Italian cities, and a very few were even performed outside Italy altogether, for instance in Germany[86] and in England.[87] His travels in the period 1702–8, when he was away from Naples, enabled him to re-establish old contacts and create new ones in new places, including Venice. On his return to Naples in 1708 the old pattern seemed to reassert itself; operas were written for Naples and Rome, repeated in other Italian towns (though not in Venice), and occasionally

---

[84] Provenzale was one of the first Neapolitans to write opera. He wrote music for parts or the whole of five operas in the 1650s and for an approximate half-dozen in the 1670s. These were not well-known outside Naples. It is possible that his first opera, *Il Ciro*, was the same as the *Il Ciro* produced at the S.S. Giovanni e Paolo theatre, Venice, in January, 1654, with additions by Cavalli, see A. Loewenberg. *Annals of Opera*, Geneva, 1955, i. cols. 30–1. A. Mondolfi Bossarelli, 'Ancora intorno al codice', *RIM*, ii. 310, suggests his *Theseo overo l'incostanza trionfante* (Naples, 1658) may have been the same as *L'incostanza trionfante ossia il Theseo* produced the same year in Venice with music officially by P. A. Ziani.

[85] *Histoire de l'opéra*, Paris, new edn., 1931, p. 188.

[86] For details of German performances, see A. Loewenberg, *Annals of opera*, i, col. 95; and L. Schiedermair, *Die deutsche Oper*, Leipzig, 1930, p. 30.

[87] For English versions of his *Pirro e Demetrio*, see Loewenberg, *Annals*, i, col. 95.

produced in German-speaking areas.[88] Evidence of the fame of his music in the first half of the eighteenth century is the surprisingly large number of autographs and manuscript copies of his operas and cantatas that found their way outside Italy and are now in foreign libraries.

It so happened that the period when Scarlatti left Naples for a while (1702–8) was around the time that a new generation of conservatory-trained opera composers began to emerge. This was the generation of Mancini, Sarri, Porsile, and Porpora (see the list on p. 17 above). It is arguable that Scarlatti's absence left a gap in the Neapolitan opera field that facilitated Mancini's and Sarri's entry into it. Scarlatti left in the summer of 1702; Mancini's first opera for the S. Bartolomeo, *Ariovisto*, was staged in November of the same year; Sarri started writing for the S. Bartolomeo in 1706. Mancini and Sarri remained in Naples most of their lives writing for their local community. The same cannot be said of the next composer on the list, Giuseppe Porsile. In an interesting article on this composer, Prota-Giurleo has drawn attention to a chapel of Neapolitan musicians set up by Charles, Hapsburg claimant to the Spanish throne, in Barcelona in 1707.[89] The Austrians captured Naples that year. A document originally in the Naples Archives mentioned salary increases in July 1708, to seven Neapolitan musicians of that chapel. Three of the musicians were singers, three were instrumentalists, and the seventh was the *maestro di cappella*, Porsile. Porsile seems to have composed just one opera, *Il ritorno d'Ulisse in patria*, performed at the Fiorentini in 1707, before moving to Spain; and he was certainly not yet the most experienced of musicians. However, he was the man selected to go, and his job was the best obtained by a Neapolitan-trained opera composer outside Italy up to that moment. In 1711 Charles was recalled to Vienna to become Austrian Emperor, and control of Catalonia and Naples passed to his wife Elizabeth, who stayed behind in Barcelona. When the whole of Spain was assigned to Philip V in 1713, Elizabeth also returned to Vienna, and with her went Porsile— though there was no immediate opening for him in the Imperial Chapel. However, Charles did not forget his *maestro* of Barcelona days and conferred upon him the title of 'actuary' of the Royal household in April 1717, and of 'court composer' in 1721. This was one of a number of ways in which Austrians began to aid Neapolitan individuals and Neapolitan music, an aid that might not have been so forthcoming if Naples had not

[88] Ibid., i. col. 115.
[89] 'Giuseppe Porsile e la real cappella di Barcellona', *GMN*, 1956, ii. 161 ff.

become part of their dominion. We note, for example, that two of Porpora's operas, *Arianna e Teseo* and *Temistocle*, received first performances in Vienna in 1714 and 1718 respectively. It has been suggested that the composer got the chance to write *Arianna e Teseo* through the influence of his patron Prince Philipp, Landgrave of Hesse-Darmstadt, head of the Imperial army in Naples 1709–13 and afterwards governor of Mantua.[90] We note that the Austrian court also began to look upon Naples as a good centre not merely to get music from but to send young musicians to. Ever since the sixteenth century, composers from German-speaking states had tended to stay in Venice or Rome if they wished to study Italian music at source. But when Giuseppe Bonno, a young composer under the patronage of the Austrian court, was sent to study in Italy in 1726 (or slightly earlier), it was to Naples that he was directed.[91]

It was in the 1720s that the travels of Neapolitans away from the city and number of commissions they received outside the Neapolitan state began to be really noticeable. Leonardo Vinci, one of the key figures of that decade, wrote almost as many operas for Rome and more northerly cities in Italy as he did for Naples itself. His career seems to have set a pattern for the most successful Neapolitan composers of later years to follow. Most of them obtained their very first opera commissions from Neapolitan theatre impresarios, but then they tended to move away from the city for shorter or longer periods. Finally a proportion of them moved away without waiting for any home promotion. Giovanni Paisiello, for example, who emerged from his conservatory in July 1763, travelled northwards before the end of the year and received his first opera commissions in Bologna, Modena, Venice, and Parma. With this 'foreign' experience to his credit, he returned and broke into the Neapolitan theatre world toward the end of 1766.

There are several other ramifications of the expansion of the Neapolitan effort, only a few of which can be mentioned here. If, as is suggested, Neapolitan emigration began sometime in the first decade of the eighteenth century and got into high gear around the third, there should be signs about the same time that Neapolitans were becoming a competitive force and possibly displacing some of the local musicians in other places. Anyone

---

[90] F. Walker, 'A chronology of the life and works of Nicola Porpora', *Italian studies*, 1951, vi. 33–4.

[91] E. Wellesz, 'Giuseppe Bonno (1710–88). Sein Leben und seine dramatischen Werke', *SIM*, 1909–10, xi. 396.

regarding the Italian opera scene over-all will probably reach the conclusion that composers associated with Naples in the first two decades of
the century seem no more impressive as a group than the group of
contemporary Italian composers historically associated with North Italy
and with Vienna. Scarlatti, Mancini, Sarri, Porpora, etc., were certainly
no more active than more 'Northern' composers like G. and M. A.
Bononcini, F. Gasparini, A. Caldara, A. Vivaldi, and A. Lotti, and
attracted no more attention than they. Quite different was the situation
c. 1750–60 when Neapolitans were in a majority among the prominent
opera composers and when only B. Galuppi and G. Sarti among young
Italians not connected with Naples seem to have been able to gain more
than local repute. Whoever wants details of the Neapolitan incursion into
local areas can do worse that examine the situation in Venice during the
first decades of the century. Venetians had long accustomed themselves to
the idea that their opera was as good as any. Foreigners in the second half
of the seventeenth century tended to assume that this city was the foremost
centre of opera in Italy—so that when, for example, St. Evremond attacked
Italian opera in his essay *Sur les opéra* [sic], it was the 'operas of Venice'
that he chose to mention at one point, not the operas of Rome, Naples, or
anywhere else.[92] Impresarios of Venetian theatres started the century cool
toward Neapolitans and toward opera originating in the Neapolitan area.
A. Scarlatti wrote two operas for the S. Gio. Grisostomo theatre in 1707,
but this does not seem to have made him a popular figure there. *Barilotto*,
a short intermezzo by Sarri, was performed at the S. Angelo theatre in
1712. In the 1720s fashions changed considerably. Leo's *Timocrate* was
staged at the S. Angelo in 1723. *Despina e Niso*, intermezzo from Scarlatti's
Amor generoso of 1714, was performed in the same theatre in 1724. Two
Vinci operas were produced at the S. Gio. Grisostomo in 1725. In 1726 four
operas by Neapolitans, three by Porpora and one by Vinci, were
performed at the S. Gio. Grisostomo and S. Samuele theatres. Thereafter
the annual rate of 'Neapolitan' productions fell somewhat, though a year
seldom passed without the Venetians having opportunity to see something
that a Neapolitan had composed. With their operas came the Neapolitans
themselves, several of whom obtained posts in Venice. Burney bears
witness to this Neapolitan entry in the following manner:

The Neapolitan school, during the present century, has often furnished the Venetians
with composers . . . Among these, besides Alessandro Scarlatti, Leo, Vinci, and

[92] St. Evremond, *Oeuvres meslées*, London, 1705, ii. 106.

Porpora already mentioned, Mich. Fini, Ign. Fiorillo, Salvator Perillo, Gaetano
Latilla, Rinaldo di Capua, Giuseppe d'Arena, Genaro Alessandri, Domenico
Paradies, Genaro Manna, Gioacchino Cocchi, Nicola Piccini, Tommaso Traetta,
and Antonio Sacchini all Neapolitans . . [93]

The movement of musicians was therefore rather the reverse of what it
had been. Gone were the days when a Venetian opera composer could
move to Naples and pick up the post of court *maestro di cappella* there, as
P. A. Ziani had done. Prota-Giurleo has informed this author of a document, once in the Naples Archives, relating to the Venetian reaction in
1745 to the news that the Neapolitan court was advertising a competition
for the vacant post of court *maestro di cappella*. Having decided to hold the
competition, the court ordered its diplomats in Rome, Bologna, and
Venice, to spread the news in their areas. The representative in Venice,
Count Finocchietti, replied that he had spoken with several Venetian
musicians about the competition but that none dared attempt it, since they
were 'certain they would not give satisfaction'.[94] The post went to a
Neapolitan, Giuseppe di Maio.[95]

History might have been very different had the major institutions of
music education in Naples and Venice been other than they were. In
Naples there were many charitable institutions looking after either boys
or girls. The four famous for their music were, however, for boys only.
In Venice there were four charitable institutions called 'hospitals' (*ospedali*)
also famous for their music, but these were for girls. [96] The fact that there
were four of each in Naples and Venice seems a point of mere coincidence.
Other points of resemblance do not seem coincidental at all and suggest
similar social and economic conditions in the two cities. Both sets of
schools began to teach music to professional standard in the seventeenth
century. Both came to accept fee-paying boarders as well as orphans. Both
acquired music teachers of the highest competence. Both reached the height
of their fame in the eighteenth century and both experienced financial
trouble and a curtailment of their activities toward the end of it. The point
about the difference in the sexes is important because boys had many more
career prospects than girls when they grew up. The conservatories trained

[93] *A general history of music*, London, 1776–89, iv. 542.
[94] Originally in the Naples Archives, Segreteria casa reale, fasc. 30.
[95] For details of this competition, see Prota-Giurleo, 'Nel bicentenario di Francesco Durante', *Il Fuidoro*, 1955, ii. 17–18.
[96] For more on the Hospitals, see especially D. Arnold, 'Orphans and ladies: the Venetian conservatories (1680–1790)', *RMA*, 1962–3, lxxxix, 31 ff.

their boys with an eye to turning many of them into life-long music professionals. The hospitals insisted their girls leave them either to marry or enter a nunnery. Among reasons why Neapolitan standing in the musical world crept up on the Venetian, this question of career opportunity must be counted.

An entire book could be written on the subject of the movements of Neapolitan composers to and from European capitals during the great eighteenth-century period—of the activities of Duni, Sacchini, and Piccinni, in Paris, for example; of Conforto in Madrid; of Porpora, Guglielmi, and Sacchini, in London; of Jommelli in Stuttgart; of Porpora and Fischietti in Dresden; of Traetta, Paisiello, and Cimarosa in St. Petersburg. It would be hard to say which of these contributed most to the reputation of Naples outside Italy. There might be grounds for saying that none contributed more than Giovan Battista Pergolesi, and he did not travel nearly so far afield. Pergolesi was an important figure in the Neapolitan operatic movement not just for his compositions alone but also for the way in which, after his death, he became its romanticized hero. All evidence to hand suggests he had a successful career from the time he left the Gesù Cristo in 1731 to the year of his death in 1736. Within that period he wrote, among other things, four heroic operas (three of them with comic intermezzos) and two comic operas. He became *maestro di cappella* to the Neapolitan Prince of Stigliano (in 1732), deputy *maestro* to the city of Naples (in 1734), and supernumerary Neapolitan court organist in 1735. A number of his compositions, including some incorrectly attributed to him, achieved popularity after his death to a degree unusual at that time in Italy where fashions favoured the most modern in music. Particularly famous among the correct attributions were the *Stabat Mater* and *Salve Regina*, also one of the intermezzos, *La serva padrona*.[97] Among the artists helping to popularize Pergolesi outside Italy were the small troupes of Italian comedians then travelling through Western Europe performing plays and short comic operas of the type usually known as intermezzos. The most popular intermezzo in their repetoire was undoubtedly *La serva padrona*. This work was performed on 1 August 1752, at the Parisian *Académie royale de musique* by a troupe under Eustachio Bambini. Its success on that occasion helped to provoke the controversy among Parisians over the respective merits of French and Italian opera

[97] For details of Pergolesi performances in the eighteenth century see especially G. Radiciotti, *Giovanni Battista Pergolesi*, *Leben und Werk*, German edn., ed. A-E. Cherbuliez, Zürich, 1954.

called the *Guerre des bouffons*. One fact about the *Guerre* that has not been
commented upon as much as others was its propaganda value for Pergolesi's
music and for Naples, the city he was associated with. There was a remarkable increase from *c.* 1752 in the number of references to Pergolesi in
French correspondence (by the Encyclopaedists especially) and in French
literature on music. Back in 1739 de Brosses had called him 'my charming
Pergolesi'. [98] Later epithets were more extravagant. Grimm in 1754 called
him 'sublime'.[99] In the 1760s d'Orville wrote: 'One knows that this
celebrated musician died very young but lived long enough for his glory.
For the Italians bestowed the title of "Divine" upon him after his death and
all nations have confirmed the title.'[1] What contributed to Pergolesi's
romanticized image was the undoubtedly sad fact of his early death,
coupled with a certain melancholy quality listeners thought they heard in
some of his music, for example in the aria 'Se cerca se dice' from his opera
Olimpiade. Rumours relating to his sad death (as well as to his life) became
exaggerated. There were reports he had been poisoned, and several writers[2]
mentioned these even though most added they were inclined to disbelieve
them. Stories of poisoned musicians were fashionable in the eighteenth
century, since a similar one got about in the 1730s in connection with
Vinci's death,[3] and we are all familiar with the supposed poisoning of
Mozart by Salieri. It is possible that Vinci, who also died comparatively
young, might have been built up as the sentimentalized hero had not
Pergolesi come and taken the spotlight off him. As it was, Pergolesi made
the greater impact upon popular sentiment and imagination.

The sentimental attitude toward Pergolesi after the mid-century was
symptomatic of a new, sentimental view of Naples and its music. This was
a period of 'sensibility' when cultured persons, especially among the
French, were inclined to profess themselves so touched by good music as
to be at times overcome by it. Neapolitan music, being in vogue through
the efforts of Pergolesi and others, tended to become associated with the
exquisite feelings that the man of sensibility sought to experience. And
Naples acquired a special glamour through its association with affecting

[98] *Lettres familières*, i. 387.
[99] F. M. Grimm, Diderot, Raynal, Meister, etc., *Correspondance littéraire*, Paris, 1877, ii. 409.
[1] A. G. Contant d'Orville, *Histoire de l'opéra bouffon*, Amsterdam, 1768, p. 39.
[2] Including J. Hawkins, *A general history of the science and practice of music*, London, 1776, v. 375;
Kelly, *Reminiscences*, i. 33; and J-C.R. de Saint-Non, *Voyage pittoresque ou description des royaumes de
Naples et de Sicile*, Paris, 1781–6, i. 163.
[3] K. L. Pöllnitz, *Lettres et memoires*, 3rd edn., Amsterdam, 1744, ii. 225.

Neapolitan music. Though Frenchmen were perhaps the most flattering in their comments, others also joined in glamourizing the city. The following is from a discussion on verisimilitude in opera that forms part of one of the *Musikalische Dialogen* of Wilhelm Heinse. It tells us nothing about Naples itself. What it does say is that a near-perfect opera would be one acted by the female singers Faustina and Cuzzoni, by the Neapolitan castrato Farinelli, and by Porpora (who was renowned as singing teacher as well as composer), and with text by the Venetian librettist Apostolo Zeno and music by Pergolesi. If all these artists could be brought together and their opera performed in Naples, the result would be, literally, out of this world.

Whoever has seen an excellent opera performed in Naples will be in no doubt that an opera can so delude a man and made him forget its improbable nature that he will believe he is seeing the true Alexander, the true Dido, and the true Hercules [on the stage]. The heaving bosoms afflicted by anguish and the copious tears rolling down the sorrowful faces of the tender and passionate Italian ladies will prove the point for him. Should there still be someone with such a matter-of-fact outlook he wishes to consider these tears sign of the wild nature of the Italians, let him observe the faces of the French and English at these operas, and their tears will tell him that he is neither a man nor less a god but a mere thinking machine without humanity. Even the figures of the castratos which are often rather unsuitable for the parts they play will not hinder the deception. If as well Faustini, Cuzzoni, Farinelli, and Porpora, have suitable parts, if at the same time an Apostolo Zeno has expressed the characters' passions in the language of the Muses, and a Pergolesi has felt its accents in his soul—oh then how little can a man know of nature who considers these characters' song unnatural! He is not worthy of feeling happiness![4]

Whoever examines late eighteenth-century literature on Italian music will notice two lines of thought in it that have relevance to our study. With regard to Naples, most writers, though not Burney, tended to accept the view that it was still the musical centre of Italy. With regard to Italian opera as a whole, Italian writers especially took the gloomy view that standards of composition and performance were falling. If Italian opera was not so good as it once was, was opera at Naples so good? And was Naples beginning to live on its past reputation? Certain foreigners visiting Naples in the late 1700s saw no Neapolitan 'decline'. Friedrich Meyer, writing of his experiences around 1783–4, was as enthusiastic as any previous writer over the beauty of the S. Carlo theatre, the stage pro-

---

[4] Publ. Altenburg, 1805, pp. 123–5. On p. 8 the editor, J. F. R. Arnold, states that the work was probably written around 1776 or 1777.

ductions, and the quality of the singing to be heard there. The orchestra apparently played with such verve that its tempi got faster and faster, and *andante* often ended up as *allegro*. But such a fault, he implied, was really the result of strength among the players rather than of weakness. And once they were accompanying a soloist, then everything blended into 'a superlatively effective harmony'.[5] The Spanish dramatist, D. Leonardo F. de Moratin, was in Naples for most of carnival 1793–4 and attended the S. Carlo opera as a matter of course. Like certain earlier visitors he was prevented by the chatter and by the size of the theatre from hearing all the music. But more important are his statements on the general condition of music in the city and the status of Neapolitan musicians in the Italy of their day. Naples, he believed, was the centre of music education. All Italians thought so. Living Neapolitan composers had not fallen from the high standards of their predecessors, and operas written for Naples were still performed afterwards in theatres elsewhere. Of all Italian composers living, who wrote primarily for the theatre, one third at least were Neapolitan; and this third included many of the most notable—Cimarosa, Paisiello, Tarchi, Traetta, Guglielmi, Andreozzi, Fioravanti.[6] Among those mentioned here Traetta was in fact dead already; Guglielmi, Paisiello, and Cimarosa, were then firmly established composers of the older generation; and Angelo Tarchi, Gaetano Andreozzi, and Valentino Fioravanti, represented a younger generation that posterity has all but forgotten everything about. Additional evidence of the fine reputation of Naples among foreigners is contained in the correspondence of Mozart and his family. From Milan, in March 1770, Leopold Mozart wrote that he and Wolfgang might have to spend the following winter in Naples 'which is such an important centre'.[7] In fact their visit to Naples was in the summer and could only be a short one. Wolfgang again thought of going to Naples in 1777 on the suggestion of the Bohemian composer Joseph Misliweczek; 'and certainly', as he then wrote, 'it is a real distinction to have written operas in Italy, especially for Naples'.[8] Finally, we should recall the opinion of the Belgian composer, André Grétry, who received much of his musical training in Rome and who later, in his *Mémoires* (Paris, 1789), declared he would ideally like to send five singing and five composition pupils to

[5] *Darstellungen aus Italien*, Berlin, 1792, iii. 361–3.

[6] Quoted in G. Roberti, 'La musica in Italia nel secolo XVIII secondo le impressioni di viaggiatori stranieri', *RMI*, 1901, viii. 549–50.

[7] *The Letters of Mozart and his family*, ed. Andersen, London, 1938, i. 174.

[8] Ibid., i. 443–4.

Naples to be educated.[9] It was di Giacomo who wondered whether, if Grétry had visited Naples and seen the conditions in the conservatories as Burney saw them, he would have been so keen on the idea.[10]

If there was a decline in Neapolitan music therefore, where is the evidence? Some might say that the best evidence for or against is in the musical scores—and this matter we wish to discuss later. It becomes increasingly difficult to talk about Neapolitans alone as the century progresses since they mixed so in with the Italian musical community as to become almost indistinguishable from it. Many of the leading authors in Italy, notably Algarotti (in *Saggio sopra l'opera in musica*, 1756), and Arteaga (in *Delle rivoluzioni del teatro musicale italiano*, 1783–5), made no distinction between Neapolitan and other composers and considered all part of the total Italian scene. Neither of these writers was enthusiastic about what he saw of contemporary Italian opera and neither was very optimistic. One notices in both cases, though especially in Arteaga's, a rather fatalistic view that it was inevitably on the down grade. This was much bound up with his theory of the rise and fall of art: 'Human affairs cannot remain for long in the same state. Like the curve described in the heavens by the planets around their central body, the path of the arts has an origin, rise, and fall, as unalterable and certain as the courses of the stars.'[11] To him the peak of perfection in Italian opera had been reached in the late seventeenth and early eighteenth centuries. This was 'the golden century of Italian music'.[12] Now that Italian opera was on the decline, do not be surprised, he said, if other nations capture a branch of that 'fortunate laurel that was destined by heaven to grow and thrive only upon privileged Italian ground'.[13] No one need imagine of course that the idea of a recent decline in art was a new one in the second half of the eighteenth century. It had more relevance though to Italians at that time than earlier. The country was no longer as prominent a source of instrumental music as it had been. In opera its singers were no longer so uniformly competent.[14] The most exciting operatic innovation of the time, Gluck's reform, was foreign to the Italian ethos. If anyone furthermore was looking for reasons why any part of Italy, say Naples, was producing fewer superb musicians than it used to, he could conveniently turn to the theory as an explanation.

[9] p. 492.   [10] *I quattro antichi conservatorii*, i. 255–6.
[11] 1st edn., Bologna, ii. 1.
[12] This is the title of chapt. 9 of vol. i (p. 275).
[13] ii. 2.
[14] Cf. p. 64, below.

The 'inevitability' of the decline of art excused a multitude of sins and saved a more thorough examination of the subject.

One reason for the decline in numbers of Neapolitan musicians was the contraction and then closure of one conservatory after another. But these numbers never actually dwindled to nothing. The nineteenth-century *collegio* carried on the function of the old conservatories and was itself later to train some fine musicians, including Saverio Mercadante and Vincenzo Bellini. The chief difference between eighteenth- and nineteenth-century Naples was the difference in the percentage of the Italian musical élite taught there. The eighteenth century was undoubtedly the greater period of Neapolitan music and music education. One of the few problems remaining is to decide if and when the great Neapolitan operatic movement of the eighteenth century properly closed. Did it finish with the death of the last great composer to come from the old conservatories (would this be Paisiello, who died in 1816, or Zingarelli, who lived till 1837?) Or in view of the continuity of teaching traditions between the two centuries, could it be said that the period never ended and that Pergolesi and Bellini belong to the same movement? The material in the succeeding chapters of this book hardly deals with anything after *c.* 1790, for by this date the amount of talent emerging from the conservatories had dwindled considerably and hereon the impact of Neapolitans everywhere seems the impact of individuals rather than of a group. Nineteenth- and twentieth-century views of when the Neapolitan movement ended have been of two basic kinds. The first is that the movement, or the 'Neapolitan school' (a phrase implying some kind of teacher-pupil relationship), ended with Paisiello and Cimarosa.[15] The second, minority, view is that the movement was continuous and unending. One of the latter's strongest advocates was Francesco Florimo, who, in his *La scuola musicale di Napoli* (1880–2), considered the school to stretch from the Renaissance, and the birth of the conservatories, right through to the time he wrote.[16] He would have the

---

[15] This view is already implicit in certain statements stemming from early nineteenth-century Neapolitan sources, see E. Taddei, *Del Real Teatro di S. Carlo*, Naples, 1817, p. 8; also the anonymous review of F. S. Kandler's *Cenni storico-critici intorno alla vita ed alle opere del compositore di musica, G. A. Hasse* (first published Venice, 1820) in the Neapolitan *Giornale del regno delle Due Sicilie* (28 September 1821, issue no. 161).

A less common belief is that Zingarelli ended the Neapolitan line, see the statement, made without explanation, that he was 'the last great maestro of the Neapolitan school' in *Dizionario Musicale Larousse*, Italian edn., Milan, 1961, iii. 418.

[16] The same attitude had previously permeated the Marchese di Villarosa's *Memorie dei compositori di musica del regno di Napoli*, Naples, 1840; see especially p. vii (preface).

school spread to include composers with any kind of link with the city. So on his list came Handel, Gluck, Schwanberg, Mozart, J. Haydn (through his connections with Porpora), and Meyerbeer (through his with Tritto).[17] If we accept this sort of proposition, we might as well say the Neapolitans leavened the entire loaf. In order not to get into difficulties trying to explain the Neapolitan characteristics of the music of composers as disparate as some of these, it seems best to limit the term 'Neapolitan' to composers with a close, personal contact with the city.[18] There is plenty here for Neapolitans to be pleased about, without having to exaggerate their influence unduly.

[17] 1882, ii. 14–15.

[18] This definition of a Neapolitan composer avoids all question of musical style. Opinions expressed this century to the effect that Neapolitan operatic music had sensuous, popular, non-intellectual characteristics are misleading in that they may lead to the inclusion within the Neapolitan category of certain composers with no direct connections with the city and the exclusion of others with direct connections.

Heroic Opera—the Texts

IN the previous chapter all the emphasis was on the musicians of Naples as though poets and literature did not enter into the question of Neapolitan opera. If anyone asks whether the Neapolitans produced as influential a school of librettists as of composers, the short answer is 'no'. And if the question is confined to heroic opera of the late seventeenth and eighteenth centuries, then the answer is that there were very few Neapolitan librettists of note. Andrea Perrucci (1651–1704), author of the important book *Dell'arte rappresentativa premeditata ed all'improvviso* (1699), is the obvious name that springs to mind when one searches for Neapolitans who wrote librettos in the late seventeenth century—and he wrote very few, the most famous being *Stellidaura vendicata* (1674), because it was set by Provenzale, and *Chi tal nasce tal vive o vero L'Alessandro Bala* (1677–8), because of Rolland's attempt to ascribe its music to Provenzale.[1] Probably the best-known librettist of Neapolitan origin in the first decades of the next century was Sebastiano Biancardi, otherwise known as Domenico Lalli (1679–1741), who spent most of his creative career in North Italy.[2] He started writing librettos for Venetian theatres *c.* 1710. Most of his subsequent work first appeared in that city, though he wrote a few texts for other places.[3] Three of his librettos are known to have been premiered at the Neapolitan S. Bartolomeo: *Il gran Mogol* (set by Mancini, 1713), *Tigrane* (A. Scarlatti, 1715), and *Cambise* (A. Scarlatti, 1719).

If we proceed to examine the situation in the mid-eighteenth century, we find Neapolitans no more interested than before in controlling the literary trends of their own or anyone else's heroic opera. This was the time when the librettist Pietro Metastasio was at the peak of his fame. Napoli-Signorelli, in his *Vicende della coltura delle due Sicilie* (1784–6), exaggerated a little in saying that Metastasio's librettos were 'almost

[1] *Histoire de l'opéra en Europe*, p. 190 n. M. Scherillo, *L'opera buffa napoletana*, Naples, edn. of 1916, pp. 37 ff., provides a synopsis of another Perrucci libretto, *Epaminonda*, produced at the Neapolitan Royal Palace in 1684 with music by S. de Luca.

[2] Reasons for Biancardi's flight from Naples in the first instance are in Scherillo, *L'opera buffa*, pp. 492–3.

[3] Ibid., pp. 498–502, gives a list of Biancardi's librettos with places and dates of first performance.

always' chosen by the S. Carlo management in the mid-century. Nevertheless Metastasio, then resident in Vienna, was far and away the most popular librettist with the high-class Neapolitan public. If the S. Carlo management did not choose his work, then they tended to take some older libretto and use that. The contemporary Neapolitan poet hardly got a chance at all. Napoli-Signorelli knew of only one who did:

But there was no one, so far as I know, who dared expose his librettos to comparison with those of Metastasio which were almost always performed [at the S. Carlo]. To my knowledge Duke Morvilli [*sic*] was the only one who managed to obtain performances of [two of] his works, called *L'incendio di Troja* and *La disfatta di Dario*.[4] These were quite successful, in spite of their weak poetry, because of the stage decorations and the music of the erudite Pasquale Cafora [*sic*].[5]

It is not the case that there were no dramatists or literary figures in Naples—Napoli-Signorelli gives considerable space to them in volume five of his *Vicende*. But it does mean very few seriously wrote for or tried to influence the high-class music theatre. 'Neapolitan opera' of the heroic kind is therefore hardly 'Neapolitan' so far as its texts are concerned. The major eighteenth-century librettists were Roman, Venetian, or came from some other part of Northern Italy. Managements of the S. Bartolomeo and S. Carlo theatres in Naples imported the majority of their librettos and used them with whatever changes of text were necessary to suit local, Neapolitan conditions. Most of these librettos had already been set to music and heard elsewhere, so they were not new at the time Neapolitans heard them. The most important point perhaps is that librettos used at Naples were not so different, in spite of adaptation, from those used in other Italian cities or even in certain cities outside Italy altogether.

If we look back to the situation in a city like Venice in the mid-seventeenth century, that is at about the time opera in Naples began, we note librettists having to write for commercial theatres whose audiences wanted pure entertainment with a comparatively large amount of tuneful music and plenty of lavish scenery. Operas were not serious works in which music and scenery came second and third to high-minded poetry. This was a period when librettists protested they had little influence over opera as an art-form. Libretto prefaces of the 1660s and '70s abound with complaints about the commercialism of the music theatre, about the

---

[4] *La disfatta di Dario* (text by C. Morbilli, music by P. Cafaro) was performed at the S. Carlo in 1756, *L'incendio di Troia* at the same theatre in 1757.

[5] P. Napoli-Signorelli, *Vicende*, v (1786). 558–9.

current disregard of the well-known rules of drama (as these were allegedly laid down by the ancients), and about the concessions librettists are forced to make to corrupt, contemporary taste. Not before the late 1680s and early '90s did the librettists' attitude change fundamentally. And then it was towards asserting their right to an equal say with the other artists in the operatic team. By improving the libretto and making it more comparable with the great dramas of the past, they hoped to make the opera a 'literary' piece as well as a musical and a scenic one.

Since the 1640s the Italian operatic scenario had normally been based on an episode, or episodes, from classical history. Except for the names of the characters, however, nothing very 'classical' remained in it. The actions of the main characters—the kings, queens, princes, and their advisors—were determined by ambitions of political power, by sentiments of love, or by both. Within their circle they plotted the downfall of rivals, formed cabals, eavesdropped and spied on each other. Equivocal behaviour, half-heard conversations, interrupted messages, were usually wrongly interpreted and led to heightened animosity and passion. Decisions were arbitrarily made and just as arbitrarily reversed. Some characters masqueraded in clothes of the other sex in order to gain entry into the circle and trace their lovers. These and other intricacies produced a plot with fast action and often with humorous moments. Strikingly out of keeping with the rest was the denouement, which had by convention to be a happy one with a minimum of bloodshed. The librettist, having involved his characters in a series of irresolvable entanglements, then had to sort them all out. At this moment in the work characters became conciliatory, agreed to marry the correct partner whom they had resisted all the way through, and allotted the kingdom or the political power to the rightful owner of it. Around the last decade of the century librettists began to change the spirit of the drama by reducing the number of separate actions and events. They allowed their characters more time to reflect on what they were doing. The number of characters was reduced from ten, twenty, or more, to an approximate six to ten—in the early eighteenth century it came down further to between five and seven. The number of humorous interludes was reduced, and so was that of the comic characters in them. These comedians—whom we have not yet mentioned—were the lower-class characters who acted the part of nurses, pages, and other servants. Other characters that were popular back in the 1640s and '50s—deities, magicians, allegorical figures— now appeared but rarely.

The obvious source of inspiration to the librettist of the new movement was the classical-style tragedy (including modern ones by Corneille and Racine). But it is worth mentioning that most writers were also attracted by poetry and drama of the previous great age of Italian literature, that of the late sixteenth century. Suggestions have been made that this late-Renaissance influence, which made itself felt in many branches of Italian literature, had a superficial rather than profound effect.[6] One thing it did do was re-awaken interest in the pastoral. Several operas with pastoral scenarios were written and performed in Italy between *c.* 1695 and *c.* 1710. Librettists used this theme rather less after *c.* 1710, but they preserved something of the pastoral's spirit for the next thirty years or so in operatic arias referring to creatures like lions, bees, and turtle-doves. This 'countryside', or 'nature-orientated', element was often imitated in the music, though not always. Italian composers of the time tended not to be over-concerned with musical pictorialism.

Adriano Morselli, Andrea Silvani, Frigimelica Roberti, Apostolo Zeno, and other Venetian librettists of the end of the seventeenth century and opening of the eighteenth adopted a confident tone in their libretto prefaces, that is in the sections called 'synopsis' (*argomento*), or 'to the reader' (*a chi legge*). Gone is the tendency to depreciate the librettist's efforts, to declare that the work of the composer, singers, or stage designer, will make up for the insufficiencies of the text and that the Venetian public determines taste and must be pleased. Writers have ceased to apologize for themselves and attempt to be more didactic. They defend themselves against the argument that the text does not obey the rules of the Aristotelean unities. They produce abundant classical quotations to prove the historical source from which the plot springs, even if that source, as before, provides little more than the place of action and the names of the chief characters. Precedents for original treatment of a historical or pastoral theme are traced to Ovid, Horace, Virgil, and other humanist sources. The name of a modern tragedian, for example, Racine, may be used in support. It is perhaps significant that Apostolo Zeno (1668–1750), the most famous writer of the new movement, was a historiographer and expert on coins as well as writer of dramatic texts. His scholarly thinking comes through in a work like *Sirita* (performed in Vienna, 1719, with music by A. Caldara) in the preface of which he proclaimed that the main chain of events followed history throughout and was not the product of his imagination.

---

[6] See J. M. Baroni, 'La lirica musicale di Pietro Metastasio', *RMI*, 1905, xii. 385.

In most of his librettos, however, he had to elaborate his source considerably to suit contemporary taste. In the preface to *Cajo Fabbrizio* (Vienna, A. Caldara, 1729) we read that one of the female characters is fictitious: 'Sestia, Fabricius' daughter who together with other Romans is made prisoner by Pyrrhus, is introduced to further the amorous intrigues, without which it seems no play is thought acceptable nowadays.'[7] In general Zeno tried hard to find that happy mean between what was acceptable to his patrons (who evidently still liked a play with romantic intrigues and complicated interrelationships) and what was reasonable according to his own, severe concept of tragedy. In the preface to *Venceslao* (Venice, C. Polaroli, 1703) we find him trying to square with himself his decision to have an improbable yet popular-style ending. The plot concerns Casimir, elder son of King Wenceslas, who kills his younger brother (thinking him to be someone else) during a struggle for the favours of the princess Erenice. The father, in spite of love for his son, feels bound to honour the law and commit him to death, and would so have committed him but for the timely intercession of Erenice and others. Casimir, for long unrepentant in his love, suddenly changes his attitude at the end of the opera and marries another lady whom the king wishes him to marry. This is a convenient about turn which allows the opera to terminate on a happy note. It is absolutely within the tradition of seventeenth-century operatic endings. What is interesting is that Zeno sees fit to defend Casimir's change of heart:

The sudden change in Casimir's character, after his act of unwitting fratricide, is contrary neither to Moral Law nor to the teachings of Poetry. A bad person becomes good only with difficulty, it is true. The depths of sin and the heights of virtue are achieved only by degrees. With the reform of reason, however, imminent danger of death, or horror with violence, has sometimes caused similar changes.

Zeno's eighteenth-century supporters and apologists placed much emphasis on the moral message his librettos were alleged to convey. The Abbate Conti extolled Zeno's ability to dramatize cases of mature judgement, forgiveness of personal injury, moderation in good times and strength in bad, unshakable friendship, conjugal love, and other virtues Zeno discovered in stories from the classics.[8] Gaspare Gozzi[9] and Napoli-

---

[7] The full text of *Cajo Fabbrizio* has been republished in A. della Corte, *Drammi per musica dal Rinuccini allo Zeno*, Turin, 1958, ii. 623 ff.

[8] A. Conti, *Prose e poesie*, Venice, 1739, i. (preface).

[9] See R. Giazotto, *Poesia melodrammatica e pensiero critico nel settecento*, Milan, 1952, p. 75.

Signorelli[10] repeated Conti's statement. A modern reader of Zeno's librettos will agree there is in them some glamourizing of virtue and of the decision to act virtuously. Acts of heroism are associated with moral rather than with physical bravery. Self-sacrifice is extolled rather than chivalry. To accent the moral content, characters pronounce little homilies on the advantages of doing right. Kings make asides to the audience (and to princely ears in that audience) to the effect that they are human and face moral problems like anyone else. The clash between personal inclination and moral law—this is a common theme in classical-type tragedies and one Zeno tried to exploit. Wenceslas's uncertainty in *Venceslao* whether or not to kill his son is a case in point. Whether the vacillations of Zeno's heroes are really the result of a deep, internal struggle—the sort of struggle that goes on within the soul of one of Racine's characters, for example—is a matter of personal interpretation. To some these vacillations will appear mere avoidance of the unpleasantness that might follow if a decision were made. Most of Zeno's characters in fact make decisions for other than moral reasons. When they fashionably talk of *virtude* and *onore*, they are really playing with these concepts to serve their immediate and long-term interests. The concepts are not well enough expressed in the language entirely to engage our sympathies for the person expressing them, and they therefore all the more readily appear a structural device to keep the drama in motion.

Anyone reviewing the situation in the 1690s and early 1700s will note the gradual elimination from opera of the nurses, pages, and other court retainers who had been its traditional clowns .By the time Zeno published his first libretto in 1695, these had already disappeared from many operas at Venice, and he simply followed the trend. There was still a place in some of his earliest librettos for a solitary servant—called Nesso (in *Eumene*, 1697), Adolfo (in *Odoardo*, 1698), Niso (in *Lucio Vero*, 1700), etc.—who descended from the comic page of earlier opera. But this servant could hardly be called comic in the accepted sense, for he had few lines to sing, no companion to banter with, and little to do other than pass messages (which he managed rather incompetently). The singers who acted this part in the first, Venetian productions must have possessed limited musical capabilities, which further diminished its importance. They were rarely permitted to sing an aria, there being in fact no arias at all for some of them. The need to stress that we are here dealing with Venetian productions is

---

[10] *Storia critica de' teatri antichi e moderni*, 2nd edn., Naples, 1790, vi. 262.

because the presence, or absence, of comic elements in opera of the time depended more on the taste of local audiences than on that of the writer. The disappearance of comic servants from many operas at Venice in the approximate period 1695–1705 was not paralleled by a similar disappearance of comic servants from opera everywhere else. When Zeno librettos were accepted, for example, by the management of the S. Bartolomeo in Naples, they had, at least up to *c.* 1720, to be adapted to allow for more comic acting. The ramifications of this will have to be discussed on a later page. The important thing to note now is that Zeno's disinclination to write comedy fitted in well with the theatrical situation in Venice, where he worked till 1718 when he was appointed court poet and historiographer at the court of Vienna.

There is no record that Zeno visited Naples. The best-known librettist of the period who did was Silvio Stampiglia (1664–1725), a Roman and founder member in 1690 of the influential Arcadian society. His arrival in Naples came in the wake of the appointment of Medinaceli as viceroy in 1696, and must be related to the viceroy's wish to make the Neapolitan opera equal to any in Italy. Of his librettos written during the Medinaceli era, three—*La caduta dei decemviri* (1697), *Eraclea* (1700), and *Tito Sempronio Gracco* (1702)—were first set by A. Scarlatti. Two others, *Il trionfo di Camilla* (1696, first set by G. Bononcini), and *Partenope* (1699, first set by L. Mancia, alias Manzi), acquired popularity. From 1706 to 1714 he was court poet in Vienna, holding the post later held by Zeno and, after Zeno, by Metastasio. By virtue of that particular appointment his name became associated with theirs and consequently also with improvements in the libretto which they were particularly responsible for. There are few references to him in mid-eighteenth-century sources, but more in those of the last quarter of the century—which argues a revival of his reputation. Precisely what he was good at was open to debate. Napoli-Signorelli thought he was one of the first authors to provide happy endings in opera.[11] S. Arteaga disputed this and accused Napoli-Signorelli of not having checked his sources.[12] In Arteaga's view—which turns out to be equally mistaken—Stampiglia was among those who purged opera of comic elements, simplified scenarios, and limited the need for complicated stage machinery. No one from Arteaga on has thought highly of Stampiglia's literary talent. The dialogue in his earlier dramas written for Naples in the

---

[11] *Storia critica de' teatri antichi e moderni*, 1st edn., Naples, 1777, p. 333.
[12] *Delle rivoluzioni*, 1st edn., i. 324–5.

period 1696–1702 contains a great many short, staccato sentences which characters toss about between themselves or pass, as asides, to the audience. The language is bald in the extreme and only attempts to rise above the ordinary when extreme emotions are aroused or gallant feelings expressed. Even at these moments Stampiglia is far from original, contenting himself to use characteristically baroque similes that others had used already. The person in any kind of difficulty compares himself to a ship seeking port or striking a rock (*scoglio*). The lover provoked beyond measure threatens to divide his bowels from his heart (*le viscere dal core*). His lady's face is compared to the sun, her eyes to the stars, her cheeks to roses, and her breasts to white snow. As for the plots, they are hardly influenced by any desire to emulate the best tragedians of the past. Stampiglia's earlier librettos are really galant comedies in which the paths of the pairs of lovers (mostly of princely rank) cross and recross until such time as the story should conveniently end. Heroism of the kind connected with manly courage is hardly known, and the hero's greatest act of self-sacrifice is to hand over his girl friend to his opponent. The climax in *Partenope* (1699) comes when Rosmira, dressed in male attire and calling herself Eurimene, challenges her former betrothed, Arbace, to a duel. By a complicated series of manoeuvres she has isolated him from Partenope, Queen of Naples, whom she suspects is susceptible to his charm. Now she is making him pay the price of his infidelity. The idea of making a man and a woman clash in a duel goes way back in Italian literature, and was to be used again by Zeno and Metastasio. What makes this particular clash unusual is its comic denouement. Arbace, well aware who his opponent really is and unwilling to fight with her, finally unmasks her not by any forthright statement about her identity but by declaring his intention to have a fight 'with bared breast':

> Ma combattere io voglio a petto ignudo.

At which point the lady is forced to disclose who she is and the story collapses into a giggle.

After a long period of absence Stampiglia returned to Naples in 1722 and stayed there till his death three years later. There is no record that he wrote any new librettos at this time, though he did revise some of his old ones to bring them up to date for new productions at the S. Bartolomeo. In view of his connections with the city, it is interesting that no one thereafter tried to suggest he was Neapolitan. Not even nineteenth-century

Neapolitans tried to suggest it—and we pick on nineteenth-century Neapolitans because of the way some of them did their best to magnify and inflate the Neapolitan involvement in eighteenth-century music.[13] If Neapolitan scholars had been at all chauvinistic about local librettos, they might have conjured up some small school of Neapolitan librettists. And they would have had the greatest librettist of the eighteenth century to pick on, for Pietro Metastasio (1698–1782) lived and worked in Naples between 1719 and 1724.

Metastasio's period of residence in Naples coincided with those formative, early years of his life when he abandoned the study of law and began seriously to write for the music theatre. A serenata of his, *Angelica*, was set to music by Porpora and performed in Naples, in 1720. Another, *Gli orti esperidi*, also with Porpora's music, was heard there in 1721. In 1723 he patched up a late seventeenth-century libretto by Domenico David, *La forza della virtù*,[14] renamed it *Siface*, and got Feo to set it to music. His first work of real importance, *Didone abbandonata*, was produced at the S. Bartolomeo theatre in carnival time, 1724. The music was by Domenico Sarri. This seems the only time in the eighteenth century when a Neapolitan theatre secured the first production of a really important libretto of the heroic or tragic kind. We guess the Neapolitans were aware of the importance of the production from the way it was reported in the official *Gazzetta di Napoli* for 8 February. The report is not long, but it is thorough by *Gazzetta* standards. Why Metastasio is not personally mentioned in it is not immediately clear.

In the evening the première was given of a new opera, Didone abbandonata, which, because of the text by a celebrated author, the music by maestro di cappella Domenico Sarro, and the cast (outstanding among whom were Cavalier Niccolò Grimaldi, excellent as Eneas, the virtuosa Marianna Benti Bulgarelli, called la Romanina, as Dido, and the virtuosa Antonia Merighi, as Jarba), drew universal applause from the members of the audience who flocked in great numbers to hear it. The beauty of the work was enhanced by the actors' costumes and by the stage designs, all in perfect taste, especially the last one depicting the lifelike burning of

---

[13] As gross an exaggeration as any was perpetrated by Genaro Grossi in an article on A. Scarlatti in vol. vi of Martuscelli's *Biografia degli uomini illustri del regno di Napoli* (Naples, 1819) in which he declared that Scarlatti had been a conservatory pupil and then a teacher at several conservatories in Naples, that he had begun his career as composer at the court of Bavaria, then moved to Vienna, then to Rome; finally, as a crowning event in his life, Naples 'called him home' (*la patria lo chiamò a se*).

[14] For more information on *La forza della virtù*, see N. Burt, 'Opera in Arcadia', *MQ* 1955, xli. 154 ff.

Carthage. The success of the total production was due to the careful and able management of the impresarios of the said theatre.

Metastasio's version of the Dido legend limits itself to the period immediately prior to and during the departure of Eneas from Carthage; and his departure is timed to coincide with the arrival of Jarba, King of the Moors, a new suitor for the hand of Queen Dido. To some extent Eneas's unwillingness to check Jarba's activities is determined by the fact that fate has decreed he shall sail away to Rome. In other words, he has no control over his ultimate actions and this limitation puts him at a disadvantage which few other heroes created by Metastasio have to cope with. Nevertheless he shares with these others the trait of being unable to resolve opposing inclinations of love and duty. His love for the queen and her pleadings drag him one way, and destiny drags him another. In his dialogue he stammers, leaves sentences unfinished, and in other ways shows his indecision. The one thing he is certain of is his virtuous character; and this he upholds even to his final exit when he sings the aria beginning:

> A trionfar mi chiama
> Un bel desio d'onore;
> (A fine wish for honour calls me to victory)

and simultaneously leaves Dido defenceless before Jarba. That Jarba has been permitted to continue court to Dido against her wishes is entirely Eneas' fault. He has saved Jarba's life on three occasions either by refusing to fight with him or by capturing him and then letting him go—because that is the honourable thing to do. Jarba, painted as black as Eneas is white, simply used these reprieves to call in more troops, plot with one of Dido's confidantes, and terrorize Dido herself.

Criticism of this sort of drama will depend on the angle from which it is viewed. It could be said, and not incorrectly, that human indecision is a technique used to activate the plot, and 'virtue' is a device used to excuse the human indecision. Eighteenth-century commentators on Metastasio's librettos tended to regard plot as a structural background for character portrayal, and the valour/virtue of the characters as the important thing. The first criticism of Metastasio appeared in the *Considerazioni sopra il Demofoonte* (Venice, 1735) of F. Rosellini, who took the librettist to task on this matter of characterisation.[15] He cited the cases of two characters, Timante and Creusa, in *Demofoonte* (set by Caldara, Vienna, 1733), a libretto presupposing as part of its background the secret marriage of the

---

[15] Cf. Giazotto, *Poesia melodrammatica*, pp. 47 ff.

alleged son of King Demofoonte, Timante, and Dircea. The marriage was a secret one because of a law forbidding princes to marry commoners. Timante was only the supposed son of Demofoonte, in fact, since he had been swopped at birth with Dircea, and neither knew the fact. Neither he nor she therefore connected themselves with a terrible decree of the oracle that a maiden should be sacrificed once a year until such time as the 'innocent usurper of the kingdom' was 'known to himself.' During the opera Demofoonte commands Timante to marry Creusa, and Timante uses every technique, including threats and force, to circumvent the order without uncovering his marriage. In so doing he offends practically everybody. At a moment of crisis Dircea is condemned to be sacrificed, and Timante is condemned along with her. At this moment a document conveniently disclosing that Dircea is Demofoonte's daughter stays the execution, though it makes Timante believe he has married his sister. Then another document discloses he is the true son of Dircea's supposed father, Matusio, and the story ends with everything forgiven. The main argument of Rosellini was that Timante's words and actions throughout the drama are too devious and contorted to permit anyone to think him a true hero and that the extremes of behaviour he exhibits are foreign to any real person. He suggested that Creusa, similarly, alters character too radically, for she plots Timante's death at one point, yet pleads for his life later. Metastasio did not answer this criticism in writing till 1747, when he was in correspondence with the publisher Bettinelli.[16] Timante, he wrote, is a 'valorous youth', subject to moments of passion but also capable of clear thought and impeccable behaviour. Creusa is a princess very conscious of her rank and beauty. Rejected by Timante, she throws herself into schemes of vendetta, yet allows reflection to modify her feelings afterwards. 'It seemed to me', wrote Metastasio, 'that this should be considered not as incongruity of character but as diversity in the situation, without which every person in the play would appear insipid and unreal'.

The majority of eighteenth-century commentators thought that Metastasio's characters were worthy examples of the type suitable in tragedy. Antonio Planelli in his *Dell'opera in musica* of 1772 asserted that one of the great advantages of modern tragedy over the old was that there was room in the modern kind for the 'supremely virtuous character'.[17]

---

[16] See *Lettere ed opere postume del Sig. Ab. Pietro Metastasio*, ed. d'Ayala, Venice, 1808, i. 248–9.
[17] Publ. Naples, p. 75.

This paragon may still have human 'weaknesses' which show from time to time, but he will not have any serious 'vices'.[18] Metastasio's character Temistocle (in the libretto of that name first set by Caldara, 1736) is just such a character regardless of the fact that he appears 'overburdened' (oppreso) by his sense of virtue and sometimes fails to live up to it. Metastasio's detractors claimed to the contrary that the true hero should always be equal to himself, maintain his poise and self-control, and preserve a fairly rigid stance before opposition. Rosellini was the first of those who compared the heroes of Metastasio and Zeno to prove that Zeno's were more vigorous and more competent. Then as now, of course, everything depended on just what was meant by words like 'virtue' and 'heroism'. In more recent times the tendency has been to assert that Metastasio's heroes are more effeminate than manly, and that they are more interested in their psychological problems than in anything else.[19] From the time of de Sanctis in the last century the notion has prevailed that there is something vaguely comic in their indecision and vacillations.[20] Giazotto, referring back to the eighteenth-century argument over the character of Timante, finds he is merely ingenuous.[21] All seem united in believing that eighteenth-century criticism placed too much emphasis on the moral and didactic qualities of the works under review.

The commencement of Metastasio's activities as librettist in the 1720s happened to coincide with a great expansion of the Neapolitan musical influence; and throughout that decade, the most formative of his career, he worked more closely with Neapolitan-trained composers than with any other group. The list below gives the first performances of his early librettos together with who set them. The composers are Neapolitan in each instance. Sometimes almost contemporaneous first productions were arranged in two cities.

NAME OF WORK:	COMPOSER:	PLACE AND DATE:
Didone abbandonata	D. Sarri	Naples, carnival 1724
Siroe re di Persia	L. Vinci	Venice, carnival 1726
Catone in Utica	L. Vinci	Rome, carnival 1728
Ezio	N. Porpora	Venice, autumn 1728
Semiramide riconosciuta	{ N. Vinci	Rome, carnival 1729
	{ N. Porpora	Venice, carnival 1729

[18] *Dell'opera in musica*, p. 79.
[19] See L. Russo, *Metastasio*, 3rd edn., Bari, 1945, pp. 133 ff.
[20] F. de Sanctis, *History of Italian literature*, English edn., trans. Redfern, London, 1931, ii. 848–9.
[21] *Poesia melodrammatica*, p. 57.

NAME OF WORK:	COMPOSER:	PLACE AND DATE:
Alessandro nell'Indie	L. Vinci	Rome, winter 1729
Artaserse	{ L. Vinci	Rome, carnival 1730
	{ J. Hasse	Venice, carnival 1730

On taking up his imperial appointment at Vienna in 1730, Metastasio tended to work with musical employees of that court, few of whom were Neapolitan, or with musicians on a visit there. This meant that Neapolitans obtained fewer 'firsts' among the settings of his dramas after 1730 than they had done before. But Metastasio kept contact after 1730 with musicians with Neapolitan connections, Hasse especially. And to the extent that both the Neapolitans and Metastasio were undisputed masters of their respective fields in the mid-century, some interrelation continued to exist between the success of the one and that of the other.

The constant demand everywhere for Metastasio's texts[22] meant a reduced demand for texts by other poets. It also had the effect of discouraging them from seeking new dramaturgical techniques that were out of line with Metastasio's own. For a while patrons were not worried by this. No one other than Metastasio so perfectly understood their desire for a type of tragedy (so-called) which emphasized sensuality and the passion of love, excluded acts of barbarism (on stage at least), and depicted a disastrous turn of events firmly righted by human generosity and compassion. No one else had the same ability to select words with minimum harshness and exploit the 'musical' qualities of the Italian language. No other poet seemed so qualified to write words for musical setting. Metastasio understood the technical processes of composition well enough to try his hand at writing music and once stated he was incapable of writing words to be sung unless he imagined the music for them.[23] Compare his correspondence with Zeno's and we find that he was much happier than Zeno was with having to write for the music theatre. Zeno wrote as though he knew nothing about music and found the techniques of writing for the music theatre conflicting with those dramatic principles he wanted to adopt.[24] Both

---

[22] Some indication of his popularity is the fact that the total number of musical settings of his librettos has been estimated at around 850, see G. Pannain, 'De Sanctis e la musica', *GMN*, 1955, i. 24. U. Rolandi, in *Il libretto per musica*, Rome, 1951, p. 82, has counted up the number of eighteenth- and early nineteenth-century settings of individual librettos and found that *Artaserse*—the most popular of all, it seems—was set by eighty-one composers between 1730 and 1795.

[23] See J. M. Baroni, 'La lirica musicale di Metastasio', *RMI*, 1905, xii. 390, n. 2.

[24] For more about Zeno's views on the compromises necessary to adapt dramas for musical setting, see especially his letters nos. 59 and 756, *Lettere*, 2nd edn., Sansoni, Venice, 1785, i. 121 and iv. 276–8.

dramatists were highly critical of the way opera was set and staged. But Metastasio, unlike Zeno, still had the grace to make generous remarks about composers if deserved and the knowledge and/or sense to make occasional practical suggestions as to how modern music might heighten the effect of his texts.[25]

If we turn now to the question of the technical problems involved in writing for the music theatre, we have first to remind ourselves that opera from its inception contained two fundamentally distinct musical styles, recitative and lyrical song (ensemble, chorus). As opera developed, the two diverged more and more. By the 1650s at the latest librettists were beginning to recognize the two styles by writing in two styles themselves, the bulk of their 'blank' verse of seven- and eleven-syllable lines (*versi sciolti*) being designed for recitative and their short, rhyming stanzas for songs. They also began to identify the lyrical sections typographically by having them inset by the printer. Composers of the mid-seventeenth century did not always follow the librettist's indications, occasionally preferring to set seven- and eleven-syllable lines in a lyrical style, and aria verses as recitative. But by the end of the century librettist and composer were usually at one over what parts of the text should be set in what manner. With the increasing distinction between the styles of recitative and aria came an increasing distinction between their functions. More and more the substance of the action or plot passed into the recitative only, while the arias became lyrical commentaries. The final result in certain eighteenth-century librettos was that the recitative bore all the action there was; and most arias could be removed without damage to the structure. Although a recitative text by Metastasio might superficially appear a self-sufficient text, it would be misleading to believe that the dramatist wrote it without calculating how it would fit into the opera as a whole. The recitative, in other words, is not the exact equivalent of a spoken drama text;[26] and arias are not just lyrical insertions. The point is that when the librettist thought out the plan of his new work, he had to take into account what the

---

[25] Note especially his advice to Hasse on how to set the recitatives of *Attilio Regolo*, (cf. p. 84 below).

[26] Metastasio once blurred the distinction between a libretto and a spoken drama by writing: 'I know by daily experience, that my own dramas are much more certain of success in Italy, when declaimed by comedians, than when sung by musicians'. Quoted in C. Burney, *Memoirs of the life and writings of the Abate Metastasio*, London, 1796, ii. 318. Burney, in a footnote on the same page, declared that, when he went to Italy in 1770, he heard of no successful dramatic representation of a Metastasio drama without music.

singers' and composer's demands for arias were and where these arias should come; and such demands could affect the dramatic plan exposed in his recitative.

One of the striking features of the typical Venetian libretto of the 1670s–'80s period is the relatively large number of short arias it contains. This number has some correspondence, though by no means an exact one, with the large number of predicaments and diverse situations the characters find themselves in during the course of the work. Librettos of the 1690s and following decades show a definite decline in the total number of their arias. The earliest surviving opera by Provenzale, *Lo schiavo di sua moglie*, 1671, has in the region of eighty-nine to ninety lyrical songs and ensembles. This is an approximate number, let it be admitted, since there are some sections on the border line between aria and recitative that may, or may not, be added to the number of songs according to one's personal interpretation. A. Scarlatti wrote sixty arias and ensembles in his setting of Stampiglia's *La caduta dei decemviri*, 1697. A later production of *La caduta*, heard in Naples in 1727 with music by Vinci, contained thirty-nine major arias and ensembles[27] plus four other lyrical items of short duration. These examples are indicative of the general trend. We do not mean to suggest here that opera contained fewer and fewer opportunities for lyrical music. The decline in the number of arias was offset by the growing length of the music of each one, thus necessitating fewer arias per opera. Related to the need for fewer arias was the reduced number of characters, which was in its turn related to the trend toward plot simplification that we have referred to already. So both literary and musical factors contributed to the new-style libretto that was emerging.

Our previous comment that the aria in many eighteenth-century operas was a lyrical commentary might imply a loosening of the ties holding aria and action together. But in another way the ties between the two were actually stronger in the early eighteenth century than they had been in the mid seventeenth. The first decades of the eighteenth were a period when it became customary for the singer to leave the stage immediately following an aria. This meant the librettist had to distribute the arias to suit characters' exits or alternatively plan the exits to suit the number and distribution of arias. By 1730, at the latest, positioning the aria before the exit was a rule of libretto writing. In order for characters to have good motivation for

---

[27] The thirty-nine items mentioned include eight arias and duets sung in comic intermezzos serving as interludes in the work.

entering and then leaving sufficiently often—for the total number of arias per opera in the early 1730s was still in the region of twenty-four or rather over—librettists could not provide too simple a scenario. There still had to be a modicum of political subplots, subsidiary love affairs, confusions of personal identity and the like, to enliven the text. These additions to the main plot could be, and often were, defended on the ground that they provided extra human interest. But they also gave opportunity for a sufficient number of (a) exits, (b) arias to satisfy the singers, impresarios, and others who demanded them.

Each act of an opera was textually divided into so many 'scenes'. Following the practice of the French classical playwrights, Italian librettists of the end of the seventeenth and opening of the eighteenth centuries began to change the scene at the point where a character walked on or off. In earlier, mid-seventeenth-century librettos scene changes had occurred rather at random. The more organized system was of course introduced gradually, and we can find some characters' entries and exits slightly out of phase with scene changes even in librettos by Metastasio, who was as rigid in the application of the system as any. By making the scene change occur at an exit, librettists also ensured that most arias came at the end of scenes. This point is important to the understanding of the chart below, which shows the number of characters on stage per scene per act of Metastasio's *Artaserse* (1730), a fine piece which exhibits the then principles of libretto construction particularly clearly. The prime function of the chart is to demonstrate how the position of lyrical items relates to the movement of characters on and off.[28] The arrangement of arias/exits/ends of scenes in this libretto is just too organized to be in any way accidental, and was obviously worked out at a very early stage of the planning. There are six characters in *Artaserse*.[29] It is usual to find in Metastasio's dramas the character list headed by a sovereign (of either sex) or by a prince close in line of succession. The prince in this case is Artaxerxes. Underneath comes a group of high-ranking persons (often four of them) intimately connected with the prince through political, sentimental, or blood ties. In *Artaserse* they are Arbace and his father Artabano, Arbace's sister Semira, and his

[28] Similar charts were made by Max Fehr (*Apostolo Zeno und seine Reform des Operntextes*, Zürich, 1912, diagrams facing p. 142) to show how characters moved on and off in Corneille's *Le Cid* and in operas from Manelli's *Andromeda* of 1637 to Metastasio's *Attilio Regolo* of 1740/50.

[29] See R. Gerber, *Der Operntypus Johann Adolf Hasses und seine textlichen Grundlagen*, Leipzig, pp. 14 ff., for an examination of the similar character lists and plots in different Metastasio librettos.

girl friend Mandane. Normally the list is completed by one or more *ultime parti*, in this case by Megabise, general and supporter of Artabano. In the chart these names are abbreviated for the sake of convenience. Other abbreviations below the horizontal axis of the chart refer to the exits of characters and to the lyrical items sung. They may be explained as follows:

A = Aria at the end of the scene followed by the exit of the singer.
E = Exit of the singer without an aria.
D = Duet followed by the exit of both singers.
a = Arietta sung at the beginning of the scene.
C = Final chorus.

Artaserse

Chart of the number of characters on stage per scene per act

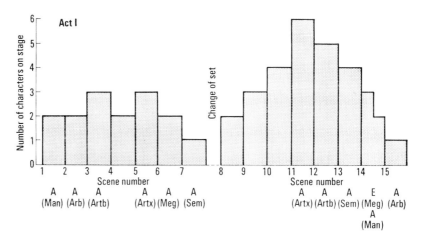

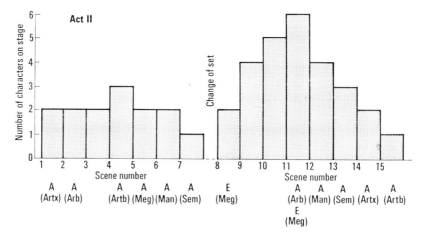

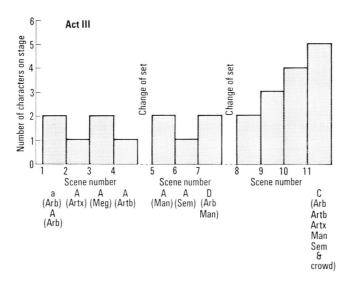

The chart shows firstly that the vast majority of lyrical items are arias, not vocal ensembles. There is merely one duet in *Artaserse*, plus a final chorus of no great length in which the crowd joins with the five main characters. The chart also shows that Megabise, the character lowest in rank, is the only one to leave the stage several times without an aria. This accords with what may be observed in other eighteenth-century Italian operas of the tragic kind, namely, that the singer's chances of leaving the stage without an aria increased if he were playing a subordinate role.[30] Again, the chart shows that each character sings his aria in turn, and that only when all characters have sung their first aria per act is anyone allowed his second. Some remarks by F. S. Quadrio in his *Della storia, e della ragione d'ogni poesia* may be relevant here:

Finally, it should also be noted that these *Ariette* [*i.e.* arias] should be distributed so that each of the top-quality singers has the same number. It is helpful to the performance of the drama that the best voices be equally displayed before the audience. It is also right that equal ground should be given to the more virtuoso singers so that their just value may appear. And, as a last point, it contributes greatly to the peace of mind essential to the singers if they are to perform well. For they often get upset in similar situations by matters of precedence and honour. At the same time care must be taken to ensure that the above-mentioned *Ariette* are not arranged so that three, or four, are placed together for one singer.[31]

[30] In general, the *ultime parti* of Metastasio's dramas come and go without many arias. Some characters in this class, *e.g.* Adreuso (in *Demofoonte*, 1733) and Sebaste and Lisimaco (in *Temistocle*, 1736), are not given arias in every act. Alcandro (in *Olimpiade*, 1733) has no aria at all.

[31] Publ. Milan, vol. iii (parte seconda), 443.

Quadrio's warning against giving one singer three or four adjacent arias seems curious in a publication appearing in 1744. A contemporary librettist with any experience at all would not have given a singer even two adjacent arias of any importance. The most he would have given would be a short *arietta* together with a major aria, the sort of thing we find in scene one of Act III of *Artaserse* where Arbace appears singing a four-line *arietta*, discourses then with Artaxerxes in recitative, then breaks out into a full-length aria just before his departure. By referring to the temperamental nature of singers, Quadrio pinpointed the reason why the arias had to be distributed as they were. The singing profession had become so viciously competitive that no *primo uomo* or *prima donna* worthy of the name could bear to see too great a concentration of interest on another.

There is further evidence that the librettist had to follow the singers' wishes. The case of Carlo Goldoni has often been cited in this connection. In 1733 he suffered the misfortune of having his tragic libretto *Amalasunta* rejected by the singers of a Milanese company because it did not obey the conventions that pleased them. According to his own evidence, which may or may not be accurate, he was advised that the first castrato, the first lady, and the tenor, expected five arias each, the second castrato and second lady four each, and the sixth singer (and the seventh if there was one) three. The fifteen arias of the three leading singers had to be distributed so that two arias expressing the same type of feeling never came next to each other. The arias of the secondary singers had to be considered as a type of *chiaroscuro*, that is, they served to bring those of the chief singers into relief. Goldoni was criticized for having let an important singer leave the stage after a harrowing episode (*scena di forza*) without an aria, also for having left another singer on stage after an aria. He was told that in an opera six or seven stage sets were normal whereas he had given opportunity for three only. His best act was the third, 'but this is also against the rule'.[32]

Many of the above points apply to other operas of the period (see the chart of *Artaserse*), so clearly we have here a set of general principles that

[32] Goldoni's account of the fate of *Amalasunta* first appeared in the complete edition of his *Commedie*, Pasquale, Venice, 1761, xi. 5–6; then again in the *Mémoires de M. Goldoni*, Paris, 1787, i. 219 ff. The *Mémoires* version is slightly different in its particulars. It says the top three singers should have five arias each, the second castrato and second lady three each, while the subordinate singers must be satisfied with anything they get. This revised account therefore lowers the aria total for the less important singers. The revision could well have been prompted by Goldoni's knowledge of the trend toward fewer arias that continued in opera after 1733, the year of his experience with *Amalasunta*.

most people then agreed with. The most puzzling point seems to be the one about a weak third act, for this does not follow on from the rules about arias. We shall have more to say on the decline of the third act later on. For the moment it is worth while examining one aspect of the third act that comes out in the chart of *Artaserse*. The line of the chart is different in Acts I and II from what it is in Act III. Scenes 1–7 of the first two acts show a roughly horizontal line with on average two people on stage per scene. In sections like these during which one person tends to enter as another exits, each scene may have an aria. Provided, furthermore, that the length of each scene does not fluctuate too much, the arias may succeed each other at reasonably even intervals of time. Quite a different technique of moving characters on and off is found in scenes 8–15 of the same two acts. Here the characters come on singly or in groups till all are on stage together. They then depart in turn. For the period when they assemble on stage, no arias occur. The lyrical items all come in the series of scenes that starts with the maximum number of characters on stage and ends with a soliloquy. Act III ends differently from the other two, for it obeys the then standard custom of having most characters on stage for the finish. The final scene ends with a short chorus after the action is over. Metastasio might have decided to bring the characters on at the same moment for this ultimate scene. What he did in several librettos was to build up the number in a series of scenes (in the case of *Artaserse* scenes 8–11) which because of the rule about arias and exits have no arias. The same final scenes provide the denouement, and there is no aria music to supplement it.

All in all the convention that singers leave the stage after an aria affected the librettist's work profoundly and is not the least reason why a libretto differed from spoken drama of the time. In view of the convention's repercussions on Italian opera, we might expect theorists of the late seventeenth and early eighteenth centuries to comment upon it. But in fact there was little published comment, so the evidence as to why it grew is insubstantial. Did the singers leave after an aria, for instance, because they liked the sensation of sweeping offstage to the audience's applause? Did they feel the need to relax after a prominent solo? Or was it generally felt among librettists that a sense of anticlimax was created if a singer relapsed from aria into recitative? The Neapolitan writer, Giuseppe Salvadori, gave the impression in his *Poetica toscana all'uso* (Naples, 1691) that aesthetic reasons were involved: 'Arias can be put at the beginning of scenes, but recitative is better in that position. This arrangement will make the aria more agreeable'.[33] Benedetto Marcello referred to the question of singers' exits in his humorous and well-known *Il teatro alla moda* (1720). It would appear from the way he wrote that the onus of responsibility for the exit aria rested on the librettist, though his remark may be slanted for the best satirical effect rather than for its accuracy: 'He [the poet] will absolutely never allow the singer to make his exit without the customary *canzonetta*, especially when, by a vicissitude of the drama, the latter must go out to die, commit suicide, drink poison, etc.'[34]

The lack of commentary on singers' exits is part of the general silence maintained by late seventeenth- and early eighteenth-century theorists on aria functions. One real reason for the existence of the aria, namely, the pleasure it gave the audience, was hinted at by Salvadori at the point where he advised that the recitative be short, 'so that the listeners can hear the ariette, which they so much desire'.[35] But to the literary intellectual, brought up on humanist theories of the need for theatre to instruct, guide, and stimulate, the creation of pleasure was only one object of opera and not necessarily the most worthy one. Only when the aria had become long sanctified by time and practice did the intellectual cease to regard it as either a necessary, practical measure to please audiences and musicians or else just unnecessary. Not till sometime before the mid-eighteenth century did statements appear on what its ideal function ought to be.

Eighteenth-century opinions on the aria will be found mainly in two types of source. The first is eighteenth-century literature on music: the music lexicon, manual of performance practice, critical essay on music, etc. The second is the eighteenth-century book or essay criticizing opera as a branch of literature and/or of theatre. The Italians produced several works in the second category that give a greater or smaller amount of information on the aria—fewer, surprisingly perhaps, in the first, though Tosi's *Opinioni de' cantori antichi, e moderni* (1723) is an important work that cannot be forgotten. German music lexicons, treatises, etc., give perhaps the clearest indication from this type of source of what the aria's function was supposed to be. J. Walther's *Musikalisches Lexicon* of 1732 states how the composer is to construct his arias and, at the same time, avoid unsuitable word setting.[36] But it fails to say how the piece is to fit into a larger unit

[33] p. 82

[34] Modern edn, ed. d'Angeli, Milan, 1956, p. 10. Quoted also in O. Strunk, *Source readings in music history*, New York, 1950, p. 522.

[35] *Poetica toscana*, p. 72.

[36] pp. 46–7.

such as a cantata or opera. J. Mattheson, in his well-known *Vollkommene Capellmeister* of 1739, produces something approaching an aesthetic theory of the aria: 'He who wishes to provide an opera with melodies should pay attention above all to the most lively expression of the passions that are depicted.' Replace the word 'melodies' with 'arias', and we understand that it is the function of the aria vividly to express the chief states of mind (affections/passions) of the characters. Mattheson complains that in opera the overriding passion is love. He admits nevertheless that love may arouse many secondary emotions: jealousy, sorrow, hope, pleasure, revenge, rage, frenzy, all of which will add variety to the work.[37] The individual aria he describes as 'a well-organized song with fixed tonality and time measure, normally divided into two parts and expressing a strong affection in a concise statement'.[38] The next conclusion in the development of thought was that the aria was an overspill of emotion resulting from a charged situation. As C. G. Krause put it in his *Von der musikalischen Poesie* (1752): 'Sometimes the feelings become so strong and the affection so great that we cannot be happy till we have unburdened ourselves of them and opened our hearts. This happens now in an aria.'[39] In the context of Italian opera the overspill came naturally at the end of the scene. We read in volume one of Marpurg's *Historisch-kritische Beyträge* of 1754 that Italian librettists were not wrong in putting the arias where they did. The listener is 'set on fire' by the content of the recitative and the aria hereafter presents itself to him in 'a not unnatural manner'.[40] The aria often functions as a 'climax' (*Bekrönung*) of the previous dialogue and action.

Whereas the author of the music treatise had, it may be assumed, a certain liking for music, the author of the book on theatre and its various branches (including opera) did not have to be a partisan of music at all. Several early eighteenth-century Italian writers on the theatre were far from enthusiastic about music, not just for itself alone but also because it restricted the librettist's freedom. Someone like Quadrio, who declared opera to be 'a bizarre labour of poetry and music', a bad work in which poet and musician 'mutually wear their brains out', would not have agreed that an aria was a suitable 'climax'. Too often in his view it gave rise to stupid situations on stage. 'This custom of desiring the *Canzonette* at the end

[37] Publ. Hamburg, p. 219.
[38] p. 212.
[39] Publ. Berlin, p. 129.
[40] Publ. Berlin, i. 128–9 n. bb.

[of the scene] is one of the reasons why the dramas are so ridiculous, for characters are often forced to leave using ideas, similitudes, and lyrical phrases that are quite out of place; and, what is worse, leave the stage to a pretty *Arietta*, even when they have to go out to die, kill themselves, or rush off in a hurry.'[41] Quadrio's remarks on the 'bizarre' nature of opera were an almost exact quotation from the essay *Sur les Opéra* of the Frenchman St. Evremond.[42] This essay seems to have furnished several Italian critics with arguments against opera as a genre. Literary critics, brought up, as St. Evremond was, to believe that art should imitate nature, found it unnatural that a character should, for example, go to death or order wars and at the same moment 'sing sweetly, quaver, and calmly execute a pleasant and very long trill'.[43] It was not until the middle of the eighteenth century that an Italian literary critic put forth a strong case for opera and suggested that the best poets 'resume the reins of power' within the operatic field.[44] F. Algarotti's *Saggio sopra l'opera in musica* (1756) is important for several reasons and perhaps especially because it is the first of several Italian books treating opera as a dramatic form with inherently good qualities. Provided that the type of music suited the moment, said Algarotti, there could be no more objection to a character singing on the point of death than to his reciting poetry in a similar situation.[45] Nothing, he maintained, was wrong with the principle of opera. What was wrong was that opera had grown too much into a musical, as opposed to a dramatic and literary, art.

Recognition that opera had intrinsically good qualities made Italian literary critics look at the aria anew. Metastasio's successful application of the principle of putting the aria at the end of the scene was probably one reason behind the new, critical support for that principle. The same year that Algarotti's *Saggio* appeared, Ranieri da Calzabigi wrote that the aria was to modern drama what the chorus was to ancient tragedy. The aria was also an improvement on the chorus, since it was sung by the protagonist, not by a crowd of spectators who sensed his mood indirectly. It

---

[41] *Della storia, e della ragione*, iii (seconda parte), 434.

[42] *Oeuvres meslées*, ii. 104–5.

[43] L. A. Muratori, *Della perfetta poesia italiana spiegata e dimostrata con varie osservazioni*, Modena, 1706, ii. 48.

[44] Algarotti, *An essay on the opera*, English edn., Glasgow, 1768, p. 11.

[45] *An essay on the opera*, p. 32. A rather similar point was made by J. Mattheson both in *Das neueröffnete Orchestre*, Hamburg, 1713, pp. 165–6, and in *Die neueste Untersuchung der Singspiele*, Hamburg, 1744, pp. 38–9.

also had the virtue of adding pleasurable variety to modern musical recitative. Calzabigi did not agree with the criticism that arias were usually 'isolated pieces sewn on without skill to the end of the scene'. The arias, quite to the contrary, were intimately connected with, and formed an epilogue of, their respective scenes.[46] Planelli, in his *Dell'opera in musica* (1772), strongly emphasized the emotional qualities of the aria. The aria text had to be 'the simplest language of the affections, containing nothing other than formulas, let us call them thus, of pain, indignation, tenderness, desperation, fear, or other such passion'. It should not contain anything relating to the narrative, to debates and deliberations, to information affecting the course of action. All this properly came in the preceding recitative.[47] The aria had to occur at the point where the passion, held back in the recitative, reached its climax.[48] Arteaga, in the *Rivoluzioni*, agreed that the aria represented an outbreak of emotion previously held in check within recitative. Each aria, beside being the termination of a dramatic situation in which one particular affection obtained, was also 'music's most perfect accomplishment'.[49]

By putting the aria at the scene ending, librettists did limit its possible content. The singer of the following aria from *Il prigionier fortunato*, II.ii, performed in Naples in 1698 with words by F. M. Paglia and music by A. Scarlatti, leaves after it without waiting for the answer the text seems to demand. The words will do, but they are not ideal for an 'exit aria'.

> Dimmi il vero
> Che se taci
> Il mio core contento non è.
> Tu mi piaci
> Mensogniero,
> Ma non quando mentisci con me.
> Dimmi, ecc.

(Tell me the truth, for my heart is not content if you remain silent. I like you, liar, but not when you lie to me. Tell me, etc.)

As the convention about exits strengthened (i.e. from *c.* 1690 onwards), librettists had to be more and more careful about suiting the aria to the exit. A character could still answer a question or express a desire to

---

[46] 'Dissertazione su le poesie drammatiche del Signore Abate Pietro Metastasio', *Poesie del Signor Abate Pietro Metastasio*, Paris, 1755, i. pp. xxxi–xxxiii.

[47] p. 85.

[48] p. 91.

[49] 1st edn., Bologna, 1783, i. 50.

implement some future policy, in which case his aria remained essential to the action. But eighteenth-century operas also contained arias, irrelevant to the course of action, during which the character stepped out of the drama and commented upon it with varying degrees of detachment. Theorists were not entirely at one over the degree of passion or detachment that the aria should express. While Arteaga, for instance, wanted it to express emotions and little else, the Neapolitan theorist Saverio Mattei liked to find in it some considered, intellectual profundity. Nothing could be more detached and intellectual than the following aria of Metastasio quoted by Mattei in his *Elogio del Jomelli* (1785):

> Tutto cangia, e il dì, che viene
> Sempre incalza il dì che fugge;
> Ma cangiando si mantiene
> Il mio stabile tenor.
> Tal ristretta in doppia sponda
> Corre l'onda all'onda appresso,
> Ed è sempre il fiume istesso,
> Ma non è l'istesso umor.[50]

(Everything changes, and the coming day follows swiftly on the dying one. But my life, while changing, remains on its stable course. Contained by the two banks, each wave pursues the previous one. It is always the same river, but the mood varies.)

Many of Metastasio's arias, like this one, contain a maxim or conceit wrapped up, often in a delightful way, to appear emotional or profound. The poetic presentation is responsible for whatever degree of success the aria contains. But Mattei praised it for its 'philosophy' and for the chances he thought it gave the composer: 'What philosophy! What maxims! What truths! And everything so easily and delightfully explained! What field is not present on which music may spread its treasures?'[51]

The static quality of the average aria, static in the sense that it was not accompanied by action, may well have been strengthened by traditional practices of acting. Tragedy was considered a genre in which actors moved with grave restraint and dignity as befitted the seriousness of their subject. Quick physical action, and a lot of it, was considered suitable only for comedy. In early eighteenth-century performances of spoken tragedy, the custom was apparently for actors to strike a pose and declaim without

---

[50] This comes from one of Metastasio's short theatrical pieces, *Il tempio dell'eternità* (set by J. Fux. 1731).

[51] Publ. Colle, p. 119.

constant changes of position. Heroic/tragic opera of the Zeno-Metastasio period was another genre in which, partly because of the arias in it, the long held pose was possible. Whether the bad acting some singers were known for was also in any way copied from the spoken theatre is a moot point. There might be some connection between the two. One of the interesting things about the following write-up of David Garrick by a London theatre critic in 1742 is its suggestion that considerable disrespect was shown by some of Garrick's colleagues toward the play. 'When three or four are on the stage with him he is attentive to whatever is spoken, and never drops his character when he has finished a speech, by either looking contemptuously on an inferior performer, unnecessarily spitting, or suffering his eyes to wander through the whole circle of spectators.'[52] Similar disrespect was shown by some singers toward the opera. No one, significantly, tried to contradict Marcello's satirical description of the typical male singer of *c.* 1720 who, Marcello said, saluted members of the audience while someone else was singing, smiled at the orchestra, and made sure everyone understood he was the singer 'Alipio Forconi' and 'not Zoroaster whom he represents'. In the ritornellos of his arias, said Marcello again, he was inclined to walk around the stage, or take tobacco, or complain to his friends he was out of voice or had caught a cold.[53] De Villeneuve, in his *Lettre sur le méchanisme*, elaborated further on what singers did during the aria ritornellos. By this time (1756) the length of these orchestral interludes had grown out of all proportion to the dramatic requirement, and singers, not knowing what to do during them, whispered to each other, and moved their lips and arms 'so stupidly that no one who is not a spectator could have any conception of it'. If by any chance a singer had an aria while no one else was on stage, then his plight was extreme. During the ritornellos he had to take a walk or let his eyes wander over the various stage decorations. Ladies had the advantage 'in these sad moments' of being able to rearrange the trains of their dresses or get a page boy or two to rearrange them instead.[54] Few among the great eighteenth-century singers were widely praised not just for their voice but also for their stage deportment. Quantz's judgement of Faustina Bordone—'she is born to sing and act'[55]—was praise indeed. Burney praised Nicolini, Senesino, and

[52] See C. Oman, *David Garrick*, London, 1958, p. 42. Quoted also in D. Heartz, 'From Garrick to Gluck', *RMA*, 1967–8, xciv. 112.
[53] *Il teatro alla moda*, ed. d'Angeli, p. 28.
[54] *Lettre*, pp. 32 n.–33 n.
[55] Marpurg, *Historisch-kritische Beyträge*, i. 214.

Carestini for what he called the 'dignity, grace and propriety of their action and deportment'.[56] Carestini was apparently among the most animated actors on the stage; Farinelli on the other hand sang his music 'as motionless as a statue'.[57] Gaetano Guadagni, the first to sing Orpheus in Gluck's *Orfeo ed Euridice*, was praised for attitudes and gestures 'so full of grace and propriety, that they would have been excellent studies for a statuary'.[58] Quite a different story concerns another famous castrato, Caffarello, who managed to get himself put under house arrest in Naples in 1741 for constant bad behaviour on the S. Carlo stage. In spite of being warned not to do so, he had repeatedly made indecent gestures, joked with the audience at the expense of other members of the cast, echoed their phrases during their arias, and refused to sing with them.[59] He was probably the originator of several of the obscene remarks made by singers on stage that were, according to de Villeneuve, put into a pamphlet and circulated round Naples in the mid-century.[60]

It goes without saying that bad and slovenly acting could largely nullify any dramatic effect that librettist and composer thought out. The wise librettist of the time was the one who realized that singers could not be relied upon to add a new dimension through acting to what was already there in word, music, and scenic effect. Metastasio for his part tried to keep stage movement to the simplest possible type of formula. Sending a revised version of his *Alessandro nell'Indie* to Farinelli in Madrid in 1754, he enclosed a 'slip of paper' on which were mentioned 'all the entrances, exits, stage business, and situations of the several characters, as I arranged them on my table in writing the opera. And this trouble is extremely useful for the performance of some dramas, particularly *Alessandro*. If no embarrassment happens, you need not look at this paper; but, if intricacy occurs, it will save you the trouble of thinking.'[61] In the largest theatres like the S. Carlo, it was necessary for singers to stand well up to the front in order to be heard properly. Given the orderly system of entries and exits of a Metastasio-type libretto, the singers could arrange and rearrange them-

[56] *A general history of music*, iv. 379.

[57] Loc. cit. Quantz thought Farinelli had a good figure for the stage but did not act from the heart, see Marpurg, *Historisch-kritische Beyträge*, i. 234.

[58] Ibid. 495.

[59] Croce, 'I teatri di Napoli', 1890, xv. 519.

[60] *Lettre sur le méchanisme*, pp. 31. n.–32 n. De Villeneuve says of the remarks: 'Ce n'est qu'un tissu d'ordures & d'obscénités'.

[61] From a letter to Farinelli in February, 1754. C. Burney, *Memoirs of the life and writings of the Abate Metastasio*, ii. 113.

selves in groupings across the stage without much prompting from a stage director. It was when singers, always conscious of their dignity, disagreed over their positions that some production control became necessary and some guide like Metastasio's 'slip of paper' proved its usefulness. Metastasio had his share of trying to solve problems created by singers' intransigence, witness the advice he gave concerning a 1748 production of *Demofoonte* at Dresden. The problem here was that the singers had taken it into their heads to consider the superior stage position to be the one on the right. 'If you ask me who should be placed on the right hand, and who on the left', wrote Metastasio, 'I must tell you I never meant to regulate that by the dignity of the personages, but by the convenience and necessity of the action'.[62] So in the argument between two ladies, one playing Dircea and the other Creusa (for details of the plot, see pp. 45–6 above), about who had precedence and therefore the position on the right, Metastasio's advice was that Dircea, an unknown princess, should show deference to Creusa, known to be of high rank, regardless of which singer was the better one. And neither stage rank nor singing ability had anything to do with who stood on which side of the other.

It has often been said that eighteenth-century heroic opera failed in the end because singers turned it into a tasteless display of virtuosity. Such a view is based on those eighteenth-century criticisms of opera, Gluck's preface to *Alceste* being the outstanding one, which suggest form and content of the aria were evolved to suit generations of singers interested in pyrotechnics to the exclusion of all else. Since Gluck's aims make excellent sense to most modern readers, his views as to the faults of heroic opera tend to receive sympathetic attention. Nevertheless, to say that singers or composers, or the musicians as a group, were primarily responsible for the deficiencies of opera is to over-simplify the issue. It is equally possible to declare that the major librettists, by moving with the times and allowing for arias in which singers could show off their prowess, willy-nilly put their stamp of approval on the art-form. And then we should not forget the patrons, who would never have permitted the growth of an entertainment that did not please them.

Not least among the reasons for the decline of the Metastasio-type opera was the behaviour of patrons at the theatre and the way it affected the singers. All the evidence suggests that Italian patrons in the second half of the century became more and more dissatisfied with the music offered,

[62] Ibid. i. 225.

allowing their affections to settle primarily on the spectacle and on the ballets serving as entr'actes to the opera.[63] Regarding the music, de Villeneuve was saying in the 1750s already that an opera was sure to please if five or six arias were successful.[64] Burney in his *General history of music* (vol. iv, 1789) declared that an opera was sure to please if 'two or three airs and a duet deserve attention'. An additional factor here, as he pointed out, was that standards of singing declined toward the end of the century and that a 'company of singers is now reckoned good, in Italy, if the first two performers are excellent . . . performers of the second or third classes are generally below mediocrity'.[65] Something of a vicious circle was in operation. Audiences were gradually taking their attention off most of the music and encouraging singers to reserve their energies for a limited number of arias/duets. The singers, hardly encouraged by the inattentiveness of audiences, worried less and less about steady quality-singing and more about vocal agility at certain particular moments. The audience in its turn gained less satisfaction from the performance of the secondary singers. There followed a general decline in singing standards. In point of fact the singing was not the only thing to suffer. As de Villeneuve put it:

The actor will never fail, be he menacing, or trying to soften the feelings of [the characters] with him, to forget the action, leaving them and coming to the front of the stage to make his roulades and ornament the most beautiful passages with a secret complaisance which the public always recompenses with excessive applause. During these moments of enthusiasm the dramatic action ceases. In a flash the atmosphere changes, without one noticing it, from theatre to concert.[66]

While nothing stated thus far takes the blame off the singers for their share in lowering standards of production and performance, it seems that they, just like others, were caught up in a state of affairs that no individual could change by his own effort. Samuel Sharp pictured the singers at the S. Carlo,

---

[63] See, for example, the Earl of Mount Edgcumbe, *Musical reminiscences of an old amateur chiefly respecting the Italian opera in England for fifty years from 1773 to 1823*, London, 1827, pp. 51–2, summarizing part of his experience in Italy in 1785: 'But the passion for music cannot be so great in that land of song as we are apt to suppose: for on inquiring in any town if the opera was good, I was uniformly answered, oh! si, bellissimi *balli*! and indeed in general the dances are more thought of, and attended to in greater *silence*, than the opera *itself*'.

[64] *Lettre sur le méchanisme*, p. 35.

[65] iv. 560. Compare this with F. Raguenet's comment on Italian opera of *c.* 1700: 'There is no weak part in any of the Italian operas, where no scene is preferable to the rest for its peculiar beauties; all the songs are of an equal force and are sure to be crowned with applause . . .' See Raguenet, 'A comparison between the French and Italian music', English version of 1709, reprint in *MQ*, 1946, xxxii. 425.

[66] *Lettre sur le méchanisme*, p. 33.

Naples, as being nowhere near a position of control over the destinies of the opera there. Mentioning that Neapolitan audiences were much quieter during the ballets than during the rest of the performance, Sharp continued:

Witty people, therefore, never fail to tell me, the Neapolitans go to *see*, not to *hear* an Opera. A stranger, who has a little compassion in his breast, feels for the poor singers, who are treated with so much indifference and contempt; he almost wonders that they can submit to so gross an affront, and I find, by their own confession, that however accustomed they are to it, the mortification is always dreadful, and they are eager to declare how happy they are when they sing in a country where more attention is paid to their talent.[67]

The new-style opera introduced by Gluck and his librettist Calzabigi in Vienna in the 1760s was notable for musical and, to some extent, also for textual innovations. The biggest break with the past was Gluck's attempt to keep the music strictly within the limits required by the drama (e.g. not allow extra arias, or arias purely for display purposes, to please singers), but expand the music within these limits (e.g. accompany most, or all, of the recitative with the strings). Calzabigi's librettos were based on myths, tended to avoid intrigues and subplots, put greater emphasis on one or two characters than Metastasio would have done in his major works,[68] and integrated the ballets and choruses into the story. The classical-type tragedy, ancient and/or French, was the librettist's chief model. Algarotti had already suggested, in his *Saggio*, using some such model as a basis for librettos; for at the back of his book he included a libretto of his own, *Iphigénie en Aulide* (in French), plus his outline for another, *Enea in Troja* (in Italian), both with strong 'classical' leanings. Calzabigi's and Gluck's reform was influenced by French opera, which had consistently and over a long period featured plots based on ancient myth or epic, and usually been planned with a view to the over-all effect, with ballet and chorus included. It had never become a singers' opera to the extent Italian opera had. Gluck and Calzabigi may also have been influenced by practical experiments on the part of the librettist Carlo Frugoni and the Neapolitan composer Tommaso Traetta to combine the French dramatic system with Italian words and Italian-style music in two tragic operas at Parma. These operas were *Ippolito e Aricia* (1759) and *I Tindaridi* (1760),

---

[67] *Letters from Italy*, p. 81.

[68] Though not more than might be found in some of Metastasio's shorter dramatic pieces, or *azioni teatrali*, with which Gluck's *Orfeo ed Euridice*, on account of its limited size, might be compared.

whose textual bases were two French librettos, *Hippolyte et Aricie* and *Castor et Pollux*, previously set by Rameau.[69]

But though ideas about changing the character of the Italian libretto were now in the air, Italians at home were slow to put them into practice. Traditional values were still strong, which is why other librettists and composers were slow to follow the leads of Calzabigi and Gluck, and why the works of these two were often divested of some of their most modern features if and when they were given a public performance. *Orfeo ed Euridice* was the first of their joint works the Neapolitans had the chance to see. It was performed six times at the Royal Palace in January 1774 in a version that seems to have agreed more or less with Gluck's intentions, and then again, in a new production with various embellishments and additions at the S. Carlo the following November.[70] *Orfeo* is, of course, a relatively short work and would not, in its original form, have filled an entire evening at the S. Carlo. What is interesting is the way in which it was transformed into a full-length work of the kind the S. Carlo patrons were accustomed to watch. In brief, the libretto was lengthened to allow for a full cast of seven solo singers (in eight roles) and for seven different stage sets. Many of the scenes have nothing to do with Gluck's masterpiece. In Act I, scene i, Eagrus, father of Orpheus, talks disconsolately to his army general Euristo, about Orpheus's despair at the loss of Eurydice. Scenes ii to v contain basically the material of the original Act I. There is then an additional scene to finish the act, depicting the 'horrid entrance to Avernus, with a view of the river Styx and of Charon's boat upon it.' Orpheus here plays his lyre to disperse a hostile crowd of spirits, and crosses the river. The first three scenes of Act II again have no connection with the original opera. Pluto hears of the entry of a mortal into the Underworld and refusing to listen to the pleas for mercy from Proserpina orders the fury Erinni to attack Orpheus. Scene iv is basically the same as the original II.i beginning with the familiar chorus 'Chi mai dell'Erebo'. There is a scenery change to the Elysian Fields at the start of scene v, when Eurydice enters lamenting her fate. Amore enters (scene vi) to tell her she will be rescued by Orpheus—though he does not tell her of the one condition of her rescue. The first part of scene vii equals the original

[69] Frugoni and Traetta used another style of French opera, *opéra ballet*, as model for their *Le feste d'Imeneo* (Parma, 1760). Two of the three acts of this work were based on sections of *Les fêtes d'Hébé* set by Rameau in 1739.

[70] For more on other adaptations of Gluck's *Orfeo*, see especially A. Loewenberg, 'Gluck's *Orfeo* on the stage', *MQ*, 1940, xxvi. 326 ff.

II.ii; the second part is none other than the first section, much altered, of the original III.i up to the point of the duet between Orpheus and Eurydice. The new Act III commences with Eurydice's words 'Qual vita è questa mai' in the middle of the original first scene of that act, and carries on from there to the end without further substantial alteration. There seem to be two reasons why the point of break between Act II and Act III was changed. Firstly, the new arrangement makes the third act short by comparison with either of the others—and this was normal in Italian opera of the 1770s. The second, and more profound, reason was a dramatic one. In Calzabigi's arrangement the argument between Orpheus and Eurydice leading to the disastrous moment when he turns to view her is contained in the one scene (III.i). The setting is a dark cavern on the way between Hades and the world above. The adapter (or adapters) of the version used in Naples makes the action of the first part of this scene take place in the Elysian Fields, so he can tack it on to the previous scene. By then having an act interval and using the scenery of a dark cavern for the second part only of the old III.i, he creates the impression of a long time span between the start and end of the quarrel. This adds credibility to Orpheus's final act of desperation in turning round to see Eurydice.

Orfeo, even in its altered form, must have seemed to Neapolitans in 1774 to be an unusual work. Only two characters, Orpheus and Amore, appeared in all the acts. Five of the others each appeared only in one. This meant that Orpheus, especially, had to carry the action to an unusual degree. There were more choruses than was normal, and dances occurred during the acts and not just at the act endings. The performance in toto was made more conventional than Calzabigi or Gluck might have liked through the insertion of ballets that had nothing to do with the subject of Orpheus. The first of these, called *Adele de Pontieú*, formed the entr'acte between Acts I and II, and was considered sufficiently important to warrant seven and a half pages of description in the opera libretto. Another ballet, in the second act interval, had a comic subject. As for the music of the opera, the libretto claimed the various additions were by J. C. Bach, 'maestro di cappella of Her Majesty the Queen of Great Britain'.[71] It is possible other

---

[71] Bach, together with Guglielmi, had already composed additional items for the version of *Orfeo* produced at the London Haymarket in 1770. Four of Bach's arias in the London *Orfeo* (see *The favourite songs in the opera Orfeo*, London, R. Bremner) passed into the Neapolitan. These were Eagrus' 'Non è vero' (London, scene 1, Naples I.i), Eurydice's 'Chiari fonti' and 'Obbliar l'amato sposo' (London, scene 5, Naples II.v), and Amore's 'Accorda amico il fato' (London, scene 6, Naples II.vi). Note the suggestion by A. A. Abert, 'Orfeo ed Euridice', *Gluck's Sämtliche Werke, Musikdramen*,

additions were by J. Misliweczek, who directed the performances. The new lyrical items tended to be less distinguished than Gluck's original, and were certainly more flamboyant and virtuoso. The recitative of Gluck's score had been accompanied throughout by the strings, whereas in the new version much of the additional or altered recitative was set in the most conventional way, with continuo support only.

If one were not familiar with Gluck's *Orfeo*, and thought the Neapolitan version an original work, one might imagine it to be some rather advanced experiment on the part of a librettist and composer influenced by French dramatic methods but still working forward from the base of traditional Italian opera. Progressive operas produced at Naples in the last thirty years of the century show at best a compromise solution to the Metastasian–Gluckian conflict. Two librettos written by Calzabigi for Naples in the early 1790s are instructive in this context because of the conservative features to be found in them. Calzabigi (1714–95) had himself been a government official in Naples for part of the 1740s, and much later, in 1780, retired there. It is remarkable how seldom his services were used thereafter by the Neapolitan court and S. Carlo authorities—a sign in itself of a comparative lack of official interest in the sort of operatic reform he had helped to initiate.[72] Sections of his *Impermestra* set by V. G. Millico were performed at the Royal Palace in January and at the house of the Russian Ambassador at the end of carnival, 1784. No complete performance occurred however.[73] His two texts that were set and performed complete at the S. Carlo were *Elfrida* (1792) and *Elvira* (1794), both with music by Paisiello. In contrast to his librettos set earlier by Gluck, these two had comparatively complex plots based on historical subjects. They possessed secondary characters but no musical choruses. Some reformist reasoning seems to lie behind the decision to avoid arias for the secondary

1963, i. (preface), p. xii, that G. Ferdinando Tenducci, who sang Orpheus in productions of the opera at Florence (1771) and Naples (S. Carlo, 1774), brought additional items to the Naples version from the Florentine.

[72] *Orfeo* was not however the only 'reform' opera by Calzabigi and Gluck to be performed in Naples. Prota-Giurleo, *Breve storia*, pp. 138–41, mentions a private *Nobile Accademia di Musica* founded there by the Marchese di Corleto. It was inaugurated with a performance of *Paride ed Elena* in 1777. Both *Paride* and *Alceste* were performed in it in 1779.

[73] According to Prota-Giurleo, *La grande orchestra del R. Teatro San Carlo nel settecento*, Naples, 1927, pp. 46–7, the work was never performed because the S. Carlo authorities balked at the cost. The words of *Impermestra* were sent by Calzabigi to Gluck in November, 1778, and later handed by Gluck to Salieri. Salieri's setting of the text, adapted for production in Paris, appeared under the title of *Les Danaides* (1784).

characters and to let these have their share of lyrical singing only in the solo ensembles, of which there are several.[74] Incidentally, Paisiello made his own reformist contribution to *Elfrida* by refraining from writing long vocalizations and other exhibitionist ornament for the singers. He had adopted the same policy already in *Pirro*, words by G. de Gamerra, produced at the S. Carlo in 1787 and again in 1790.[75]

Progressive operas with texts by other writers are usually to be spotted through some obvious Gluckian or French feature such as a plot based on mythology with accompanying mythological scenery (e.g. a part of the underworld) or the prominent use of chorus and perhaps dance as well. Jommelli's first opera for Naples after his return from Württemberg, *Armida abbandonata*, words by F. S. de Rogatis, 1770, is of this type. *Fedra*, produced at the S. Carlo in 1788 with words by L. N. Salvioni and music by G. Paisiello, is another. *Oreste*, produced in 1783 with music by D. Cimarosa, is also worth mentioning, not because it is a particularly good or modern opera, but because of the reformist spirit with which its librettist, the Neapolitan court poet Luigi Serio, went about his task. Croce printed in his *I teatri di Napoli* a long statement from Serio to King Ferdinand written in February 1783 about the opera (produced that August). Some of Serio's remarks are reminiscent of Gluck's, in the *Alceste* preface printed in 1769, and show that the abuses Gluck complained of did not all disappear in the next fourteen years.

The dramas of our day provide little interest, not for the lack of merit in the poetry, but because of the great void existing between the recitatives and the arias ... [and] because of the wilfulness of the singers . . . and because of the negligence and ignorance of the same, who utter the words without art and without the right expressiveness. Thinking to put a stop to such disorders, I have tried to reduce the recitatives to the minimum number possible, and have put choruses into the drama to regain the listener's attention. So that these [choruses] do not become mere ephemeral, noisy pieces, I have tried to unite them to the action . . . Usually, arias are nothing but an insipid warbling . . . I have managed to place the arias, especially those belonging to the chief characters, in such positions that the composer is forced to relate [the music] to the poetry and the singers to explain the passions.[76]

If we look at the opera itself, we find that the number of choruses (four) is large for Metastasian opera, perhaps, but not for Gluck's. In other respects

---

[74] For more on these works see G. Lazzeri, *La vita e l'opera letteraria di Ranieri Calzabigi*, Città di Castello, 1907, pp. 93 ff.

[75] See also Paisiello's remarks about his *Alcide al bivio*, quoted on p. 86 below.

[76] 1891, xvi. 327.

too it is not so modern as Serio may have imagined to himself. There was nothing so unusual, for example, in his wish to cut down on the recitative. Late eighteenth-century adaptations of earlier librettos almost always involved a cut in the recitative text, and new librettos were shorter than those written in the first half of the century partly because of their shorter recitative. The arias in *Oreste* happen to occur in order for the various characters—which makes one wonder if the expression of the passions were the sole factor determining their position. Serio does not seem to mind if characters, even the important ones, leave without arias. The same fact may be noticed in other librettos by other contemporary writers—and it means that in general Italian opera plots no longer had to be so carefully woven round the exits as had once been the case.

Two other features of *Oreste* requiring comment are the ensembles for soloists at the end of each act,[77] and the minute third act of three scenes only. These features were again in line with trends in Italian opera. There are many ways to demonstrate how they fit in with the general pattern. One method is to take versions of Metastasian librettos adapted for Naples and other parts of Italy and see how the late eighteenth-century versions were modified to allow for more ensembles and shorter third acts, rather as *Oreste* has. If we take a libretto such as that of *Demofoonte*, we find that this work originally had one duet, at the end of Act II, and one chorus, at the end of Act III. The penultimate scene of Act II was for three characters, Demofoonte and the two lovers, Timante and Dircea. Demofoonte sang an aria at the end of it leaving the others to sing the last scene with the duet at the finish. In one of the earliest revisions of this work, for production at the S. Gio. Grisostomo theatre, Venice, in 1735,[78] the act ending was shortened. The adapter cut out the final scene and closed the act, after what used to be the penultimate scene, with a trio. So Demofoonte lost his aria but sang instead in an ensemble. It is necessary to pay attention to this device of telescoping together two or more scenes. When late in the century fashions were such that Metastasio's librettos had to be shortened considerably if they were to be used at all, this particular device was among the most frequently adopted—with the inevitable, and obviously desired, result of fewer scenes, fewer arias, but with more and bigger ensembles.

Late versions of *Demofoonte* also show the tendency toward a greater reduction in the size of Act III than of the other two acts. Metastasio did not

---

[77] Act I ends with a duet, Act II with a quartet, and Act III with a quintet.
[78] Music by Gaetano Maria Schiassi.

put less interest into this third act than into the rest. Nevertheless when the opera was staged at the S. Carlo, in November 1770, with music by Jommelli, Acts I and II each lost only one of their original total of lyrical items, but Act III lost four. One possible cause of this cut-back in the size of the third act, which we emphasize again was general, may have been suggested by Arteaga in his *Rivoluzioni* where he introduces a hypothetical discussion between an impresario and a librettist in which the one orders a new work from the other and states what it shall contain. The last act, the impresario says, is not something the librettist should go to too much trouble over. 'What I know is that, once the second ballet is over, the audience leaves and the players and singers are not willing to strain themselves further.'[79] If ballets were not in fact the cause, then the only other suggestion we can make is that heroic opera might perhaps at that date have been parodying comic opera, whose third act in the 1770s–'80s period withered away to nothing.[80] Comic opera is the subject of later chapters, so comment upon it can be deferred for the moment.

[79] 1st edn. ii. 195.
[80] Heroic opera also arrived at a stage where the third act could be discarded if desired. Paisiello's *Fedra* of 1788 is one of the early cases of a full-size Italian heroic opera in two acts.

Heroic Opera—the Music

VARIOUS methods present themselves for dealing with the music of Italian heroic opera. The one adopted here is to take the different types of music—recitative, arias, etc.—and trace the stylistic developments of each in turn. Recitative is put first, for the rather negative reason that it has always been considered the least interesting part of the music and to put it after the aria might create a sense of anticlimax. Eighteenth-century Italian recitative is divided into two basic types: 'simple' (in a declamatory style with thorough-bass accompaniment)[1] and 'accompanied' (with orchestral accompaniment and perhaps with orchestral interludes). The bulk of the recitative is of the former kind, save in a few works written toward the end of the period by Gluck and others interested in the reform of Italian opera. And it is this simple kind for which commentators have never been able to evince much enthusiasm.

Dissatisfaction with recitative was first expressed as early as 1626, when Domenico Mazzochi inserted certain lyrical sections into the score of his opera *Catena d'Adone*[2] to counteract, as he put it, 'the tediousness of the recitative'. No stylistic development in simple recitative between 1626 and 1700 made it more exciting for later listeners. If anything, simple recitative became more and more functional and less and less expressive. Remarks on the subject by eighteenth-century writers show that many of them either could not take it at all, or else could take it only in small quantities. Tosi, in his *Opinioni* of 1723, was one who criticized it saying: 'Much more might still be said on the compositions of *Recitative* in general, by reason of that tedious chanting which offends the ear . . .'[3] De Brosses, during his visit to Rome in 1740, played chess in the theatre, chess being marvellously designed, as he put it, to 'fill the vacuum of these long recitatives, and music [being designed] to break too strenuous

---

[1] Since the nineteenth century this type of recitative has been commonly known as 'dry' (*secco*). There seems no reason why the original eighteenth-century term 'simple' (*semplice*) should not be used, and it is the term used throughout this book.

[2] Publ. Vincenti, Venice, 1626.

[3] This is from the translation of J. E. Galliard, published under the title *Observations on the florid song, or sentiments on the ancient and modern singers*, London, 1743, pp. 74–5.

a concentration on chess'.[4] Jean-Jacques Rousseau defended the principle of recitative on the grounds that a succession of airs without intervening pauses was ineffective, yet admitted that he found Italian recitative often of excessive length and therefore boring.[5] Eighteenth-century simple recitative may well have seemed tedious not just because there was so much of it but also because its musical formulas became so hackneyed and conventional. Well before the end of the seventeenth century its chief musical characteristics became rooted in convention, and so they stayed. Its invariable time signature was $\frac{4}{4}$. The vocal part, designed to approximate a type of musically heightened speech, was composed on the general principle of one syllable one note—which was a black note (crotchet, quaver, semiquaver, less commonly demi-semiquaver) each time. The part moved over a relatively narrow range and contained few wide melodic leaps except where an unusually expressive phrase was sought after. The music was bound by no principle of over-all thematic structure or key; and key-signatures, which did sometimes occur in stretches of seventeenth-century recitative, went completely out of fashion after *c.* 1710. The thorough-bass line, slower moving than the voice, proceeded legato and in an irregular rhythm. Changes of bass note and accompanimental chord were often placed to occur on the penultimate syllable of a phrase. Prominent cadences were usually 'broken',[6] *i.e.* the voice finished before the continuo. Two among the various melodic cadence formulas were particularly common. The following example shows them both sung together:[7]

EXAMPLE I
Sarri, *Partenope*, I, ii
(Performed at the Teatro S. Bartolomeo, Naples, 1722)

---

[4] *Lettres familières*, ii. 357–8.

[5] *Dictionnaire de musique*, Paris, 1768, p. 409.

[6] Tosi, in his *Opinioni*, 1723, p. 47, used the term *cadenza tronca*, which was translated by Galliard, *Observations*, p. 75, as 'broken cadence'.

[7] J. F. Agricola, in his German translation of Tosi, published as *Anleitung zur Singkunst*, Berlin, 1757, pp. 154–5, provides variants of the vocal cadence formulas, from which it appears the upper

Problems relating to the performance of this type of cadence have received plenty of attention before. One of the well-known difficulties is to decide upon the continuo harmony of the penultimate bass note, the G in the above Example. One of the developments in recitative writing of the 1730s–'40s period was the change in the bass of the cadence formula involving a displacement of the final chords V–I by one crotchet and the insertion of a crotchet rest under the last beat of the vocal phrase. In this way chords V and I both came after the vocal phrase ending, and there was no chance of a clash of harmony between the penultimate chord and the vocal line above it.[8]

Recitative developed other formulas peculiar to itself. Successions of secondary sixth chords had been known in seventeenth-century recitative, but they became much more common in that of the eighteenth. The practice of starting a recitative on a consonant first inversion chord had already begun by the 1680s, but, once again, was commoner still after 1700. The third inversion of dominant and secondary sevenths became a prominently used discord, noticeable too because composers often failed to resolve it in the conventional way they would have adopted in a lyrical item. None of these what we might call harmonic formulas made recitative expressive in any sense, and a case might be made for saying that they were used so often because they added a rough and ready effect, a type of unprepared, casual quality, that was the calculated opposite of artistry.

The improvisatory quality of simple recitative was heightened by the tendency on the part of composers around the end of the seventeenth and start of the eighteenth centuries to remove traces of lyricism that recitative had previously contained. Change favoured the type of recitative which sounded slick, fast, had few memorable phrases, and a slow rate of harmonic change. Seventeenth-century composers had known perfectly well how to produce the type of recitative without arresting feature. But they varied it with a more lyrical and emotional kind, containing musical features that were noticeable and appealing to the ear: vocal phrases

soprano part in Example 1 could have been sung as e♮"–d"–c" rather than e♮"–c"–c". How the phrase would have been sung in Naples at the time of Sarri's *Partenope* is an open question.

[8] S. H. Hansell, 'The cadence in 18th-century recitative', *MQ*, 1968, liv. 234, points out that the musical examples of broken cadences in Galliard's and Agricola's translations of Tosi (published in 1743 and 1757 respectively) differ in the particular that Galliard's cadences are of the older kind, without rest in the bass, while Agricola's are of the more modern. Hansell asserts in the same article that one of the differences of opinion that supposedly occurred in Naples in the approximate 1730s–'40s period between the two composers and teachers, Durante and Leo, may have been over the introduction of this cadence rest.

individually moulded, with a comparatively wide range and perhaps with a melisma or two; quick chord changes; and an occasional arresting modulation. It was this type of recitative that went out of fashion, to be preserved primarily in cantatas and other pieces in what was known as the 'chamber' style. The kind therefore retained in opera was usually the other, with its formulas, preferred obviously because no thought was required to compose it and because, in Italy at least, it was not listened to. As so often happens when some procedure is followed long enough, theory finally came to support the new, inexpressive recitative. C. P. E. Bach's well-known statement on recitative in his *Versuch über die wahre Art, das Clavier zu spielen* (1753) is one example; and although it was obviously influenced by his knowledge of German music, including his father's, it does to some extent summarize the major difference between the old and the new in Italy too: 'Not long ago, recitatives used to be crammed with endless chords, resolutions, and enharmonic changes. A special kind of beauty was sought in these harmonic extravagancies . . . But today, thanks to our intelligent taste, exceptional harmonies are introduced in the recitative only rarely, and then with sufficient motivation . . .'[9]

In response to an increased demand by both amateurs and professionals, several music dictionaries and lexicons were published in northern Europe in the eighteenth century containing useful and not over-technical references to opera. Articles on recitative rarely dealt with its harmonies, perhaps because their authors considered this amply covered in thorough-bass treatises. However, these articles became steadily more informative in other ways. Johann Sulzer, in a long article in his *Allgemeine Theorie der schönen Künste* (Leipzig, 1771–4), laid down fifteen ground-rules of both simple and accompanied recitative setting which can be easily assimilated. Many of his rules imply little more than that the music should follow the sense of the words. Others are explicit on particular facets of musical technique. Here is a short summary of them:[10]

(1) The beat is irregular and has to follow the sentence structure. However, German and Italian recitative is notated in a regular $\frac{4}{4}$ time.

(2) There is neither tonal centre nor regular modulation as in closed musical structures.

---

[9] English edn., trans. Mitchell, New York, 1949, pp. 420–1.

[10] Another list of the features of recitative is in J. Mattheson, *Der Vollkommene Capellmeister*, Hamburg, 1739, p. 214. For a thorough, technical examination of recitative, see above all Marpurg's *Kritische Briefe über die Tonkunst*, Berlin, 1762, ii. 253 ff.

(3) Melismatic ornaments must not occur.

(4) Each syllable must be set to one note.[11] When exceptions are made to this rule, care must be taken to ensure that each syllable can be enunciated clearly.

(5) Musical and verbal accents must coincide.

(6) The speed of the music must accord with the natural flow of the words.

(7) The rise and fall of the notes must follow the verbal sense and expression.

(8) Pauses must occur only where the word sense permits.

(9) A change of key does not require a vocal cadence unless the sense requires.

(10) When questions, passionate pronouncements, and commands, occur at a cadence, the accent must fall on the chief word of the phrase and not always on the last syllable of all.

(11) The harmony must relate to the text.

(12) The dynamic markings must be related to word meaning.

(13) Expressions of tender feelings, and especially of sadness and pity, lasting over one or more sentences, may be set as *arioso* for the sake of beauty and variety.

(14) A regular, measured beat may be adopted in a limited number of other passages.

(15) So-called 'accompanied' recitative is suitable in places where the text is full of passion, yet broken up and with its words detached from each other.[12]

Not all the 'rules' fit the case each time, but given the vast amount of recitative written this is to be expected.

While rules 1–12 above referred to eighteenth-century recitative generally, rules 13–15 referred to features of recitative accompanied by the orchestra (*recitativo accompagnato/obbligato*). The term *arioso*—see Sulzer's rule 13—meant at that period a short, freely structured yet lyrical section attached to recitative. Sulzer described arioso as 'a very simple aria' but still thought it part of recitative.[13] He could have added that well before the time he was writing (that is, since *c.* 1720) it had

---

[11] Most singers seem to have performed recitative without adding ornament of their own. Note however Burney's comment in *Memoirs of the Abbate Metastasio*, iii. 387 n., that the castrato Luigi Marchese (1755–1829) 'has revived this primitive custom of *gracing recitative*'.

[12] ii. 945–6.

[13] i. 80.

become customary to accompany arioso with the orchestra and associate it with accompanied recitative rather than with simple. The further we go before *c.* 1720, the more confusing the situation becomes so far as arioso is concerned. In the mid-seventeenth century style and function of aria and recitative were far from rigidly divided, and many musical sections came into a very ambivalent classification zone. Late seventeenth-century Italian opera still contained free lyrical sections in addition to the arias in closed forms. Some of these free sections were similar in style and, more important, possessed similar weight and substance to the aria proper. Others were short, perhaps minute insertions which appeared to fulfil the function of varying the recitative. Composers then made no absolute distinction between the various styles, so that just as it was possible to have free sections in the style of an aria, it was possible to set an aria in the style of a (musically interesting) recitative.[14] Toward the end of the century free lyrical sections gradually lost favour, especially those with mere continuo accompaniment. This was part of a general process resulting in a much more rigid difference between the style and functions of aria on the one hand and of recitative on the other. As if to compensate for too absolute a division, accompanied recitative became more and more popular as a change from the simple; and it was primarily within the framework of accompanied recitative that the lyrical arioso continued to exist during the approximate period 1720–70.[15]

Accompanied recitative entered Italian opera sometime around the mid-seventeenth century, though one's choice of a 'first' depends on one's judgement as to when the occasional semi-lyrical passages supported by strings then to be found in opera are recitative and when arioso. Towneley Worsthorne quotes part of a passage from Act III of Cavalli's *La virtù degli strali d'amore* (1642) that might be thought to be accompanied recitative.[16] Later in the same act there is another passage, more obviously declamatory than Towneley Worsthorne's example, supported by the strings playing in alternate bars semibreves and fast, repeated semiquavers in Monteverdi's *concitato* manner. In neither case is the time absolutely free. The type of

[14] A fine, late example of this type of aria is 'Sia di Cerbero i latrati', in Porpora's *Agrippina* (1708), III.xiv.

[15] It becomes hardly valid to categorize arioso by its association with accompanied recitative once Gluck began writing operas in which accompanied recitative largely replaced simple. Gluck's adoption of orchestral accompaniments for recitative was not paralleled by a vast increase in the number of ariosos.

[16] *Venetian opera in the seventeenth century*, Oxford, 1954, pp. 68–9.

accompanied recitative that is in free time, that is, really simple recitative but with the strings replacing the continuo, did not become a common feature of Italian opera till towards the very end of the century; and this author has seen several operatic scores of that time still without trace of it. The strings in this type of recitative acted in several ways. They played the legato chords the continuo would have played. They also played detached chords, left rests in the accompaniment where no change of chord was necessary, and sometimes added their own instrumentally-conceived phraseology. By retaining the other type that was more lyrical and in measured time, composers ensured that within the orbit of recitative they now had two styles to work with.[17] The point to be made here is that eighteenth-century composers felt free to move from one to the other just as it suited them. They also preserved the essential recitative or improvisatory quality of the whole by not allowing the sung passages in a semi-lyrical style to outweigh the remainder. This means that accompanied recitative was rarely transformed into free song with declamatory episodes, of the type exemplified by 'Che puro ciel' from Gluck's *Orfeo*.

Differentiation between the various types of lyrical and non-lyrical music becomes more and more difficult when we come to recitative with long orchestral ritornellos. This was normally called *recitativo obbligato*. A. Scarlatti and composers of his generation rarely placed into their recitatives long ritornellos that could compare in length and substance with those of arias. An orchestral solo in a Scarlatti recitative was usually no more than a short, epigrammatic phrase covering a bar or two. Composers of the 1730s and later were more venturesome. Burney reported during his visit to Rome in 1770 that the composer Rinaldo da Capua had the reputation there of having originated accompanied recitative; but all that da Capua himself laid claim to was being among the first to introduce long ritornellos into recitatives 'of strong passion and distress, which express or imitate what it would be ridiculous for the voice to attempt'.[18] Precisely how accurate da Capua's claim was is still open to investigation. His first operas were composed in the late 1730s, which seems a little late for the initiation of the practice. Before saying anything else, we must emphasize that the ritornellos da Capua refers to fulfil the same function as those

---

[17] Rousseau, *Dictionnaire*, pp. 410–2, distinguished between the two calling the one *récitatif accompagné* and the other *récitatif mesuré*. Marpurg, *Kritische Briefe*, ii. 255, disapproved of the term *mesuré* arguing that recitative that was 'measured' was recitative no longer.

[18] *The present state*, pp. 285–6.

attached to arias, that is, they primarily portray the state of mind of the character, or the prevailing mood of the moment. They are not there to accompany action or fill up time to let a singer get into position, which was another function the orchestral ritornello could and did begin also to fulfil.[19] Some clue to the first introduction of ritornellos with the former function may, possibly, be found in those very few operas of the first part of the eighteenth century with a tragic and not a happy denouement. And it is not too much of a digression to examine one or two of these operas now.

Among the works in question is *Arsace*, with words by Antonio Salvi, produced in Venice early in 1718 with music by Michelangelo Gasparini[20] and repeated in Naples the following autumn with music by Sarri. The character parts of Arsace and Statira were played by Nicola Grimaldi (called Nicolini) and Marianna Benti Bulgarelli respectively in both sets of performances. In the opera Arsace, loved by Statira, Queen of Persia, is put to death on her orders after conviction of leading a revolt against the state. Demented at the thought of being responsible for his death, she finally commits suicide (after the close of the opera). In the Naples version (which seems more important than the Venetian for a reason that will become clear in a moment) there is no chorus or aria at the end, when she exits for the last time, so it terminates with recitative. The last lines of the final scene are a short lyrical verse for Statira followed by blank verse for her and her advisor Megabise. Sarri set the lyrical verse as arioso (largo, $\frac{12}{8}$ time) accompanied by unison strings which also play a four-bar introductory ritornello, and the blank verse as accompanied recitative. The next opera requiring mention is Metastasio's *Didone abbandonata*, produced in Naples in 1724, in which Nicolini and Bulgarelli were once again the chief stars and Sarri was the composer (see above, p. 44). *Didone* was one of three Metastasio librettos with a tragic denouement.[21] It was one of two by him that ended with blank verse, and was unique in his oeuvre in having a soliloquy as its final scene. At the end of this scene Dido rushes into the flames of the burning city of Carthage to avoid falling into the hands of her enemy Jarba and possibly having to marry him. Like Statira, she has a short, lyrical verse slightly before her last exit. Due to the correspondences

---

[19] The early cases of long ritornellos in Handel's operatic recitative seem primarily of this category, though, as at the start of Bertarido's recitative in I.vi of *Rodelinda* (1725) (Chrysander edn., 1876, p. 20), they may also be descriptive of the mood and place of the action.

[20] This version of the opera had earlier been produced under the title of *Amore e maestà* at Pratolino in 1715.

[21] *Catone in Utica* and *Attilio Regolo* were the others.

of cast, composer, tragic denouement, even format of the ending, between
Arsace and *Didone*, it seems certain the former opera was an influence upon
the young Metastasio. As for Sarri, there is no doubt he remembered his
Arsace when writing the final scene of *Didone*. The same, non-lyrical style
is chosen both times for the final accompanied recitative. The lyrical verse
is again set as free arioso, in a minor key, and with the strings accompanying
in unison. Once again it has an opening unison ritornello. Its time signature
is again a triple one, though changed from $\frac{12}{8}$ to $\frac{3}{4}$. The *Didone* arioso goes:

EXAMPLE 2
Sarri, *Didone abbandonata*, III, xxi
(Performed at the Teatro S. Bartolomeo, Naples, 1724)

(I go . . . but where to ? Oh God ! I stay . . . but then . . . what do I do ? Do I therefore
have to die without finding pity ?)

Among the more significant things about this passage is its time signature.
By writing the music in triple time, Sarri separated it from the surrounding
recitative in $\frac{4}{4}$. He may have been influenced here by old, seventeenth-
century practices, for composers active in his youth so often set this kind

of short strophe in triple time. The next versions of *Didone* were Porpora's produced in Reggio Emilia in 1725 and Vinci's in Rome in 1726. The latter seems to have become famous for the quality and number of accompanied recitatives contained in its last act.[22] This act, regrettably, is not with the remainder of the music now at the National Library in Vienna. Some indication of what Vinci probably wrote is in a pasticcio version produced by Handel at London's Covent Garden in 1737 and preserved in manuscript at the British Museum.[23] The point is that there are sufficient general similarities between the ending of this MS. and Sarri's *Didone* to suggest that whoever wrote the former was at least aware of Sarri's score. The Vinci/Handel version, like Sarri's, commences with a ritornello for unison strings in the minor key. The accompaniment to the arioso starts in unison (though half-way through it breaks into full harmony). In both cases the quaver movement of the orchestra stops on the final 'senza trovar pietà?'. The important novelty of the Vinci/Handel ritornello and arioso is their $\frac{4}{4}$ time signature, which creates a sense of closer connection between this music and the surrounding recitative than exists in Sarri's setting. This closer connection furthermore has the extra result of making the ritornello sound not out of place as a recitative device.

The next move was to dissociate ritornellos (in $\frac{4}{4}$) from lyrical music altogether and attach them, where necessary, to non-lyrical recitative. Da Capua's claim must be viewed in this context. His claim has this much to be said for it that lengthy ritornellos (like those in arias) became common in accompanied recitative around the early '40s. This was the period when recitative began to incorporate other developments found within the aria, notably the constant use of dynamic nuance, the greater use of the crescendo, etc. Nor should we fail to mention the appearance at this time of wind instruments in recitative. These instruments seem to have been introduced initially into particular recitatives in which a distraught character was suffering from hallucinations or ghostly visions.[24] The winds' function was to produce a type of unearthly phantom call. The same effect (from the wind) had already been applied in lyrical music,[25]

---

[22] See Algarotti, *Essay*, p. 38; also Arteaga, *Delle rivoluzioni*, 1st edn., i. 289.

[23] Add. MS. 31607.

[24] Early instances are in Jommelli's *Astianatte* (1741), and *Merope* (1741), and in Terradellas's *Merope* (1743). For more comment on the Jommelli cases, see H. Abert, *Niccolo Jommelli als Opernkomponist*, Halle, 1908, pp. 135–6.

[25] e.g. in the middle section of the aria 'Larve, fremiti' from III. viii, of Vinci's *La Caduta dei decemviri* (1727).

and must have been suggested by the instruments' particular tone qualities.

The best description of accompanied recitative of the mid- to late eighteenth century, and one that gives some idea of how varied it had become, is John Brown's in *Letters upon the poetry and music of the Italian opera* (Edinburgh, 1789). Stating that musicians tried to put music of the highest quality into accompanied recitatives, he went on to say that the vocal line was not moulded merely, as was that of simple recitative, to imitate spoken dialogue. Its metre could be distorted, but not actually violated, if the composer felt that greater expressiveness could be obtained in so doing. The role of the orchestra was that of 'describing' the emotions felt by the character. The voice, Brown suggested, was more important than any other part, because—and this was a very eighteenth-century concept—the 'pathetic powers of music' were best left to it. The style of the vocal part could fluctuate between declamation and song.

Often, in the middle of a very agitated Recitative, on the occurrence of some tender idea, on which the mind is supposed to dwell with a kind of melancholy pleasure, the music loses, by degrees, the irregular character of Recitative, and resolves gradually into the even measure and continued melody of Air—then, on a sudden, at the call of some idea of an opposite nature, breaks off again into its former irregularity.[26]

The declamatory sections, let it be added, remained by and large in the traditional style associated with such music, but the lyrical sections and ritornellos kept in line with modern developments in the style of the aria.

The other matters requiring comment are the dramatic use, and the number of, accompanied recitatives in opera. Adjectives like 'agitated' and 'melancholy' in Brown's description confirm that the accompanied recitatives usually came at the more poignant or tragic moments. Since characters tended to brood and churn out their most intimate thoughts in private, the soliloquy was one favourite place for the accompanied recitative. And given that the soliloquy, in the Metastasian libretto format, often came first or last of a group of scenes acted in a single setting, the accompanied recitative often came at one or both of these positions.

In early eighteenth-century opera, in which accompanied recitative occurred sparingly, it is noticeable how the recitative was often placed immediately after a change to a 'gloomy' stage set, such as a prison, a desolate or remote place, a night scene. It was against this sort of back-

[26] pp. 21–2.

ground that the character was most likely to give expression to his melancholy thoughts, his terror, or his hallucinations. On the other hand there
were advantages in placing the accompanied recitative in the last of a
group of scenes, for here it might, together with the aria that in this
circumstance almost inevitably followed it, produce an effective, even
climactic, finish. Hasse and then Jommelli were among the first to exploit,
with any degree of regularity, the dramatic advantages of accompanied
recitative in the last scene of an act. Jommelli went further in some of his
later works and produced a complex type of finale with several alternating,
accompanied recitative and lyrical passages, or else an aria surrounded or
broken up by recitative sections.

Metastasio's letter of 1749 to Hasse regarding the number and position
of accompanied recitatives he would wish for in *Attilio Regolo*[27] has been
commented upon on several occasions. The opera is based on the story of
the Roman general captured by the Carthaginians who is forced to return
home on parole to arrange an exchange of prisoners and who goes back
to Carthage having persuaded his compatriots not to accept the proffered
terms. Metastasio suggested four occasions in the work suitable for
accompanied recitative. Only one was a soliloquy. This was for Regulus
in II.vii, while he awaited a crucial decision of the Roman Senate on its
Carthaginian policy. The others came where either Regulus' daughter,
Attilia (in I.ii), or Regulus himself (in I.vii and III.x) harangued an
individual or the crowd. III.x is the final scene of the opera terminating
with the hero's exit to return to Carthage and certain death. Metastasio
thought that here Hasse might accompany the hero's words with the
strings, and those of the other characters with the continuo only.[28]
Ritornellos, he wrote, might be inserted into the first part of the soliloquy
of II.vii when Regulus expresses his doubts and fears. But the moment the
hero abandons these 'unworthy' thoughts and springs to his feet, the
quality of the music must change; 'the rest of the scene requires resolution
and energy' and needs no ritornello to support it. The letter makes it clear
that Metastasio had two major concerns. The first was that accompanied
recitative had to be used with caution because its various embellishments,
great or small, tended to make it slow-moving. The second was that such

---

[27] The letter was published in translation in Burney, *Memoirs*, i. 321–8.

[28] The device of contrasting the words of the hero with those of the other characters by the use of
accompanied and simple recitative is found in the final scene of *Catone in Utica* as set by Vinci (1728).
Catone and *Attilio Regolo* were both Metastasian librettos with tragic endings. Did Metastasio
remember the Vinci setting as he wrote, many years later, to Hasse?

recitative lost much of its dramatic value if it was over-used. He admitted there might be places in *Attilio Regolo*, besides those he mentioned, where the orchestra could be used, but warned that 'this ornament should not be rendered too familiar'.

Each composer was free to choose how many accompanied recitatives he wanted—within certain limits. While Hasse stuck close to Metastasio's specifications in his setting of *Attilio Regolo* (1750), Jommelli in his (1753) increased the number to seven and, incidentally, emphasized the part of Attilia more than Hasse had done by enlarging her share of the accompanied recitative total. The general trend of the period was of course toward an increased number of accompanied recitatives. And it is also true to say that the average length of each recitative tended to grow as the eighteenth century proceeded. German scholars in particular have praised Hasse and Jommelli for the part they played in raising the proportion of accompanied to simple recitative and have regarded this as one of the most modern signs to be found in mid-century Italian opera.[29] Their attitude is understandable, since Gluck's reform involving the use of accompanied recitative to the virtual exclusion of simple was just around the corner, and since we can see in retrospect that the extinction of simple recitative was an ultimate certainty everywhere. The argument favouring a maximum use of the orchestra was that it could reinforce, in a way the continuo could not, any phrase that required elaboration or expansion. And its presence ensured the possibility of emotive recitative at all times. The arguments against would have run rather as Metastasio outlined them. The constant use of the orchestra cheapened the effect and made its appearance at a really dramatic moment less spectacular. A composer with a bad sense of timing could make a scene actually less effective than it would have been with continuo accompaniment only.

There are no signs that Neapolitans in the early decades of the eighteenth century were advanced in their thinking on accompanied recitative. But neither were they particularly conservative. Sarri's *Didone abbandonata* contained what was for that time the unusually large number of six recitatives with orchestra (one occurring in each of the last scenes of the three acts). Other operas were performed in Naples in the '20s with three or four, though one or two was a more normal number. Maybe because of arguments against the over-use of such recitative, or because conditions in the theatre did not allow for too much experiment, the average number

---

[29] c.g. R. Haas in G. Adler (ed.), *Handbuch der Musikgeschichte*, reprint, Tutzing, 1961, ii. 724–6.

and size of accompanied recitatives in each opera increased slowly during the following decades. Jommelli's *Armida abbandonata* (1770), composed after he had returned to Naples from Württemberg (where he had composed operas with several and very resourceful recitatives), contained ten accompanied recitatives altogether. This number is above average for an opera composed for Naples around that period. *Armida* was a successful opera nonetheless.[30] It was repeated at the S. Carlo in 1771 when Jommelli's *Ifigenia in Tauride* failed to please and had to be taken off, and again in 1780. So there can have been no rooted objection on the Neapolitans' part to the increase in the use of the orchestra *per se*.

The fact remains that from the mid-century on, non-Italian audiences favoured recitative with the orchestra to a degree most Italian audiences did not. Jommelli was not the only Neapolitan composer either to exploit or else discover the advantages of a considerable use of accompanied recitative while he lived outside Italy. Paisiello was another. Paisiello left Naples, where he was known primarily as a composer of comic opera, for St. Petersburg in 1776. It was in Russia that he came to understand the value of accompanied recitative clearly. He wrote about his 1780 setting of *Alcide al bivio*, a short *azione teatrale* by Metastasio, in this manner: 'I have worked very hard on it, since I wanted to get away from the inconveniences created in Italian theatres, and have completely excluded vocalizations, cadenzas, and ritornellos, and set nearly all the recitatives with orchestral accompaniments.'[31] His claim to have set 'nearly all' recitatives as *accompagnati* turns out to be a slight exaggeration, since there are many simple recitative passages. The score suggests he may have begun with the intention of making substantial use of the orchestra, for the first recitatives are mostly accompanied. But for a reason that seems unrelated to the drama, the recitatives in the middle of the work are mostly simple— perhaps he ran out of time to compose them otherwise—while those towards the end are the most mixed. Regardless of Paisiello's claim, *Alcide* does show considerable advance in his use of accompanied recitative for dramatic purposes. In fact he had little immediate chance to build upon his experience with this work, since the operas he wrote during the rest of his Russian stay (up to January 1784) seem—so far as can be ascertained—to have been comic in every case. Because accompanied recitative was

---

[30] The young Mozart, during his Neapolitan visit of 1770, saw this opera and judged the music 'beautiful, but too serious and old-fashioned for the theatre'. *The letters of Mozart*, ed. Andersen, i. 211.

[31] Quoted in A. della Corte, *Paisiello*, Turin, 1922, p. 60.

associated with poignant or melancholy moments rather than with humorous ones, the need for it in comic opera was comparatively limited. On his return to Naples Paisiello began to write heroic operas for the S. Carlo as well as comic operas for the smaller theatres. Though these heroic works (commencing with *Antigono*, 1785) do show signs of progressive maturity, they do not contain that increased proportion of accompanied recitatives that the experiment of *Alcide* might lead us to expect.

Perhaps it is unfair to suggest that Paisiello should necessarily have done more with recitative than he did, given that one of the bases of Italian heroic opera was, or at least had been, the separation of action (in recitative) from music (in arias and ensembles). By multiplying and enlarging the accompanied recitatives, composers upset the balance between words and music that a previous generation had constructed. Again, if more emphasis was put on the orchestra, correspondingly less of the music's total value could be contained in the voice part—and in a country like Italy, where vocal technique reached high standards, there was bound to be argument on the relationship of the human voice to the orchestra. One place where the voice could be given the opportunity to be expressive was the aria—expressive here in the sense that the voice could suitably imitate or mirror an affection or state of mind. Eighteenth-century descriptions of the aria often state that it should express the affection uppermost at the moment; they usually disregard characterization, which we might think equally important. Even on the question of the affections, answers are not so clear as we would like them to be. Italians were generally less communicative about how to imitate affections in music than their German contemporaries; and in fact the information given by Monteverdi in his eighth madrigal book about the soft, moderate, and agitated feelings in music, and especially his practical advice on how to imitate a feeling of agitation,[32] remains about as clear a statement on the principle involved as we are likely to find in Italian writings. There were several eighteenth-century manuals by Italians that emphasized performance details—such as continuo harmonies, graces, turns, and other embellishments—all creating the mood and affecting the listener correctly. In this they complemented the large, mid-century German treatises such as Quantz's on the flute, and C. P. E. Bach's on the clavier, which also examined the application of the theory of affections in relation to the manner of performance rather

---

[32] Translated by O. Strunk, *Source readings*, pp. 413–15.

than to the basic features of a composition (the beat, time signature, mode, etc.). What strikes one about such treatises is that they took the matter of the affections largely for granted as though it were too obvious to merit preliminary discussion. Yet it was upon a fundamental understanding of the affections that the rules of composition and/or performance were built up.

The tendency of some mid- and late eighteenth-century authors to classify aria types according to musical style and the feeling aroused was based on an assumption of the doctrine's validity. This manner of classification was new in the sense that it was sufficiently simple to be understood by the average amateur; which may be why modern writers have so often quoted their comments as an easy introduction to the understanding of the eighteenth-century aria. There was de Brosses's classification of the arias in three groups: the first depicting violent action or else a strong force in nature, a stormy sea, high winds, etc; the second containing some delicate thought, or perhaps comparison, drawn from pleasant objects like zephyrs, birds, or murmuring waves; the third group tying itself closely to the action and expressing human emotions in a simple, non-virtuoso style.[33] According to Goldoni's evidence the leading castrato, leading lady, and leading tenor each expected an *aria patetica*, *aria di bravura*, *aria parlante*, *aria di mezzo carattere*, and *aria brillante*.[34] In J. Brown's *Letters upon the poetry and music of the Italian opera* occurs the often quoted classification of arias again into five main groups: *aria cantabile* (to do with 'sentiments of tenderness'), *aria di portamento* (suitable to express 'sentiments of dignity'), *aria di mezzo carattere* (a type serious and pleasing yet not so dignified or pathetic as the former ones), *aria parlante* (particularly to express agitation or passion), and *aria di bravura* (for display purposes).[35] The terms *rondo* and *cavatina* which he mentioned related merely to the structure of arias and not to their content. Others had slightly different ideas on aria classification and terminology, which shows how details were open to interpretation.[36] To us it is clear that composers did tend to select certain types of style for certain types of aria. But whether they thought about their system or were taught in their conservatories to apply one remains unclear. Brown may have provided us with an inkling of the truth in his *Letters*, where, having

[33] *Lettres familières*, ii. 369 ff.

[34] Goldoni, *Commedie*, Venice, 1761, xi. 6.

[35] pp. 36–40.

[36] J. A. Hiller, *Anweisung zum musikalisch-richtigen Gesange*, Leipzig, 1774, p. 213, mentions the following types: *Aria di bravura*, *Aria di strepito*, *Aria d'espressione*, and *Aria cantabile*.

given his own list of aria types, he then stated he had met several Italian composers who knew nothing about any such classification system. He concluded that the various types of aria sprang from natural order or from, as he put it, 'distinctions of a higher kind'. Which could be a sophisticated way of saying that common sense dictated which of the styles a composer had at his command would best suit the words. Other factors which affected the composers' choice included the claims and demands of the singers— Goldoni's experience with *Amalasunta* is some indication of this (see above, p. 54). A further influence on the composer was the example set by the aria music of his contemporaries. This is a point we shall return to later.

The fact that these lists of aria types were compiled, or at least put down on paper, well after the start of the eighteenth century ties in with what we were saying in Chap. II about comment by theorists on aria functions and how this comment began to appear *c.* 1740. Had there been equal interest in discussions on the aria back at the end of the seventeenth century, no doubt there would have been attempts then to classify aria types.[37] Such lists would have been possible to make. The point is that opposites of feeling inspired the composer then as later to use opposites of style, and these are relatively easy to pick out. In Provenzale's operas of the 1670s it is easy to see how the emotions of hopelessness or tenderness on the one hand, and rage on the other, tended to inspire the composer to employ opposite types of music: the first in a 'white' notation, usually in $\frac{3}{2}$ time, with simple melody, and with a thorough-bass accompaniment that followed the style of the vocal part; the second in a 'black' notation, generally in $\frac{4}{4}$, a busier style, this, with fast moving bass, some vocalizations for the singer, a compact and tight 'trio' accompaniment, and a more instrumental flavour to the music as a whole. Extreme differences are as easy to identify in the operas of the next decades, exemplified by A. Scarlatti's written during his first residence in Naples from 1683 to 1702. Conspicuous are the bravura styles, usually in $\frac{4}{4}$ and remarkable for the accompaniments of fast, repeated notes or broken chord passages. The $\frac{12}{8}$ time signature, which first appeared in Italian opera around 1670, was used extensively by A. Scarlatti, G. Bononcini, and others from the mid-1690s to provide an *amoroso* or pathetic effect, or suggest a pastoral scene. Certain short canzonetta-type arias were also written in $\frac{12}{8}$. One of the most lively

[37] There is no suggestion here that exactly the same lists would have been compiled as were compiled later. M. Bukofzer's warning in *Music in the baroque era*, New York, 1947, pp. 329–30 n. 27, that Brown's particular classification should not be applied to Handel's arias, is most valid.

styles was the one in $\frac{4}{4}$ characterized by a chain of quaver notes in the bass, each note different in pitch from the last. Composers used $\frac{3}{8}$ time to create effects similar to those already described and others besides. They realized that no style was more easy-flowing than the one with a chain of medium-paced semiquavers in this particular time. No style, in complete contrast, was more emphatic and jerky than the one with a succession of short-longs (♪♩) enlivened occasionally by a hemiola device.[38] Some arias in $\frac{3}{4}$ will be found in operas of this period, but they form a small minority. They tend to be medium- or quick-paced, but otherwise do not fit into any one aria group. The $\frac{3}{2}$ time signature, which had been such a feature of lyrical passages in mid-century Venetian opera, was rarely employed after the early 1690s, the crotchet finally and conclusively becoming the common time-unit rather than the minim.

It is not unknown for an author, having made a summary of aria styles, to warn that many arias pass outside any neat classification.[39] The truth is that there are several criteria for measuring stylistic and qualitative differences, and all may have validity. One very different line of approach from that taken in the last paragraph is to measure the modernity of an aria and its style in relation to the rest of the opera and to the period, an approach certainly appropriate in works of the 1690s and early 1700s in which the contrast between old and new produced a curious stylistic dichotomy. The most conservative type of aria was short, supported by the continuo alone, with ritornellos not sufficiently developed to allow much breathing space for the voice, and with a similar, non-virtuoso style for both voice and accompaniment. This non-virtuoso style was often based on dance patterns and/or simple, reiterated metrical rhythms. By comparison a more modern and easy-flowing style was adopted in other pieces, especially in those with prominent ritornellos (which allowed for correspondingly longer rests for the voice) and with well-developed orchestration. Melodies in these arias were more elongated, more repetitions occurred—especially of terminal phrases—and modulations were managed with greater finesse. While it is not true to say that contemporary instrumental music was solely responsible for new trends, the modernity of these arias with a strong, independent instrumental

---

[38] The curious alternations of $\frac{3}{8}$ and $\frac{2}{4}$ bars in 'Bel piacere è godere' from Handel's *Agrippina* (Venice, 1709) are a sophisticated variant of the $\frac{3}{8}$–$\frac{3}{4}$ rhythms in other arias of this category.

[39] See Bukofzer, *Music in the baroque era*, pp. 328–9, who sees five main aria types in Handel's operas, four based on dance patterns and one on the concerto.

part or parts suggests a cross-influence. Something of the stylistic dichotomy can be gauged from two arias in Scarlatti's *La caduta dei decemviri* (1697). The first of these is no bad aria, but it seems constricted by comparison with the other. Its effect was obviously intentional, because Scarlatti was an experienced composer by the time he wrote this opera. The two arias are for the same character, so the singer's capabilities had nothing to do with the choice of style.

EXAMPLE 3
A. Scarlatti, *La caduta dei decemviri*, III, vii
(Performed at the Teatro S. Bartolomeo, Naples, 1697)

io   tu   la tua da - ma.   E for - se del cor

mi - o   a - ma - ta an-cor son i - o,   E forse anch' il   tuo

ben Suo ben ti chia -   ma.   E forse anch' il   tuo

ben Suo ben ti chia -   ma,   suo ben - ti chia -

- ma.   O se *etc.*

(Oh, if only we could one day hope, I to embrace my sun, you your lady. Perhaps I am still loved by my dearest, and perhaps your sweetheart also calls you her dearest)

EXAMPLE 4
A. Scarlatti, *La caduta dei decemviri*, II, i

(Love, spread your wings, and enter the heart of my dearest one)

A similar contrast of style can be seen in the earliest operas of Neapolitans like Sarri and Porsile who commenced their professional careers in the first decade of the eighteenth century. Something of the same appears, incidentally, in Handel's *Agrippina*, written for Venice in 1709, in which the biggest arias for Poppaea contrast with her minute 'Tuo ben è'l trono'[40] with its primitive *da capo* form and its artless melody less reminiscent of Handel than of Venetian composers working perhaps thirty years earlier. This sense of constriction to which we refer is not something that remains in Neapolitan arias for long. Scarlatti's arias written during his second period of residence in Naples, 1708–25, for example, have an evenness of quality

[40] Chrysander edn., 1874, p. 76.

not found in his earlier work of *c.* 1700. They breathe easily for a number
of reasons, some stylistic and some structural: the modulations are more
carefully prepared and more slowly completed than those in earlier arias,
the musical phrases take longer to settle on to the cadences, there are more
ritornellos, the vocal part is more elaborately structured, the number of
repeats of words and musical phrases has increased. The point to stress at
this juncture is that this sense of expansiveness applies to most arias regardless of style or instrumentation.

A study of the instrumentation of the aria shows that this also tended to
become more uniform over the first decades of the eighteenth century. If
we go back for the moment and examine earlier practice, say in the 1670s–
80s, we find that the orchestra in many opera scores of that time is never
divided in more than three parts, two presumably for violins and one for
continuo. The instruments are rarely mentioned by name, and it is uncertain whether larger ensembles were employed in performance. Another,
fuller stringed orchestra in five parts was common to several operas by
Venetian composers, as it was usual in Lully's. In the specific case of
Neapolitan scores, we note that those known to be by Provenzale contain
three orchestral parts as a maximum. The early operas by Scarlatti have
many sections supported by a fuller stringed orchestra than the one
Provenzale indicated. The string orchestra, however, is now normally
divided not into five but into four parts (two violins, viola, continuo),
which is a more modern practice. These same scores seem neither more nor
less adventurous than those written by Northern Italians in what they
specify for wind instruments. It was during the last two decades of the
century that wind instruments were allowed to play a prominent and
individual role, possessing a like degree of independence to what older-
type wind instruments possessed in very early opera, for example in
Monteverdi's *Orfeo*. Several parts in scores of the period suggest a wind
instrument of some kind, but the specifications are missing. In other cases
a trumpet is mentioned. The words *fagotto*, *oboè*, and *flautino*, begin to
appear frequently in scores composed at the very end of the century. The
normal accompaniment to an aria of this era consisted of continuo alone
or continuo with one, two, or three string parts, and perhaps with a wind
instrument or two doubling the strings or providing an *obbligato*. The end
of the century was a period of considerable experimentation in orchestral
colour, and one in which many different combinations within the then
opera orchestra were tried out. Items with interesting combinations within

Scarlatti's *Il prigionier fortunato* produced at the S. Bartolomeo in 1698 are here mentioned in order of singing:

(1) 'Quell 'esser misero'   Recorder, violins, cellos, continuo.
     (aria, I.iii)
(2) 'Miei pensieri'   Solo viola, cellos, continuo.
     (aria, I.v)
(3) 'Belle fonti che correte'   Two groups each consisting of cellos, *Leuto e*
     (duet, II.ix)   *basso solo* [*sic*].
(4) 'Povera pellegrina'   Two solo violins, solo cello, *ripieno* group consist-
     (aria, II.xi)   ing of violins, violas, cellos, and *contrabassi soli*.
(5) 'Datti pace o sventurato' Two violins, violas.
     (aria, II.xiv)
(6) 'Aprir io voglio il petto'   Two solo lutes, violins, *cembali*.[41]
     (aria, III.viii)

It is clear from (4) above that the full *concerto grosso* was at the disposition of opera composers. (2) and (4) show that the leading viola and cello players had opportunities for solos—such as, incidentally, their mid-eighteenth-century successors rarely enjoyed. (3) and (6) prove that lutes formed part of the resources of the continuo group as they had done in opera productions early in the seventeenth century. (3) is interesting too because it is a duet in which each of the singers is accompanied by his own group of continuo instruments. As the singers alternate or amalgamate, the instruments do the same. This is an appropriate moment to say that, when the orchestra was first seated in the S. Carlo in 1737, the two *cembali* and other instruments forming the continuo were placed in two groups at opposite ends.[42] If this were also the placing in the older S. Bartolomeo pit, then (3) above would have produced an interesting stereophony.

Taking a more general look at the instrumentation of opera scores, we note a development in favour of a larger average number of instrumental staves per aria. This means among other things that arias accompanied merely by continuo went out of fashion. By the early 1690s Scarlatti was already composing more arias with violin part (in addition to the continuo) than without. In his latest operas written after *c.* 1710 he hardly ever limited his resources merely to continuo. As this average number grew, so the majority of arias was allotted two instrumental parts, then

---

[41] The violins and harpsichords are here notated on a single stave with bass clef. Probably the term *violini* refers to all members of the violin family in this case, the cellos supporting the bass and the violins playing one or two octaves higher.

[42] See Prota-Giurleo, *La grande orchestra del R. Teatro San Carlo nel settecento*, Naples, 1927. pp. 7 ff.

four. The increase meant that the great differences in the number of parts between one aria and the next, a feature of late seventeenth-century opera, narrowed, and a more uniform type of orchestration emerged. As a warning against assuming that analysis of instrumental resources presents no problem, it should be stated that a common custom of composers in the late seventeenth century was to add an orchestral ritornello in three or four parts as a type of prologue or epilogue to an aria supported by continuo alone. Thus the full body of strings was on call during an aria even though it was not actually required to accompany the voice. Should such ritornellos be deemed to be an integral part of the aria—as they may be— then the number of arias supported by the full string orchestra mounts proportionally. In general the tendency was to bring this full body in for more and more of the ritornellos, so that its sound gradually infused the whole of the music and it finally contributed to the average increase in the number of parts already mentioned. Another, related warning concerns the differences between 'staves' and 'parts' since the two are not synonymous and since the extra staves did not always mean an increase in real parts in the piece. Again, vocal soloists other than basses used in the late seventeenth century to sing their arias without unison support from an instrument. But by the second decade of the next century, the first violins, especially, were often called upon to play in unison with the voice.

The changing relationship of the instruments to each other and to the voice is a further point to be examined. Take the case of the *basso continuo*. In all those passages in which the continuo was the only accompaniment, the harpsichord players were soloists whose function was to provide harmony and right-hand melody. However, with the greater involvement of the orchestra in the aria, they became, more and more, accompanists providing just harmonic support. This 'support', let it be said, was still essential, not least since the person at the first harpsichord was normally the composer or director of the performance. The greater involvement of the orchestra also meant that less of the burden of the accompaniment fell upon the continuo, and composers began to experiment with silent bars for the continuo while other instruments carried on playing. H. C. Wolff points to C. F. Pollaroli's *Onorio in Roma*, first performed in Venice in 1692, for its arias with violin support and without the traditional bass.[43]

---

[43] *Die venezianische Oper in der zweiten Hälfte des 17. Jahrhunderts*, Berlin, 1937, p. 99. The English translator of Raguenet's *Parallèle des Italiens et des Français* credited Pollaroli with the invention of this particular technique, see *MQ* 1946, xxxii. 424 n.

Experiments of this kind became fashionable. Marcello, in his *Teatro alla moda* of 1720, refers to them in several paragraphs of which this is one: 'The arias then should proceed without the bass, and so that the singer may be kept on the note, the violins shall be made to accompany him at the unison, and some bass notes may then in such a case be given to the violas, but this is a matter of choice.[44] There were several ways of lightening the bass, and composers often instructed the lower strings to continue but the harpsichords to be silent, or the harpsichords to play from the lowest harmony line, that is the viola or cello line, and the double basses to be silent. These were additional techniques to the one of composing without *basso continuo* altogether.

The relationship of the instruments to the voice was bound to be affected by the technical proficiency of both of them. New techniques on the strings enabled players to execute passages that could not be done by, or else were thought not suitable for, the singer. Violin parts, especially, were designed to show off the players' new ability to cross the bow over several strings from note to note, to play arpeggios with ease, to shift the hand above third position. Neither the leaps nor the range that a stringed instrument was capable of were vocally feasible; and composers understood the voice too well to make it compete with the strings in these ways. Nevertheless the voice could execute many passages as nimbly and quickly as any stringed or wind instrument. The singer could control his breathing as carefully as could any wind player. And the ability of the singer to rival, even surpass, the instrumentalist in certain types of bravura was one of the chief reasons why the incursion of instrumentally-conceived passages into the aria was so general and unresisted.[45] Burney's anecdote of Farinelli and the trumpeter is important in this regard. According to the story the singer and the player extemporized each night during the performance of a particular aria, their extemporization ending with a combined shake in thirds. Their performance became competitive, and one night the trumpeter sustained the shake until he was utterly spent, stopping then on the assumption that the singer would be forced to do the same. But Farinelli carried on without breath and produced further virtuoso passages.[46] The story suggests that top-ranking singers could equal or

---

[44] Ed. d'Angeli, pp. 18–9.

[45] H-P. Schmitz, *Die Kunst der Verzierung im 18. Jahrhundert*, Kassel, 1955, p. 14, suggests the influence was two-way, the singer having the example of players in fast passages, the player the example of the singers and their cantabile in slow.

[46] *The present state*, pp. 205–6.

surpass anything a *clarino* trumpeter could then produce. The incident occurred, again according to Burney, in Rome when Farinelli was seventeen. This would make the date 1722 or 1723. Since most of the big, written-out solos for *obbligato* trumpet occur in operatic scores written before this date, it seems that the incident took place toward the end of the Italian *clarino* trumpeter's heyday. It is not clear from Burney's account whether the improvised passage was a vocalization or a cadenza. A cadenza might seem the more obvious alternative, but a vocalization it could have been since some late-baroque arias had vocalizations with cadenza-like qualities and with support from an *obbligato* instrument. A good case is the one in 'Ondeggiante agitato il pensiero' from Scarlatti's *Il prigionier fortunato* (1698), an aria whose first section has thirty-two bars all told. Thirteen of these thirty-two bars are a vocalization with solo trumpet support. The player starts it off with short phrases each echoed by the singer at the same pitch. After this sparring the two performers settle on high A and F sharp (the trumpeter being on top) and they then perform a long shake in semiquavers.

EXAMPLE 5
A. Scarlatti, *Il prigionier fortunato*, III, vii
(Performed at the Teatro S. Bartolomeo, 1698)

This is finally interrupted by a single D in the bass, obviously the harpsichordist's signal, heralding the re-entry of the orchestra and the end of the vocalization. The chances of extemporization within this section are many. The soloists could well delay the start of the shake by adding extra phrases to the earlier part, and the harpsichordist could delay his chord, thus letting the shake last longer.

The 1690s seems to have been the period when composers swung decisively in favour of the *da capo*. In a lengthy study of A. Scarlatti's early operas, A. Lorenz points to *Pirro e Demetrio* (1694) as the particular work of his in which 'the seal is set on the dominance of the da capo form.'[47] Lorenz's contention was that *da capo* form was accepted by so many

---

[47] *Alessandro Scarlattis Jugendopern*, Augsburg, 1927, i. 144.

because ternary form was an intrinsically satisfying one in itself.[48] This cannot be the only reason, or else *da capo* arias would have been in a majority in much earlier opera too. The only comments printed in the 1690s on the shape of the aria that have so far come to light are Salvadori's in *Poetica toscana*. It is quite clear from this book that the author accepts the convention of the *da capo*. He states that the first two lines of a four-line aria verse are to be repeated—he does not say they are to be repeated at the end, but he must mean this since all the aria verses he quotes end with the return of the first sentence.[49] Though there was no need for the music to follow the words and return to the opening too, there seems little reason why the verses should persistently have this idiosyncrasy unless the musical structure were somehow related. The interesting thing is that though Salvadori accepts the verse formula as normal, he does not say why it is normal. And on this point we are still guessing. One fact to note is that the *da capo* structure became the convention at a time when arias with two or more strophes set to the same music were going out of fashion. The repeat of the first section at the end of a *da capo* aria allowed a second hearing and so acted in a way like a substitute strophe. It could be that the elements both of structural balance and of repetition were among the reasons underlying the popular choice of *da capo* form. Tosi, in his *Opinioni de 'cantori* (1723), hints that this particular form became popular because of the desire 'to show the Capacity of the Singer, in varying the Repetition'.[50] He declared that singers took the opportunity to vary the three sections of the *da capo* aria with successively more elaborate ornament. From what he writes, and from other evidence,[51] it is clear that the repeat of the first section, which was the most ornamented part, was the climax of the piece. Whether singers were, or were not, responsible for making the *da capo* initially popular, it is certain they thereafter helped ensure its general acceptance for a long period. For the form allowed them an opportunity to show how they could vary a given vocal line, and audiences probably liked to compare their different renditions.

[48] Ibid., i. 61.

[49] pp. 76 ff.

[50] *Observations on the florid song*, p. 91.

[51] Including eighteenth-century aria manuscripts with the ornament written in. Note the aria 'Son qual nave' by R. Broschi with the embellishments sung by his brother, the famed Farinelli, quoted in H-P. Schmitz, *Die Kunst der Verzierung*, pp. 76–93. Schmitz notices (p. 31) that there are no additional embellishments notated in the middle section and comments that 'the middle section of the aria [is], as usual, decorated hardly at all.'

Not altogether irrelevant to this discussion on varied repetitions are Grosley's remarks on what happened if an aria was encored. Grosley was in Italy toward the end of the 1750s.

At the operas in Italy, clapping an *arietta* is a signal for an *encore*. The orchestra then returns to the prelude, and the *castrato* walks about in a circle, and sings the favourite *arietta* the second time. This is sometimes repeated even to the fifth or sixth time; and in these repetitions it is, that the singer exerts every resource of nature and art, to surpass himself at each repetition, by the variety of gradations which he introduces into the trills, modulations, and whatever belongs to the expression. Slight and quick as some of these gradations may be, not one of them escapes an Italian ear . . . [52]

It is natural to relate this to what is already known about mid-eighteenth-century performance practice and the constant wish of soloists of the period to embellish their parts. In the context of opera it is also necessary to remember that audiences in theatres like the S. Carlo attended many performances of one production (see above, p. 9), so singers had to devise what methods they could to hold the audience's interest. If a soloist were lucky enough to be called upon regularly to sing encores, then the need for variation grew proportionately. Not least among the reasons why mid-century singers and audiences could give their entire attention to embellishment and other matters relating 'to the expression' was the fact that *da capo* structures were so well understood, and composers kept so overwhelmingly to the convention, that few needed to think about it. A curious sense of comfort indeed may have been derived from complete knowledge of the *da capo* form and of other, stable elements, for example the positioning of the aria just before the end of the scene. At the same time knowledge must have created a heightened awareness of any deviations from the standard formulas. So if by any chance an aria was performed that was not in *da capo* form, and gave the singer no varied repeat, the impact was probably greater on the Italian audience of the time than it could be on a modern audience accustomed to very different operatic traditions.

Another sign of satisfaction with *da capo* form was the general absence of printed criticism in Italy against it. Not till the 1770s–'80s did the aria's form come under attack, mainly on the grounds that it made nonsense of the words. Tosi had expressed the earlier complaisance of his fellow Italians when he wrote that the invention of the first section repeat 'cannot be blam'd by Lovers of Musick; though in respect of the Words it is some-

---

[52] *New observations on Italy*, ii. 234.

times an Impropriety',[53] meaning thereby that in the aria the music came first. One of the earliest things composers and librettists had to learn about *da capo* form was that if the first section was to appear again at the finish, then the text of this section should contain a main clause so as to make perfect sense. R. Gerber has singled out the aria 'Gran tonante' from I.x of Scarlatti's *La Statira* (1690) as a case of unsatisfactory use of the *da capo*.[54] Scarlatti here was presented with a verse containing a conditional clause followed by a main one. In the aria as we have it the first and third music sections cover the conditional clause, the second covers the main. The most suitable aria verse was one with a main clause for each of the two music sections to be composed, and the aria verse-form that emerged to suit the *da capo* normally had this feature. While this got rid of one type of impropriety with respect to the words, it did not remove others. A repeat of the first section was still nonsense if it contradicted the meaning of the second. Again, if the words of the first part were treated too thoroughly by the composer and those of the second were skimped, then the repeat merely accentuated the imbalance. That the first part did grow out of all proportion to the second is evident from even the most cursory of glances at scores of the 1740s onwards. Curiously, *a–b–a* form arias in scores of the late seventeenth century often contained a longer *b* section than either of the *a*'s. The custom of placing more and more musical emphasis on the first part was an eighteenth-century phenomenon. An early sign of the composers' greater interest in *a* than *b* was their organization of the former into a standardized binary structure, while the latter remained less organized. This two-part organization of *a* came into being in Italy during the approximate 1705–15 period. The first half of the aria text was set twice in its entirety with optional ritornellos at the start and middle and with a standard ritornello at the close. The first run-through of the words brought the key from the tonic to a related key, while the second brought it back to the tonic. Perhaps this arrangement was so that the music could expand without unorganized proliferation of word repeats. It also demonstrated the wish of that generation of composers for clear, standardized musical structures. Earlier methods of expanding the music of the vocal line, especially the trick of inserting a ritornello after the initial vocal phrase and then making the voice go back to the start (the so-called *Devise*), were now not so necessary and tended to fall into abeyance.

[53] *Observations on the florid song*, p. 91.
[54] *Der Operntypus Johann Adolf Hasses und seine textlichen Grundlagen*, Leipzig, 1925, p. 30.

This does not explain why composers failed to make so compact an arrangement in the case of the second part. Perhaps the first part was considered
more important because it had to make the initial impact on the audience
and because the singers' wish to embellish the repeat put undue emphasis
upon it.

One of the ways singers were expected to add to the pleasurable quality
of the aria was through the improvized cadenza. According to Tosi there
were three of these per aria, one at the end of each part.[55] By cadenza we
do not mean just an embellished rendering of a cadence point—for the
embellishment of cadences was a common practice long before the
eighteenth century—but a cadence arrested by an orchestral pause during
which the soloist added whatever trills and runs came to his fancy. Quantz
had definite views about when such pauses became common.

Perhaps the surest account that can be given of the origins of the cadenzas is that
several years before the end of the previous century and in the first ten years of the
present one, the close of a concertante part was made with a little passage over a
moving bass, to which a good shake was attached; between 1710 and 1716, or
thereabouts, the cadenzas customary at present, in which the bass must pause,
became the mode. Fermatas, in which one pauses *ad libitum* in the middle of a piece,
may well have a somewhat earlier origin.[56]

The same dates for the origin of the cadenza were given by J. F. Agricola,[57]
who may have taken his information from Quantz. Whether they are
correct remains an open question. There is a curious statement in Raguenet's
Parellèle des Italiens et des Français of 1702 suggesting that final cadences
were of some length—in which case pauses were possible then. The appropriate section from the English translation of 1709 states that Italian singers
will 'execute passages of I know not how many bars together, they'll have
echoes on the same passages and swellings of a prodigious length, and then,
with a chuckle in the throat, exactly like that of a nightingale, they'll
conclude with cadences of an equal length, and all this in the same breath'.[58]
Another problem is to determine the position of the pause. Did Quantz
mean that by 1716 the pause came on the $^6_4$ chord of the classical cadence
formula with which we are familiar from Mozart's and Beethoven's
concertos? A noticeable characteristic of arias by Neapolitans—Scarlatti
especially—in the second decade of the eighteenth century is the rest in all

[55] *Observations*, pp. 128–9.
[56] *On playing the flute*, English Edn., trans. Reilly, London, 1966, pp. 179–80.
[57] *Anleitung zur Singkunst*, p. 196.
[58] *MQ* 1946, xxxii. 426.

parts just prior to the final cadence. When a fermata occurs over this rest, the suspicion seems confirmed that this was the position of the cadenza. A pause over the subsequent $^6_4$ chord does not seem nearly so apposite or likely from the musical point of view.

EXAMPLE 6
A. Scarlatti, *L'amor generoso*, I, ii
(Performed at the Royal Palace, Naples, 1714)

We know for sure that the $^6_4$ chord was the position of the pause for the cadenza by *c.* 1750. Tartini tells us so in a rather roundabout way in his *Traité des agréments de la musique*.[59] It so happens that the abrupt pause before the cadence formula disappeared from Neapolitan arias in the 1720s. And it could be that this was the period when the cadenza shifted its position on to the final cadence phrase itself.

The melodic and harmonic progressions used in final cadences are to be found basically in whatever aria of the period we care to look at, and clearly these were inculcated in students as fundamental formulas of good composition. Tosi mentioned three types of final cadence. He did not bother to discuss the harmonies as the cadences were perfect in each case. The melody of the first type fell by step from the third degree of the scale on to the tonic; the second also had three notes—tonic, leading-note, tonic; the third was distinguished by a drop of a fifth on to the last, tonic note.[60] Tosi surprisingly described this third as 'at present the most prevailing', though independent study suggests it was usual only in music for bass singers—a definite minority among the Italian singing profession and employed usually to sing comic roles. What Tosi did not mention was that the final note of the cadence was customarily on a strong beat, so needed a last word

[59] Ed. Jacobi, Celle & New York, 1961, p. 118. Jacobi, p. 39, considers the *Traité* to have been compiled between 1752 and 1756.
[60] *Observations*, pp. 126–7.

with stressed final syllable. But librettists often provided a final line suggesting a feminine cadence, with accent on the penultimate syllable. This
conflict of accents may have been the cause of the common, seventeenth-
century cadence formula found in the works of Cavalli, Cesti, and others,
and exemplified by the upper of the two vocal parts (below) from a duet
in an early opera by Scarlatti. The detail to notice is the last, unaccented
syllable placed on the penultimate, unaccented note and not on the final,
accented one.

EXAMPLE 7
A. Scarlatti, *L'onestà negli amori*, I, xii
(Performed at the Bernini Palace, Rome 1680)

Scarlatti and his contemporaries gradually dropped this cadence formula
over the 1680s–'90s, and tended more and more to write strong, masculine
final cadences whatever the word accent. Librettists now had to learn to
write aria verses whose two sections had a final line ending with a stressed
syllable.[61] Quadrio was one who recognized it was the poet's duty to
please the composer on this occasion: 'Then it will be observed that in all
the arias truncated lines [*versi troncati*] please composers not a little and
sound very well at the end of the cadences.'[62] That he was talking about
cadences with a final stressed syllable is clear from the short verse he
quoted as example:

> Il mio core a chi la diede,
> Serva fede:
> Nè già mai si cangerà.

(May my heart be true to the one sworn to me. Indeed, it shall never be swayed)

A discussion on the appositeness of melodic phrase to word accent leads
conveniently to the subject of melody in arias written by Neapolitans in

---

[61] For late instances of conflict of accent at the cadence, see the aria 'Per queste amare lacrime' from
III.vi of Pergolesi's *Salustia* (1731), Caffarelli edn., 1941, p. 161.
[62] *Della storia, e della ragione*, iii (seconda parte), 445.

the 1720s–'30s. Vinci and Hasse, like Scarlatti, were often prepared to fit the musical phrase to the line rather than to the sense of the verse and mix up their word phrases to suit an attractive tune. But the young composer emerging in the 1720s showed respect for the verse by not adding extra words of his own—Scarlatti quite often added the particles *sì* and/or *nò* to spin out his text—and by writing melodies that emphasized the natural lilt of the poetry and the basic feminine nature of its rhythms. Much of the success of the new melodic styles depended on certain formulas which were overworked but which, when employed by good composers, ensured a delightful melody as fresh today as it was then. Some of these formulas (as employed in music in $\frac{2}{4}$ or $\frac{4}{4}$) appear in the following extract, the first vocal section of an aria from Vinci's *Artaserse*. The opera was first produced in Rome in 1730. In Naples it was heard in 1731, 1738, and again in 1743.

EXAMPLE 8
Vinci, *Artaserse*, II, ii
(Performed at the Teatro delle Dame, Rome, 1730)

(You drive me out indignantly, you shout at me severely. I despair of seeing mercy in you, if you feel no pity at these moments)

Noticeable features of this melody are the ♪♩ ♪ rhythms and the short, terminal figures (which in this aria have the rhythmic notation ♫♪ though in many arias they appear as ♫♪). Both contribute to the obvious lilt this tune possesses. Small grace-notes are more in evidence here than in any previous Musical Example in this book—from which the reader may correctly conclude that the art of gracing with appoggiaturas has during the 1720s become more than ever an essential element of the aria. Another characteristic of this melodic style is the run down the scale on to the final cadence note from the octave (in some arias it is from the sixth degree). The balance of high and low notes in this melody, as in many others, helps contribute to its buoyancy. Finally, the balanced phraseology of 4 bars–4 bars–8 bars is to be noted. Composers writing at the start of the century sometimes produced melodies as balanced as this. But it was during the approximate period 1720–5 that they seem to have become particularly conscious of the value of balanced phrasing. This was the period when the shapely tune seems to have become a particularly desirable object and objective. By shapely tune we do not necessarily mean a square one. Even in the above Example the final 8-bar phrase is subdivided into 2+6, not 4+4. In some Vinci arias the phrases are of various lengths (of both an odd and even number of bars), but the over-all balance of the melody is maintained. The judicious repeat of a phrase now and again contributes here to the sense of form. In general melodies have become 'ordered'; there is an apparent simplicity about each phrase and about the arrangement of the phrases; but there is also a certain sophistication in the arrangement that raises the level of the melody above the primitive and makes it artistic rather than just popular.[63]

The music above also demonstrates how much of the substance is concentrated on the top, melodic part. Composers *c.* 1700 were not preoccupied to this extent with pure melodic appeal—unless they were writing simple arias of the canzonetta type. Vinci's accompaniment is very elementary. The strings are laid out on four staves, yet not more than three real parts are playing at any one time. As happens in many other arias of the period, the first violins support the voice; the second violins provide what middle line there is; and the violas play the bass line an octave up. The arrangement ensures that no distraction occurs to take the mind off the melody; there is no trace of counterpoint, no obbligato instrument to compete with the voice. To further the impression of pace within music with a slow rate of harmonic change, composers of this period and later often used repeated quavers (or crotchets) in the bass, and there is trace of this technique in bars 20–3.

Certain trends in the aria ran parallel to those in the instrumental concerto. In the concerto the older arrangement allowing a solo group of players to alternate with the *tutti* was gradually replaced by a new one permitting one player to dominate in the solos. Developments in the aria gradually led to the transference of any soloistic work for instruments to the ritornellos only. An obbligato role for an instrument during the vocal sections therefore, becomes an incident to note—and the oboe obbligato during 'Lieto così' in I.xvi of Pergolesi's *Adriano in Siria* (Naples, 1734)[64] is one striking example. Vocal and instrumental parts both show signs of new advances in performance technique. The new vocal virtuosity is clear in bravura arias where the vocalizations are longer than ever, the leaps are bigger, and the range expands to two octaves or over. By contrast the vocal span in A. Scarlatti's bravura arias had rarely exceeded an octave and a fifth and usually was narrower than that.[65] The upper strings had moments in the bravura aria too when they could demonstrate some of the latest, fashionable techniques on their instruments: fast rushes up and down the

---

[63] For more on some of the melodic styles in operas composed *c.* 1730 by Neapolitans, see Gerber's *Der Operntypus J. A. Hasses*, pp. 45 ff. Gerber divides the melodic styles in Hasse's operas into four. Very roughly, these styles relate to the four main time-signature and speed combinations: fast-medium duple or quadruple time, fast-medium triple, slow triple, and slow duple or quadruple. Musical Example 8 above would fit into the first of his categories.

[64] Caffarelli edn., 1942, pp. 68–73.

[65] For an analysis of vocal ranges in Scarlatti's operas, see Lorenz, *Alessandro Scarlattis Jugendopern*, i. 183 ff.

octave scale, rapid arpeggios over three or four strings (especially where there was occasion to imitate the motion of water, rivers, or waves on the sea). While the upper parts demanded more performance skill than formerly, the lower ones became if anything technically easier. A notable decrease in technical difficulty may be observed in the brass parts which tended to descend in pitch. So the trumpet, playing notes lower down the order of the harmonic series, could no longer produce the elaborate and ornamental melodies that earlier composers had required of it in the high register.

While the bravura aria was the most flamboyant of all aria types, it was not necessarily the one most admired. De Brosses said the songs that pleased most were the simple ones 'tied to their subject',[66] and maybe an aria like Pergolesi's famous 'Se cerca, se dice' from *Olimpiade* (1735) was the kind he had in mind. However exciting the virtuoso aria was to the general public, some listeners seemed to prefer the more heartfelt qualities of the least spectacular items. In the mid-century when men affected an extreme sensitivity to music and its nuances, the simplest of the arias by Pergolesi and other composers writing in the same general style seemed to affect the heart in a way no other music they knew could. The ability of this song or melody to make the spirit yearn, sigh, and feel a thousand indefinable sensations was one reason why many Frenchmen came to acknowledge the superiority of Italian operatic music over their own. The particular style employed in 'Se cerca' and similar items has already been discussed elsewhere.[67] Suffice it to say that the rhythm of the opening ♪♪♪♪♪♪♪♪ is really a variant of the ♩♩ ♪ rhythm noted in Musical Example 8 above. The use of the short rest to detach one short phrase from the next—the technique will be observed in bars 17–20 of the above music—was particularly common at this period, and in the context of the style we are talking about tended to communicate the impression of hesitancy or poignancy. In other music and in other situations in heroic opera it was primarily a rhetorical device or else, of course, just a practical pause or breathing space.

A final though essential point to make about 'Se cerca' is that it is in a minor key—and arias in minor keys were from the 1730s on in such a small

---

[66] This is the third group in de Brosses' classification, see p. 88 above.

[67] H. Hucke, 'Die neapolitanische Tradition in der Oper', *International Musicological Society*, *8th Congress*, New York, 1961, i. 266 ff. The reduced score of Pergolesi's 'Se cerca' is printed in the Caffarelli edn. of *Olimpiade*, 1942, pp. 111–14.

minority that they had special significance. Lorenz has already pointed out that a much older composer like Scarlatti started his career writing as many arias in the minor as in the major, but that as he grew older he gradually came to prefer the major.[68] The liking for the 'happy' effect of the major was still more in evidence in the late 1720s and '30s when composers whittled the number of lyrical items in the minor down to perhaps two or three per opera. Not only were there fewer of these items; composers now used fewer minor keys. G minor and C minor were the ones commonly used; D minor and F minor were occasionally selected. On the sharp side E and B minor were the only ones employed at all and then very seldom. As if to offset the restrictions composers imposed on themselves in this regard, they often switched from major to minor for short passages within arias in the major. The device was not a new one. However it was now used more extensively than before and helped create that effect of poignancy Italian composers managed so well. Its emotive properties were felt by de Brosses whose remarks on the subject betray his particular sensitivity: '[Italian composers] hardly ever compose in the minor mode; almost all their airs are written in the major; but into these they mix, without anyone expecting it, some phrases in the minor which surprise and strike the ear to the point where the heart is affected.'[69]

It seems to have been sometime during the second decade of the eighteenth century that Italian composers began, as a matter of regular practice, to write down grace-notes and short trill-signs in vocal parts. The number of bowing slurs and staccato signs for the strings now increased too. It is clear that these indications reflected what performers were already doing. The composer, in other words, was as much concerned with keeping pace with performers' mannerisms as with curbing their right to create them. Whenever ornaments were written down, they were incorporated into the initial act of composition and no longer left to the performer's discretion. Some singers may have felt that the composer was here challenging their right to embellish freely. Tosi was particularly irate about the new practice of notating appoggiaturas by means of grace-notes and asked why, if composers thought they knew so much about singing and embellishment, they did not write out every other ornament as well.[70] At least a small grace-note was recognizable as an ornament. But what about the big notes? Leopold Mozart was later to warn that performers

---

[68] *Alessandro Scarlattis Jugendopern*, i. 175–6.   [69] *Lettres familières*, ii. 380.
[70] *Observations on the florid song*, pp. 38–9.

sometimes mistook an appoggiatura written out in ordinary notation for part of the unadorned melody and added another appoggiatura to it.[71] The point is that as the only ornament signs (involving pitch) used by Italian opera composers for many years were those for the short trill and the simple, one- or two-note appoggiatura/acciaccatura, all other ornament they wished to notate had to be written in big notes. When they incorporated such ornament, performers were spurred on to elaborate further. Each group in fact reacted to the deeds of the other.

The evidence present is enough for us to draw some conclusions about the 'revolution' in music attributed by Burney, Arteaga, and other authors of the end of the eighteenth century to Italian composers living near the beginning of it. These writers would have their readers believe that the revolution overthrew all 'Gothic' complexity in music, all taste for contrapuntal contrivancies, canons, and fugues. Instead, what was said to emerge was musical simplicity and clarity, beautiful melody, and a perfect affinity between music and text. Many of these writers, especially those least informed, seemed to think that the true musical Renaissance occurred not in the fifteenth and sixteenth centuries at all but toward the end of the seventeenth or beginning of the eighteenth. It was primarily in the seventeenth century, according to Arteaga, that the forces of change gathered strength. Now was the time when it was learned

to subordinate each of the diverse and multitudinous elements which [music] contains to all of them, and to concentrate entirely on the great goal of depicting and of stirring the heart; there was more study of the close relationship that must exist between word sense and musical sounds, between poetic metre and beat, between those affections expressed by the characters and those created by the composer. Fugues, counterfugues, and canons were considerably reduced in number . . . [72]

However much contrapuntal devices enriched the harmony and showed the resourcefulness of the composer, said Arteaga, they usually spoiled the simplicity and energy of the passion expressed. A. Scarlatti and L. Leo were among those who realized this and so took part in the 'happy revolution'. Pergolesi was the one, however, who 'carried theatrical melody to the highest level of excellence that has been attained so far'.[73] The reason for Scarlatti's inclusion among the reformers may be that he was thought of as a kind of father-figure to the Neapolitan 'school' of composers and so gained credit for what the school did. Scarlatti's style was no more, no

---

[71] *Gründliche Violinschule*, English edn., trans. Knocker, London, 1948, pp. 179–80.
[72] *Delle rivoluzioni*, 1st edn., 1. 287–8.   [73] Ibid., 289–91.

less contrapuntal than that of many composers of his generation. In general his style maintains that neat balance of interest between linear part-writing and vertical chord progression that characterizes other music of the late-baroque period. The lower parts of his arias, as a German might say, *konzertieren* rather than *begleiten*. Very different was the homophonic style prevalent in the late 1720s when the upper parts monopolized any horizontal, melodic interest the music contained. Burney was probably right, therefore, in not ascribing to Scarlatti any major part in the overthrow of counterpoint. Burney thought Vinci was the true revolutionary; and though he was probably wrong in having the reader believe Vinci was the one composer responsible, he did right in selecting someone whose first operas appeared about the time when the signs of change occurred. This composer, said Burney, 'was the first among his countrymen, who, since the invention of recitative by Jacobo Peri, in 1600, seems to have occasioned any considerable revolution in the music drama'. In the seventeenth century composers forgot that

the true characteristic of dramatic Music is clearness; and that sound being the vehicle of poetry and colouring of passion, the instant the business of the drama is forgotten, and the words are unintelligible, Music is so totally separated from poetry, that it becomes merely instrumental . . . Vinci seems to have been the first opera composer who saw this absurdity, and, without degrading his art, rendered it the friend, though not the slave to poetry, by simplifying and polishing melody, and calling the attention of the audience chiefly to the voice-part, by disentangling it from fugue, complication, and laboured contrivance.[74]

The strength of this reaction against counterpoint should not be underestimated, especially in a land like Italy. In the realms of music criticism it meant that a composer was least likely to gain applause for his technical competence and most likely to gain it if he took the shortest cut to 'affecting the heart'. The following passage attributing to Paisiello some of the credit for relegating 'rules'—which we must take to include technical device and counterpoint—was the highest flattery that could be paid him. Whether the author, Luigi Cassitto, was accrediting him with precisely the reforms which Burney accredited Vinci with is not clear—if Cassitto was, then he was just wrong. More important is the fact that both authors, and Arteaga, emphasized the value of melody, the need to stir the passions, and the need to avoid any ostentatious show of technique. Before Paisiello, so Cassitto said,

[74] *A general history of music*, iv. 547.

the arias were all of the same type, the pastoral song and the solemn one being no different from each other, and the same style expressing both anger and tenderness. Furthermore, perfection in composition was bound up with labyrinths of rules, and the dramatic action appeared absurd and badly managed because of such extravagances. It was left to Paisiello to get rid of such defects, for he knew that science consists in expressing the many and varied passions of the human heart by harmony and melody, and knowing how to measure the degrees of the passions judiciously.[75]

This eulogy, published in Naples in 1816, is interesting because it suggests a tide of opinion against the ostentatious use of techniques still prevailing at that date. It was an opinion that could not be dismissed by composers, nor by those who taught them (compare the comments on Nicola Sala on p. 20 above).

Mixed up with this question was the Italians' other obsession: the supremacy of melody. This is not the time to go into eighteenth-century arguments about the origins of melody, for example in Rousseau's *Essai sur la musique française* (1753), though there is a connection. Pronouncements on melody by late eighteenth-century Italians tended to emphasize its fundamental affinity to words. Since music and words had not dissimilar properties of rhythm and sound, the one was held by many writers to complement the other.[76] Perhaps because of the strong humanist influences prevalent at the time, some authors re-stressed an idea expressed in the Renaissance that public utterances of early Greek politicians, philosophers, actors, etc., were sung, the singing heightening the effect of these utterances.[77] If so profound an impact were to be made on modern audiences as had been made on the Greeks, then the harmony and suavity of music had again to be joined with the clarity of words—just as the Greeks had managed. The discovery or invention of a vocal style that reflected word meaning and moved the heart could thus be held to be the final goal and achievement of any composer.[78]

---

[75] From the *Elogio storico* in G. B. Gagliardo (and others), *Onori funebri renduti alla memoria di Giovanni Paisiello*, Naples, 1816, pp. 18–19.

[76] For anyone studying opinions in Naples, the remarks on the parallel between music and language by F. Galiani, secretary to the Neapolitan embassy in Paris in the 1760s and recalled to Naples in 1769, are perhaps most interesting of all. See the MS. (F. Galiani varia, XXXI.A.10) in the library of the Società di Storia Patria, Naples. Part of the opening section of the MS. is quoted in V. Monaco, *Giambattista Lorenzi e la commedia per musica*, Naples, 1968, p. 96.

[77] See Arteaga, *Delle rivoluzioni*, 1st edn., ii. 3, and D. Antonio Eximeno, *Dell'origine e delle regole della musica*, Rome, 1774, p. 156.

[78] Cf. the short, anonymous account of the Neapolitan school of composers in *Giornale del regno delle Due Sicilie* (24 Oct. 1821, issue no. 183). The Neapolitans, it says, reduced 'melody to rules

The argument that words and music were naturally associated may have contributed to the Italians' comparative lack of interest in the symphony and concerto at the very time, toward the end of the century, when these were being developed in more Northern countries. The eighteenth-century Italian aria had many stylistic and structural affinities to contemporary chamber and orchestral music, so many more composers trained at, for example, Naples could conceivably have concentrated on instrumental music than did. Example 9 below is just one small piece of evidence of the parallel development of the symphony and the aria. Though coming from an opera not known to have been performed at Naples, it is selected for containing a number of useful pointers to new trends *c.* 1740 and for being by an interesting though, this time, none too well known Neapolitan composer, Gennaro Manna. The extract, from a *da capo* aria, comprises the first run-through of the first four lines of text, plus the succeeding ritornello. The music is marked allegro.

EXAMPLE 9
G. Manna, *Siroe re di Persia*, II, viii
(Performed at the Teatro S. Giovanni Grisostomo, Venice, 1743)

analogous to those constituting the grammar of every spoken language . . . The principle of their system lay in the rediscovery of the melodic shape [*concetto melodico*] and the rhythmic movement best suited to express the sense of the words'.

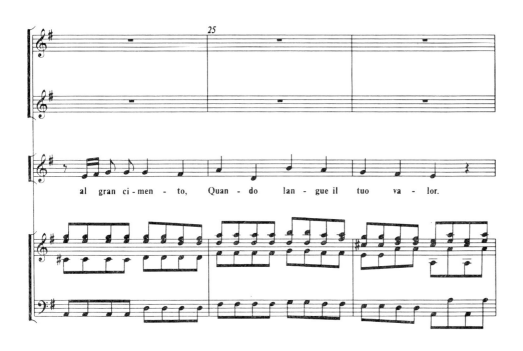

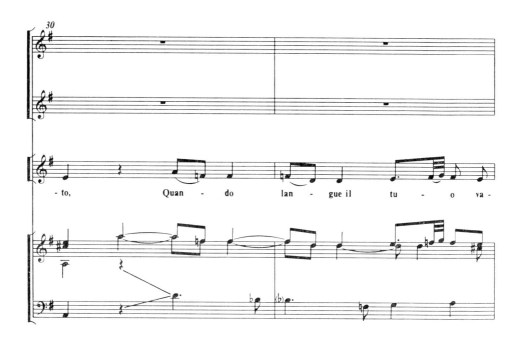

- lor,   il   tuo   va   -   lor.

(If you have no idea how to combat fate, oh innocent and unfortunate one, I can take the great task upon myself when your valour fails)

The switch from major to minor in bar 30 reminds us of de Brosses' comment on this very technique (see above, pp. 110–11). It was probably inspired by the words, *langue* especially, and happens to be to a common 'flat' key, namely D minor. The minor phrase has structural as well as expressive functions. We find in certain arias written by Pergolesi in the 1730s that a change to the minor can occur in both halves of the binary structure constituting the setting of the first part of the text. The phrase in such cases usually appears towards the end of the two sections and occurs in the minor of the major keys then reached—which are, respectively, dominant and tonic. Manna follows the same procedure in 'Se pugnar', adding the whole four bars in the minor also to the opening ritornello. The difference between Pergolesi's treatment and Manna's in Example 9 seems to be one of emphasis. The switch to the minor is more dramatic in the latter case, the texture in bar 30 suddenly lightening, the bass lifting, the melody becoming smoother than that in the preceding passage. The more lyrical nature of this melody, in comparison with the opening, is also a point to notice. The phrase as a whole has, because of its individuality and position, the characteristics of a primitive 'second subject'; and it is highly reminiscent of similar, incipient subjects in, say, C. P. E. Bach's keyboard sonatas written at this time. Manna's music shows signs of that more diversified texture that becomes a common feature of pre-classical and classical music in general. There are several changes between fully and barely harmonized passages, between legato and semi-staccato accompaniments, between periods of uniform rhythm in all parts and others of diverse rhythm.

Two other features of Example 9 are worth a mention. The first is the repeated chords of the end of the cadence in bar 22. Such emphatic reiteration of the final chord of the cadence appeared in a few of Vinci's latest arias, and afterwards became a prominent feature of arias marked allegro. The cadences selected for this manner of treatment were those at the end of important ritornellos, also at the finish of what might be called the preliminary statement by the voice. In Example 9 this statement covers bars 17–22. The cadence at the end of it is interesting since the tonic has already been well established during the opening ritornello where no other keys other than the tonic minor have been touched upon. Manna, and others like him, obviously considered the vocal section to be a new beginning, so that the tonic had to be established once again. The second feature of note in Example 9 is the climactic treatment of the cadence in bars 34–6. As the cadence approaches, the strings break into repeated semi-quavers, the texture thickens, the tone gets louder, and there is some hint of a crescendo. There is a sense of drive here missing from cadences of earlier arias. The orchestral surge into the following ritornello is perfectly contrived.

This last point leads naturally on to the question of crescendos and decrescendos. Signs for the crescendo and decrescendo appeared, like other expression marks, after these practices had become common. There were certainly many occasions between the 1720s and '40s when crescendos were executed in operatic music. What may be one of the earliest, written indications of a crescendo in Italian opera occurs in Vinci's aria 'T'apri o cielo' from his *Caduta dei decemviri* (Naples, 1727). The first ritornello opens with several bars of static B flat harmony, repeated quavers in the lower parts, and a gradually ascending phrase for the violins playing semiquaver trills. The first five bars are marked successively *pia, mez. for, for, più forte*, and *for^mo*. The 'cellos play the bass of bars one and two, and the *tutti* basses enter on the 'for' to add extra weight at the right moment. Similar openings with a rising top line and static harmony suggest a crescendo even if the score makes no mention of it. Although a graded series of *pia, mez. for, for*, signs indicated the crescendo well enough, it was a clumsy method; and composers soon began to use the term *rinforzando* instead. Since the publication of Abert's book on Jommelli, it has been assumed that this composer was the first to write the phrase *crescendo il forte* in an operatic score, namely in *Artaserse* of 1749.[79]

The fact that the fashion for relatively constant changes of dynamics came at a time when melodic embellishment was a prominent feature of opera was not entirely coincidental. A crescendo over three or four bars containing no change of harmony was a method of ornamenting that passage and giving it life which it lacked otherwise. It was a very easy effect to create, as easy as turning a trite melody into something more immediately arresting by adding a few trills and grace-notes. Associating dynamics with melodic ornament is perfectly defensible in the mid-eighteenth-century context. We have only to look at mid-century publications on performance practice to realize that dynamics were then considered as essential a part of ornamentation as the pitch ornaments were. The affection of a passage was allegedly controlled both by the gracing of the melody and by constant variation in the dynamic level.

The comparative unity of style and texture within the aria section therefore started to break up in the '30s–'40s period. Diversity of colour provided by the wind instruments was another factor turning the aria into a variegated piece. There was no single decade in which all heroic operas in Italy for the first time exhibited more arias with wind support than without. What is clear is that the proportion of arias supported by strings and wind increased over the mid-century period until, *c.* 1765, this proportion was the major one in practically all operas. While the normal role of the wind back in the '20s–'30s had been to double the outer strings in the ritornellos and play sustained chords supporting the harmony, the wind now gained an extra function. The new kind of solo was generally different from the old-fashioned *obbligato* in its short length and non-virtuoso character. Note the short solos for bassoon and flute in the Example below.

---

[79] Abert, *Niccolo Jommelli*, p. 215. The question however remains open. The phrases *crescendo f* and *crescendo* appear in Eneas' aria 'Se resto sul lido' from I.xviii of Jommelli's *Didone abbandonata* (1746) as preserved in the Naples Conservatory MS.7.7.23. Provided this MS. is the same date as the opera, *Didone* has the edge over *Artaserse*.

EXAMPLE 10
Traetta, *Ifigenia in Tauride*, II, ii
(As performed at the Teatro della Pergola, Florence, 1767)

(What can I do? This is the question!)

Here flute parts have independence from bassoons, bassoons independence from horns. The bassoons begin the section by doubling the top melody, not playing the bass as was their more normal task. Individual instruments have both soloistic and accompanimental duties within a short passage. The solos—and this is generally true of wind solos of the period—are arranged for pairs of instruments running in thirds. Here is an important pointer to new orchestral and stylistic techniques. Melodies in parallel thirds were no new thing in mid-eighteenth-century music, of course. The difference between their use now and before was one of degree. The sensuous sound of parallel thirds excited the later composer a little more than it had done the earlier. In music like the Traetta Example above, the liking for the third is manifest even in the chord layout—witness the heavy doubling of the third in bar 13. We cannot leave the subject of thirds without observing how they softened the dissonant quality of the accented appoggiatura. The expressiveness of many a phrase in music of the second half of the century depended partly upon this doubled appoggiatura at the third. It was a common feature of cadences. How often we meet this cadence figure in operatic music of the 1770s–'80s above the bass progression IV–V–I or else just above V–I.

EXAMPLE II

The opening of the Traetta Example (no. 10) above is representative of a small group of arias—written notably by Jommelli and Traetta among the Neapolitans—in which the orchestra shows signs of taking the music over entirely. The orchestra moves compulsively forward, the voice tending to follow the lead of the orchestra rather than vice versa. Now that new and exciting methods of treating the orchestra were available, a composer with a flair for orchestration might have been inclined to let the role of the voice change to a type of *concertante*. It is not coincidental that Jommelli and Traetta, the two composers mentioned, were also noted for being among the keenest to chip away the conventions of Metastasian opera and move toward a new (more Gluckian) form in which shape and style of music were more analogous to dramatic action. Other opera composers emerging in the '50s–'60s—Sacchini and Piccinni among them —were slower to change theatrical conventions. To someone admiring the profundities of Gluck's music and its appositeness to drama, the continuing pursuit by some Italians of pure vocal music within a series of self-contained arias might appear reactionary or empty-headed.[80] Ultimately though, one must judge whether a series of arias on the stage is or is not a thing of beauty in itself, and not accuse a composer of not producing music naturalistically timed and styled to suit action when that was not his intention. Given the almost intolerable conditions in a theatre like the S. Carlo, where audiences chattered and paid minimal attention to the show, the wonder is not that the average composer failed to see the need for drastic change but that he managed to keep his end up so well within the limits prescribed by custom.

In the last chapter some circumstantial evidence was presented about the decline of heroic opera in the second half of the century. The quality of singing declined, it seems. Audiences listened to fewer and fewer arias and turned their attention to ballets. We have no recorded impressions of audience attitudes at the S. Bartolomeo, Naples, to compare with later attitudes at the S. Carlo. So it is difficult to know whether these attitudes changed quicker in one generation than the next. Mattei suggests that a real change of attitude among Neapolitans occurred between the dates of Jommelli's visit to Naples in 1757 and his return there in 1769. By the time of his return there was, said Mattei, a 'taste for music that was effeminate [*molle*], and flabby [*snervata*], a dislike for everything costing effort, and a liberty in capricious singing'.[81] If this were true, it would help explain why composers favoured music that accentuated showmanship, great rhythmic drive, and a good deal of dynamic contrast—because these were the type of feature that might best gain the attention of the reluctant listener. The accusation that musicians set out merely to tickle the ear, never flatter the heart, is one often met with in publications of the second half of the century, and could again be related to the above-mentioned trend. Metastasio was already complaining along these lines in 1750. By accusing the musician of neglecting to move the heart, he and others were suggesting a decline in music from the Vinci-Pergolesi era.

. . . in Italy, at present, there is a taste for nothing but extravagance, and vocal symphonies; in which we sometimes hear an excellent violin, flute, or hautbois; but never the singing of a human creature. So that music is now to excite no other emotion than that of surprise . . . Composers and performers being only ambitious

---

[80] So see the criticism in G. Adler (ed.), *Handbuch der Musikgeschichte*, reprint 1961, ii. 739, that Italian heroic opera in Gluck's time showed the Italians' preference for the 'conventional, the easily comprehensible, the purely musical'.

[81] *Elogio del Jomelli*, p. 90.

of tickling the ear, without ever thinking of the hearts of the audience, are generally condemned in all theatres.[82]

The arbitrariness of music, its lack of relevance to the drama, its capricious interpretation by the singers, were all favourite complaints from now on. Gluck's *Alceste* preface, when it appeared, merely added grist to the mill. There was some confusion over what had actually gone wrong with heroic opera. Those who looked to the artists to improve matters wondered whether they were sufficiently interested in the 'philosophy' of opera-making. Algarotti popularized the notion that composers, dancers, etc., should work as a team led by the poet to create a combined art-work. Each should not work independently of the others to steal the show for himself.[83] Planelli was also concerned about the apparent division between the arts and the lack of a common aim. But to envisage a common aim required both intellect and sympathetic understanding; and musicians were not noted for being among the most intellectual of men, while the intellectuals did not help the musicians by pretending to be superior.[84] Arteaga was another who criticized the composer for tickling the ear and not moving the heart. It was he who brought the discussion down to earth by complaining that too many arias were beginning to sound the same.[85] One reason was that a musical motive perhaps most suitable in a love aria was employed to suggest kindness, devotion, mercy, friendship, 'passions so different one from the other'.[86] Because composers were now muddling all the affections, much of vocal music was being divorced from its poetic source, and new words could be added to an old aria originally inspired by something quite different without anyone being the wiser. To make his point he put at the end of his book a piece of vocal music which, he thought without claiming certainty, was by Astaritta. Underneath the vocal part three sets of words were printed, the first being the original text from Farnaspe's aria in I.ii of Metastasio's *Adriano in Siria*. The other two, one of them in French, were placed beneath simply to prove the contention that the nondescript music fitted the sense of either as well as it did the original. There was no similarity between the three texts other than their metre and verse length.

If the truth were to be told, one good reason why music sounded dull and lacking in variety was because too many composers were copying each

[82] Burney, *Memoirs*, i. 375–6.   [83] *Essay on the opera*, pp. 31–2.

[84] *Dell'opera in musica*, pp. 121–2.   [85] *Delle rivoluzioni*, 2nd edn, ii. 254.

[86] Ibid., 309.

other. To keep up with the times, as much as for any other reason, composers always looked over their shoulder at recent precedent. There was nothing new in this attitude or policy—which could produce generally beneficial results given the right circumstances. But these right circumstances did not necessarily obtain any longer. Quantz was of the opinion that the new styles were just too easy to imitate. Modern opera was easier to write than the old, for less technical skill was required in the new styles. Young Italians realized that to write opera was to make a mark quickly, so into the operatic field they plunged, relying on their ability to imitate other composers, and without themselves having gained a technical mastery of their craft. They were also quite capable of passing off another composer's work as their own—especially if they were abroad.[87]

A certain amount of blame for the universal desire to imitate may also be laid to Metastasio's account, not through any conscious action of his but because he was too successful. The popularity of his work meant there was a constant demand for new settings of old texts. Composers setting his librettos were faced not just with normal, recent precedents in musical style and form in general, but with actual settings of the same words by equally worthy masters. In the case of the simple recitative this hardly mattered; the lyrical items were the problem. Rather different was the situation with relation to other texts—to Zeno's, for example, whose aria poetry was never revered like Metastasio's. When Zeno's work was revived, the arias as often as not were replaced by new ones by the local hack poet. The great arias by Metastasio were rarely replaced. So what did composers do in the case of an already famous aria like 'Se cerca, se dice'? The opening words:

> Se cerca, se dice,
> L'amico dove'è?

(If he searches and asks, Where is my friend?)

may make many people imagine a rhythm similar to the ♪|♪♪♪ᵧ♪|♪♪ of the Pergolesi version. Several other Italian composers chose variants of this selfsame rhythm (in duple or quadruple time).[88] Here are the openings of two other versions:

[87] *On playing the flute*, p. 20.

[88] See J. G. de Laborde, *Essai sur la musique ancienne et moderne*, Paris, 1780, iii. 193: '. . . one notices that [Pietro Guglielmi] is perhaps the only one who has composed music to the beautiful air *Se cerca se dice* from Metastasio's Olimpiade in a manner quite different from that first created by Pergolesi.' A footnote below also excepts Sacchini's version of the aria from the generalization.

EXAMPLE 12
Leo, *Olimpiade*, II, viii
(Performed at the Teatro S. Carlo, Naples, 1743)

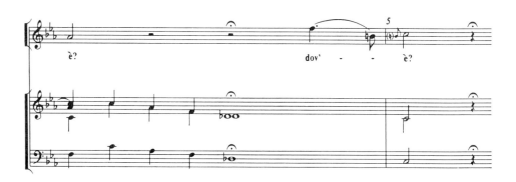

EXAMPLE 13
Cimarosa, *Olimpiade*, II, viii
(Performed at the Teatro Eretenio, Vicenza, 1784)

Other similarities exist between different versions, showing that musicians had some common understanding about the general nature of this aria. The words were soberly set, without elaborate vocalizations or embellishment. The voice usually entered at the very beginning, so there was no opening ritornello. Leo's choice of F minor for his setting could have been influenced by Pergolesi's choice of C minor. Traetta's setting, as found in the Florence MS. of his *Olimpiade* (1767), is in E♭ major, and several later versions are in this key.[89] When it came to deciding on a musical form for this aria, composers had to bear in mind that Metastasio's stanza was of twelve, not the more normal eight, lines. Perhaps the slight abnormality of this verse pattern was responsible for some interesting deviations from the normal *da capo* form. Some kind of two-part structure was often selected on this occasion. Many later versions composed in the 1770s and '80s contained a slow section followed by a fast one.

The case of this aria shows there can be a relationship between the unusual shape of a musical item and the unusual poetic structure. Which in turn may make us beware of crediting the composer alone for whatever deviation from the norm we happen to find. The words, too, may predetermine the reoccurrence of particular musical motives or sections in different parts of an opera. May it be said that such recurring or reminiscence motives were not the regular thing in Italian heroic opera, but they will be found on occasion.[90] Obvious cases of musical reminiscence occur in settings of Metastasio's *Alessandro nell'Indie*. The story centres on the love of two Indian rulers, Poro and Cleofide, at the time of Alexander's Asiatic campaigns. In I.vi the two swear eternal love and faithfulness cemented by Poro's short song:

> Se mai più sarò geloso,
> Mi punisca il sacro Nume,
> Che dell'India è domator.

(If ever I am jealous again, may the sacred God who is lord of India punish me)

In the next scene Cleofide announces her decision to visit Alexander, which at once arouses Poro's jealousy and suspicions. She tries to calm him in a full-length aria beginning with the following lines:

[89] In Piccinni's 1st *Olimpiade* (1768), 2nd *Olimpiade* (1774), Mislíweczek's *Olimpiade* (1778), and in the Neapolitan MS. of Paisiello's *Olimpiade* (1786) where the aria also appears in C major.

[90] For differing views on recurring motives in Scarlatti's operas, see Kretzschmar, *Geschichte der Oper*, p. 166, and Lorenz, *Alessandro Scarlattis Jugendopern*, i. 190–1.

> Se mai turbo il tuo riposo,
> Se m'accendo ad altro lume,
> Pace mai non abbia il cor.

(If ever I disturb your calm, if ever I fall for another, may my heart never know peace)

which we can see are closely allied in verse structure to the preceding. Later in the act after Cleofide arrives at Alexander's camp in the hope of securing his downfall through her feminine guile, Poro suddenly appears dressed as Asbite, emissary of Poro, whose true identity is known only to Cleofide herself. The two start to argue in front of Alexander, who finds it embarrassing and walks off.[91] In the last scene of the act the lovers have the stage to themselves. Each reminds the other of their previous vows, and a duet begins with Poro singing the opening three lines of her aria

> Se mai turbo il tuo riposo,

to which she replies by singing his words

> Se mai più sarò geloso, etc.

The duet then becomes a battle of mutual reproaches. The text invited some musical connection between one or both solos and the duet, and composers for fifty years or more commonly related them regardless of the fact that once the work had been set two or three times it was no longer original to do so. What each composer had to decide was whether to let Poro and Cleofide sing the same or different material in their solos. In earlier versions the solos generally were so connected; in later ones they were usually distinct. Other points at the composer's discretion included key signatures. All three items in Vinci's version of 1729 are in B♭. Handel, to take the case of a non-Neapolitan for the moment, wrote a version of this opera, called *Poro*, in 1731. In this setting Poro's solo is in E♭, Cleofide's in B♭. The difference seems due to the different ranges of the two singers involved, Senesino who sang Poro possessing a lower range than Strada who sang Cleofide. The difference is turned to good musical account at the beginning of the duet where Poro starts Cleofide's tune in E♭, Cleofide replying with his higher up in B♭, which is the dominant key and the one to which the music naturally modulates at this moment.[92]

---

[91] This is what happens in Metastasio's original version. His revised version makes Alexander leave earlier, before the argument.

[92] See the Chrysander edn., 1880, pp. 18–21, 34–7.

Even more fundamental, though, to the question why too much of the music of heroic opera started to sound the same was the contraction in the number of styles selected. From the second decade onwards there was an increasing tendency to avoid rhythms reminiscent of popular tunes and dances, and musical effects associated with comedy. This was not a point that eighteenth-century commentators made much of. Mattei gave a hint of it when he praised Jommelli for seeing and combating 'the common defect of giving the secondary characters styles worthy of the sock and not of the buskin, and filling their arias with trifles from the comic theatres'.[93] He was presumably not thinking of comic effects in music designed to raise a laugh—these were the property of comedians in comic opera and intermezzos. He may have been thinking of certain types of popular music associated with the man in the street and therefore held too undignified for the princely character. Study of time signatures selected by composers will give some idea of what was then considered dignified. The $\frac{12}{8}$ time signature was used fewer and fewer times in heroic opera in Italy after *c.* 1720. For a while yet it remained associated with, and was used for, pastoral effects. But we find it so rarely in scores of the '50s onwards that we can safely say Italian composers by then no longer thought of it in relation to heroic tragedy.[94] $\frac{6}{8}$ became rare too. $\frac{3}{8}$ and $\frac{3}{4}$ were used certainly, though the number of items in these times was always proportionately smaller than the number in $\frac{4}{4}$ or $\frac{2}{4}$. There seems to have been a reaction against triple times with a rhythmic lilt like ♩♪♪ ♩♪♪ and a trend in favour of slowing all triple times down. This means that the $\frac{3}{8}$ presto became a device normally reserved for comic opera, while in heroic opera its employment was limited to certain hearty choral items and ensembles with sections in several time signatures and speeds—such ensembles being by the late eighteenth century heavily influenced by procedures in comic opera anyway. If light music was more suitable for comedy, then the more elaborate kind was good for tragedy, and heavily embellished styles were associated with the latter. There is a paradox here, for too ornate embellishment, and certain types of embellishment like staccato semiquavers or semiquavers in triplets, could and often did add a piquancy and frippery to the music, counteracting its dignified features. For some reason the $\frac{4}{4}$ allegro was thought suggestive of the heroic pose suitable for a prince. This

---

[93] *Elogio del Jomelli*, p. 108.

[94] This time signature was still relatively common in Jommelli's heroic operas, but decidedly rare in those of younger Neapolitans, e.g. Piccinni, Paisiello, Cimarosa.

time permitted a style with a strong, though uncomplicated, rhythmic emphasis. Unfortunately, the later the period the more this style was depressingly overworked. It allowed among other things for fast vocalizations—by the late eighteenth century preferred overwhelmingly to those at slower speeds. It permitted orchestras to show their mettle in the execution of rapid passages and in the precision of their attack. Example 14 (pp. 136–42) is one instance of the style, taken from Piccinni's second *Olimpiade* of 1774. The aria 'Superbo di me stesso' was one that might have been described by Brown as a mixture of *di portamento* and *di bravura*.

The first point to note about Example 14 is the number of short orchestral phrases that break up the vocal line. They are particularly common in Piccinni's allegro arias of the late 1760s—though by 1774 there are signs his style has sobered down. They erupt through the gaps in the tune, add contrast and a certain jittery tension, and also inflate the music's length. A second point concerns the phraseology. Because of the increased length of the sections of the average aria, it was natural for the music of each section to tend to fragment and form sub-divisions within itself. This is a development that has often been commented upon in the contemporary instrumental sonata and symphony. The composer, instead of viewing the section as a single musical period (rather as Vinci had done in Example 8, see pp. 107–8 above), aimed at some kind of balance or symmetry of the phrases within the sub-unit. See, for instance, the opening statement (bars 18–32) of Example 14, and note especially how the vocalization beginning bar 28 extends the phrase and contributes to the balancing of bars 25–32 with bars 18–24. Beauty of each and every phrase was not Piccinni's aim in his longer arias, especially those in fast time. If any of his fast arias can be said to possess beauty, then this beauty resides in the occasional, warm melodic phrase that crops up arbitrarily; that is, it is not always related to the words. The affecting phrase 'di me stesso' of bars 53–4 of Example 14 comes into this category. Various factors contributed to the heartwarming qualities of a phrase. One was the effective use of the downward appoggiatura in such a way that it did not press the whole phrase unduly in the same direction. The phrase, in other words, needed a balance of high and low notes if it was not to sound heavy. Another was the occasional use of chromatic notes. Mild chromaticism appears in bars 62–6 of Example 15 below, a passage that seems particularly effective because of the diatonicism of the surrounding music. The composer of this version of 'Superbo di me stesso', Joseph Misliweczek, was no Neapolitan; but he

EXAMPLE 14

Piccinni, *Olimpiade*, I, i

(Performed at the Teatro S. Carlo, Naples, 1774)

(Proud of myself I'll go with that dear name imprinted on my forehead as it is on my heart.

Greece will then say that we held in common deeds, thoughts, affections, and finally names as well)

was popular at Naples, having at least eight of his operas produced at the
S. Carlo between 1767 and 1778,[95] beside directing the performances of
Gluck's *Orfeo* there in 1774. His setting of 'Superbo' is chosen also to re-
emphasize the similar nature of different settings of Metastasio's verses—
note the same key, time signature, the similarly emphatic and rather
prosaic opening vocal line, the forte orchestral ritornello that follows it,
in both the Piccinni and Misliweczek versions (see Example 15, pp. 144–6).

At this point there arises the question of the contraction of the aria's form
and the decline in popularity of the *da capo*. It is easy to see why the *da capo*
form ultimately came to be criticized. The size of the second, middle
section was one target for attack. This section never grew proportionately
to the first, and many mid-century composers tended to treat it as a bridge
between the first section and its repeat. Perotti likened this second section to
a pigmy by the side of a giant.[96] It was never intended to be a neat, complete
entity in itself, as the other was; and while it sometimes provided a fine
contrast with the first section, composers were sometimes guilty of care-
lessness in its composition, caring less here than in other places for the
logical progression of chords or the cohesion of style. The orchestration of
this section may have been affected by the fact that this was the area where
the keys remotest from the tonic were touched on. Brass instruments
without valves could not easily adapt themselves to remote keys; wood-
wind instruments still had problems of intonation. These could be among
reasons why the wind earmarked to play in an aria often remained silent
in its middle section. As for the first, or main, section, the fault here was not
merely that it was too long in relation to the other. Its repeat made the
differences proportionately greater. Commentators could easily poke fun
at the way composers spun out the words of the first part to last the length
of the music, repeating them, shuffling them about in new orders, and
distorting them by writing long vocalizations on suitable open vowels.
Saverio Mattei, with obvious malicious intent, got hold of a setting of
Metastasio's *Alessandro nell'Indie*, and finding in it the first aria that suited
his purpose, Poro's 'Vedrai con tuo periglio', attacked it by removing the
words from the score and then printing them, repeats, reshufflings, and all,
so that everyone could see how the composer had distorted them. Everything to do with this setting came in for attack: the vocalizations, the

---

[95] *Bellerofonte* (1767), *Farnace* (1767), *Romolo ed Ersilia* (1773), *Artaserse* (1774), *Demofoonte* (1775), *Ezio* (1775), *La Calliroe* (1778), *Olimpiade* (1778).
[96] G. A. Perotti, *Dissertation sur l'état actuel de la musique en Italie*, French edn., Genoa, 1812, p. 19.

EXAMPLE 15
J. Misliweczek, *Olimpiade*, 1, i
(Performed at the Teatro S. Carlo, Naples, 1778)

overemphasis on the words of the first part and lack of emphasis on the remainder, the quarter of an hour lost on the cadenza 'so that the silly singer may receive satisfaction'.[97] Arteaga copied Mattei and introduced into the first edition of his *Rivoluzioni* a similar criticism of a setting of 'Vedrai'.[98] One of Mattei's points was that four statements of the first part of the verse were several too many. Gluck had earlier made the same criticism in his *Alceste* preface. What no one would guess from reading Gluck or Mattei was that Italian composers were already taking measures to cut down on four statements of the words. By the 1760s it was becoming common practice to shorten the over-all length of the aria by repeating merely the second half of the first section.[99] Occasionally the more radical step was taken of cutting out the second half of the first section altogether. This meant the first section consisted of an opening ritornello (in most cases) and just one major statement of the words set to music ending in a related key. When it came to the repeat of this statement, composers had to write it out in full, changing the key so that the piece might end on the tonic. What has happened here is that the form of the aria has been modified into one close to that of the concerto first movement as composed by, say, Mozart. The initial ritornello and first verbal section form the equivalent of a double exposition, the middle section the development, and the repeat the recapitulation. Whether the aria form influenced that of the concerto, or vice versa, is an interesting question that others might examine. Abert thought rightly that, if the aria was properly to come into line with the new instrumental music, any discrepancies of style and orchestration between its first and middle sections had to be evened out, and believed that Jommelli in his last operas and especially in *Ifigenia in Tauride* (1771) was working toward this manner of uniformity.[1]

Mattei claimed he sent his criticism of the aria to Piccinni who was then composing, or about to compose, his second version of *Alessandro nell'-Indie*. This opera was produced at the S. Carlo in 1774. If Mattei's own

---

[97] 'La filosofia della musica o sia la riforma del teatro', *Opere del Signor Abate Pietro Metastasio*, de Bonis, Naples, 1781, iii. pp. xxxii–iv.

[98] ii. 45.

[99] This involved the use of the *dal segno* sign. The use of the *dal segno* to signify a return to a point after the aria's opening goes back to towards the beginning of the eighteenth century. In A. Scarlatti's last operas we often find the composer writing out a shortened version of the opening ritornello after the middle section and then instructing (by means of a *dal segno*) the performers to return to the first vocal entry. The means to shorten the first section of an aria were thus already there, but were rarely employed yet to produce drastic cuts.

[1] *Niccolo Jommelli*, p. 394.

words are to be believed, the results were important and great credit should
be given him for his initiative.

> [Piccinni] committed himself to please me in everything he had not yet written.
> He began to leave [the words of] the arias in their entire and natural order, almost
> all the arias he composed in rondo form, but among these the marvellous plan of
> the first and second parts of 'Dov'è, s'affretti per me la morte' aroused interest and
> surprise in everyone. From then on even the first sopranos who were determined
> to sing full-length arias with four statements of the first part have sung all their
> arias in rondo form, and the other old type is out of date [è rimasta a'mottetti]. But
> now we have fallen from one type of uniformity into another. Beside these shortened
> rondos [arie scorciate a rondò], true rondos in the French manner have been introduced
> which, instead of helping us along the path, have done much damage . . . [2]

Mattei therefore distinguished between the 'shortened' rondo on the one
hand and the 'true' one, of the kind exemplified by the aria 'Che farò
senza Euridice' in Gluck's *Orfeo*, on the other. 'True' rondos seem to have
entered heroic opera in Italy during the early 1770s, and their appearance
there occurred simultaneously with an increase in the number of rondos
appearing in Western European instrumental music.[3] The majority of
arias in Piccinni's second *Alessandro* are either in the 'concerto' form
described in the last paragraph or in 'abridged sonata' form, that is, in two
main sections each starting on the tonic and each tending to contain all or
most of the stanza. One advantage of this form was that the composer had
the chance, if he so wished, of giving all words equal emphasis and letting
the stanza end the right way up, its final words coming at the finish. Since
'Dov'è, s'affretti per me la morte' seemed to Mattei to be a shortened rondo
and seems to us to be in abridged sonata form with somewhat lengthened
second section, we wonder if his term *arie scorciate a rondò* in fact meant
arias in two main parts each containing most or all of the text. Unfortunately
his remark that singers suddenly demanded rondo arias does not fit with
the evidence of Italian opera scores of the second half of the '70s, in which
there are arias in two-part form certainly and a few in 'true' or 'simple'
rondo, but these do not always constitute a majority. Nor should we infer
that arias with two run-throughs of the text were unknown before Mattei's

---

[2] *La filosofia*, p. xxxv (footnote).

[3] According to M. S. Cole, 'The vogue of the instrumental rondo in the late eighteenth century',
JAMS, 1969, xxii. 425 ff., the fashion for the rondo was greatest in the approximate 1773–86 period.
In Italian heroic opera scores the term rondo is often designated in the French way, that is as *rondeau*.
Both this and Mattei's statement above suggest that Italians regarded the rondo form as originating
from French sources.

initiative. They were already common in Italian comic opera and were not unknown in heroic opera either (see the remarks below on the *cavatina*). So when Piccinni received Mattei's comments, he may well have smiled to himself and found it none too difficult to 'commit himself' to get away from the *da capo* principle.

Mattei perhaps considered it advantageous to be credited with influence over Piccinni at this moment. For *Alessandro*, as he suggested, was considered no ordinary, run-of-the-mill opera; its great success was exceptional in a theatre (the S. Carlo) whose audience had by 1774 grown to be largely preoccupied with social pleasures. Other evidence exists of the success of this work. The Abate Galiani wrote in February that year to Madame d'Epinay saying that Piccinni's opera had 'surpassed everything that has been heard in the way of good music till now' and that it had outclassed Gluck's *Orfeo*, heard in January at the Royal Palace.[4] This puts *Alessandro* in a new perspective. Piccinni's triumph seems to have confirmed loyal Neapolitans in the belief that their local opera was superior to Gluck's more radical kind. Far from coincidental to this story is the fact that Piccinni was first approached to go to Paris (there to confront Gluck) shortly after the *Alessandro* production.[5]

The trend everywhere away from the *da capo* must be interpreted as a desire for freer aria designs. It seems to have gained impetus earlier north of the Alps than south. One remembers Frederick the Great's objection back in the 1750s to the four statements of the first part, and how his Berlin court composer C. Graun tried to please him by composing most arias in *Montezuma* (1755) in the form of cavatinas.[6] *Cavatina* was the diminutive of *cavata* and came into use after the latter. For origins of the term *cavata* we turn to Salvadori's very useful *Poetica toscana* and find therein two types of aria mentioned, the *aria naturale* and the *aria cavata*. The first was a short lyrical verse intended as an aria by the poet and so set by the composer. The second was a line or two of blank verse coming at the end of a recitative section and set by the composer not, as he would do normally, as recitative but as aria, that is in a lyrical style. In this case the aria was 'extracted' (*cavata*, from the verb *cavare*, to draw off, to excavate) from verse material not originally designed for that purpose.[7] If we look at

[4] *Correspondance inédite de l'Abbé Ferdinando Galiani*, Paris, chez Truettel et Würtz, 1818, ii. 256–7.

[5] A. della Corte, *Piccinni*, Bari, 1928, pp. 73–4.

[6] Alb. Mayer-Reinach in *Denkmäler Deutscher Tonkunst*, 1904, xv. pp. ix–x.

[7] pp. 74–5. Cf. also the remarks on p. 49 above.

various dictionaries and musical commentaries of the first part of the eighteenth century, we note that Walther in his *Lexicon* of 1732 seems to have understood the origins of the term well when he declared it to be a type of short, concentrated and lyrical finish to recitative.[8] Matheson, in *Das neu-eröffnete Orchestre* (1713)[9] and *Der vollkommene Capellmeister* (1739),[10] and Krause, in *Von der musikalischen Poesie* (1752),[11] both seem under the impression, on the other hand, that a cavata was a lengthy piece containing greater breadth of idea than the average aria or arioso. It is possible that this became the more usual interpretation of the term in the mid-century. Around this period composers were wanting a term for the occasional short aria or arietta they were writing; and rather than choose cavata (which might have implied a large piece) for that purpose, they chose its diminutive cavatina.[12] Henceforth cavatina became the commoner of the two expressions. Eighteenth-century authorities that referred to the accompaniment of the cavata/cavatina all seemed agreed that it was accompanied by orchestra and not just by continuo. One writer, Rousseau, thought the cavatina was often to be found in obbligato recitative, which would put it in the class of those ariettas/ariosos associated with accompanied recitative generally. However, large numbers of cavatinas (so-called) have no such recitative connections. By calling the cavatina an air without a middle section (*seconde partie*) or reprise,[13] Rousseau was obviously comparing it with the *da capo* aria and saying it was like an aria's first section. The precise degree of similarity varied, but it is true to say that many cavatinas in opera of the 1760s–70s were copy-book versions of the first section of the conventional *da capo* aria, with its two run-throughs of the text, two-part musical form, and surrounding ritornellos. As for the size of the text, Salvadori made it clear that the cavata's original size was small—one or two lines at most. But Matheson and Krause thought the cavata's text was long, Krause for example saying it could consist of ten lines or more.[14] It is interesting that the cavatinas of Graun's *Montezuma* are comparatively short musically but contain long verses— allowing for few repeats of words, which was as Frederick the Great wanted. So here the diminutive form of the expression referred to the

---

8 p. 150.   9 p. 183.
10 p. 213.   11 pp. 128 ff.
12 Logroscino's comic opera *Il governatore* (1747) is the earliest score mentioning cavatinas that this author has seen. There may of course be earlier examples of cavatinas (so-called).
13 *Dictionnaire de musique*, pp. 76–7.
14 *Von der musikalischen Poesie*, p. 129.

musical rather than to the textual length. On the other hand most Neapolitans seem to have thought that the diminutive referred to both. So the average cavatina by a Neapolitan composer had a short text and many repeats of the words, about as many in fact as were found in the first part of a contemporary aria in the usual *da capo* structure.

Such was the fashion for the *da capo* form that composers active in the first half of the eighteenth century usually cast their duets and solo ensembles in this form too. Such formal similarity between aria and ensemble was but one sign that the latter had become in essence an extension or enlargement of the solo aria rather than a development or evolution of earlier ensemble types like the madrigal. Another point of resemblance was that many ensembles were really solo songs whose melody was shared out between several singers. In these there was little ensemble singing as such. Dent pointed out many years ago how the copyist of the septet in Scarlatti's *Eraclea* (1700) tried to save space writing out all the vocal parts on one stave. Since most of the vocal writing formed a single line only, he found this easy save for the few overlaps where he 'mutilated the music'.[15] There are other cases where an editor may save space compressing the vocal parts on to one stave, and provided he returns to full score where the voices start singing in ensemble his action is justified. It may be argued by some that the more satisfactory duets and ensembles are those to which this can least be applied and where there is the fullest rather than the thinnest possible vocal sound. For in operas like those fashionable in the early eighteenth century with so many solos and, by comparison, so few ensembles, any ensemble without ensemble work is a missed opportunity. In many cases composers did distinguish between arias and ensembles making voices in the latter start singly or in small groups and then gradually amalgamating them. A sense of cumulative build-up could be imparted by this means that was not possible in the aria. Whether they were able to bring the voices together depended on the text and whether the librettist had arranged for (*a*) more than one character to sing the same words, or (*b*) pairs or groups of rhyming lines for various characters that suggested an analogous musical pairing. Sometimes interesting results were gained by contrasting one group of characters with another, and it was this type of ensemble that perhaps showed best how dramatic nuance could be attained within the strict conventions of heroic opera. As an example we quote part of a quartet from Porpora's *Flavio Anicio Olibrio* (Example 16).

---

[15] *Alessandro Scarlatti*, p. 55.

EXAMPLE 16
Porpora, *Flavio Anicio Olibrio*, II, ii
(Performed at the Teatro S. Bartolomeo, Naples, 1711)

(Olderico Ricimero	Glory beckons me on to new triumphs.
Teodolinda Placidia	Glory beckons you on to new triumphs.
Ricimero	My dear one!
Olderico	My life!
Placidia	What do you want?
Teodolinda	What are you asking?
Olderico Ricimero	Be not so severe.
Teodolinda Placidia	If you are following Mars, leave love alone.)

The dramatic situation at the moment of the quartet is as follows: Ricimero and Olderico are Goths who are going to give battle to the Roman, Olibrio; Ricimero's sister, Teodolinda, believes in victory for the Goths; Placidia, a Roman lady captured by them, hopes for their defeat. Placidia is Olibrio's lover, but Ricimero is also in love with her. Olderico is in love with Teodolinda, but she prefers Olibrio. Both men in the quartet are therefore taking a despairing farewell of the lady they prefer, and the ladies are getting rid of them by urging them into battle. Each lady is as suave as the other, but the audience appreciates their aims are not quite identical. Note incidentally the composer's delay in amalgamating all four voices till near the end of the section.

So long as composers desired subtlety through the understatement of characters' differences, where these were expressed simultaneously, the conventional ensemble gave them the chances they sought. What the mode of the period prevented was any musical exploitation or exaggeration of the conflicts where characters disagreed. Ill-mannered retorts, interruptions, words uttered out of turn, were the requisite of the comic rather than of the serious ensemble. And though we should not make too much of the differences of characterization between the two types (since they were of degree only), it is correct to say that characters in the serious ensemble were more united in the way they musically expressed their thoughts, more prepared to let one remark follow on in orderly fashion from the last and let the melody and harmony of their parts cohere, than those in the other. What was disappointing was that more touches of realism could not be introduced when characters felt themselves opposed to each other. The duet in III.viii of Handel's *Orlando* (1733) in which

Angelica, pleading with Orlando for the life of her lover, stops in tears while he carries on, unrepentant, to finish the piece alone,[16] is the sort of realistic touch for which there are few if any parallels in Neapolitan operas of the period.

The other point to be made in connection with the Porpora music above is that the register of the voices puts much the most emphasis on the higher clefs. Olderico's part was originally written for a woman soprano. Other writers have pointed out how opera at Naples and elsewhere in the eighteenth century was written for solo casts with a preponderance of sopranos and contraltos, with one or two tenor parts at most, and usually without any for bass (comic parts excepted).[17] The problem for the modern director is how to distribute the male character parts originally consigned to castratos—or even to women, such was the vogue for high voices. He must decide whether to give them to female singers or male altos, or to transpose the parts down and give them to tenors or baritones. While questions of stage propriety perhaps sway the argument in favour of transposition, questions of musical propriety sway it the other. The likelihood of changing the musical quality if certain parts are transposed is great in ensembles in which either the melodic continuity depends on the level of the melodic pitch or pitch is an essential factor of colour effect. Dramatic nuance can be destroyed by transposition too. Musical analysts are rarely at one on any problem, but it is at least arguable that an essential element of the quartet above is the continuity of melody between the parts of Olderico and Teodolinda, that to transpose Olderico's part down an octave isolates the male character group from the female (when they are in fact singing to each other), and that by keeping Olderico's part at the written pitch the two groups of Olderico-Teodolinda (two sopranos) and Ricimero-Placidia (tenor-mezzo contralto) better maintain their separate identities.

Burney's comment that a 1770 opera in Italy was sure to please if 'two or three airs and a duet deserve attention' (see p. 64 above) suggests much responsibility put on the composer and original performers of the duet. For the number of duets, and with them larger ensembles, was of course small by comparison with the number of arias. The undeniable fact that the duet/ensemble was not the routine item that some arias were, for it was written with some care, becomes understandable if we assume

[16] Chrysander edn., 1881, pp. 93–5.
[17] e.g. Hucke, 'Die neapolitanische Tradition in der Oper', p. 263.

from Burney that audiences reserved part of their attention for it. The ensemble evolved as quickly and radically as any item. During the century it gradually lost its dependence on the aria as model. It threw off the shackles of the *da capo* form earlier than arias as a group did. It began to be influenced by the ensemble and act finale of comic opera. By 1760 at the latest the act finales of comic opera consisted of several loosely-connected sections in different time signatures and speeds. A limited number of serious ensembles now began to exhibit similar forms. The difference between them lay in the dramatic concept. The comic ensemble, and especially the comic act finale, was becoming an action piece during which characters introduced new factors into the plot and moved on, off, and about the stage. The serious ensemble, like the conventional aria, was still a moment of comparative inaction during the drama. The first heroic opera at Naples generally thought to contain action finales on the comic model is Paisiello's *Pirro* (words by G. de Gamerra) performed at the S. Carlo in 1787 and again in 1790. The finales to its Acts I and II are big items for six characters. This does not mean that all or even a majority of subsequent operas in Naples had such finales, but it is a sign of the loosening of conventions. The point is really that because the structure of the large ensemble was by 1787 one of progressive musical sections without a necessary reprise, the infiltration of a progressive action into it was an almost inevitable process that someone had to think of sometime. Once adopted, the 'action' ensemble was always available as a dramatic resource if required.

   J. A. Hiller observed that four voices could make a chorus as well as a quartet. In choruses, he said, all sang the same words, but in quartets individual voices had individual words as well as words held in common. Musically, this meant that choruses spent most of their energies singing together; quartets permitted more solo passages.[18] As we see it, most musical items with the title of *coro*, whether sung by soloists or by a team of extras, were pieces of strictly homophonic music—short, four-part songs, in fact—supported by an orchestra that provided ritornellos and some thickening and elaboration of the texture during the singing. Whereas composers were not unhappy in the solo ensemble to flirt with a little contrapuntal ingenuity now and again, they were less keen to do so in the chorus—though we know of some imitation points and even short canons in choruses by composers like Leo and Jommelli who had a particular penchant for such things. Many of the choruses in heroic opera at Naples

---

[18] *Anweisung zum musikalisch-richtigen Gesange*, p. 215.

in the second half of the century are interesting less for their music than for the fact that they were sung by the boys of the conservatories. The rather simple music that most of it is bespeaks either limited rehearsal time or limited voices. Dramatically the most the chorus does is set the scene, where for example there is a scenery change, a pause before a battle, etc., or picturesquely round it off, especially at the very end of the opera. As for the chorus taking a positive and individual role in the plot, that comes only with the invasion of French and Gluckian concepts into Italian opera, about which we said something in the last chapter. The sort of occasion we have in mind is the scene in Armida's wood in III.v. of Jommelli's *Armida abbandonata*, 1770, where Rinaldo is confronted by two different choruses in turn. These represent Armida's spirits attempting first to lure him in and disarm him (sung by sopranos, altos, and tenors) and then, as demons, to frighten him away (sung by tenors and basses). Flutes and strings support the first chorus; oboes, horns, and strings, the second. Here is the type of choral item that is sufficiently rare in opera at the S. Carlo to make the investigator sit up and take note where he finds it.

IV

The Orchestral Items

To give faithful rendition of the music of eighteenth-century opera in the way its original creators would have found familiar requires the use of a suitably sized and constituted orchestra. There have been several pieces of research so far into the constitution of eighteenth-century orchestras. The facts about the one at the S. Carlo have been well documented by Prota-Giurleo,[1] and, since so many eighteenth-century Neapolitan state archives were destroyed in World War II, it is unlikely that much remains to be discovered on the subject. No harm is done in reminding the reader of the main facts about this orchestra and their implications. It was one of the larger theatre ensembles then in existence. Assembled for the first production at the inauguration of the theatre in 1737 were 45 players altogether: 24 violins, 6 violas, 3 cellos, 3 basses, 2 harpsichords, 2 oboes, 3 bassoons, 2 trumpets. The orchestra grew rapidly in size to 70 players in 1741, then was cut back to 55. There were further fluctuations in the numbers engaged—a mere 47 in 1753 and 49 in 1759—determined by the finances of the theatre and the impresario's decisions on where to effect economies. We learn from the surviving Naples Archives, independently of Prota-Giurleo, that there were 59 players in the orchestra in 1780.[2] The breakdown shows 32 violins, 4 violas, 3 cellos, 5 double basses, 4 oboes, 2 clarinets, 2 bassoons, 4 trumpets, 1 drum, and 2 harpsichords. Here is the first record of either clarinets or drums in the orchestra, though it is conceivable that drummers were engaged from the military on previous occasions. No flutes or horns are mentioned, but Neapolitan scores of the time contain plenty of evidence of their use. So the oboists may have doubled on the flute where necessary and the trumpeters on the horn. The sound emitted by the orchestra must have emphasized the high and low notes. From Prota-Giurleo's lists and our own it is clear that the violins constituted more than half the complete assembly, also that the number of double bass players equalled or exceeded that of the cellists. Burney

---

[1] *La grande orchestra del R. Teatro San Carlo nel settecento*, Naples, 1927.
[2] From a letter signed by the then court *maestro di cappella*, Pasquale Cafaro, Naples archives, Casa reale teatri, f. 1517.

noted and deplored this imbalance between cellos and basses during his visit to Naples in 1770. That year there were 5 basses and but 2 cellos in the S. Carlo orchestra, and Burney commented that the double bass was an instrument played so coarsely in Italy 'that it produces a sound no more musical than the stroke of a hammer'.[3] One imagines what its effect must have been like in those many allegro arias with fast, repeated quavers in the bass part.

By comparison there is little information on the orchestras of the smaller Neapolitan theatres in which comic opera was performed.[4] All that this author has discovered in the Naples Archives are some names and numbers of players in the orchestras of the Fiorentini and Nuovo for the 1799–1800 season, a rather late date. They can nevertheless be compared with Prota-Giurleo's numbers for the S. Carlo orchestra as reorganized by Paisiello c. 1796. These S. Carlo numbers were: 25 violins, 4 violas, 2 cellos, 6 basses, 2 oboes, 2 clarinets, 4 bassoons, 4 horns, 2 harpsichords.[5] The names of 23 players appear on the Fiorentini's orchestral list for the 1799–1800 season, though no mention is made of the instruments involved. The orchestra at the Nuovo consisted of 14 violins (and violas), 2 cellos, 2 basses, 2 oboes, 1 bassoon, 2 trumpets, 1 harpsichord, and 2 *maestri di cappella* (of whom one was Gaspare Spontini).[6] The last-mentioned *maestri* were of course the composers who directed the first few nights of their own operas probably from the harpsichord position. According to whether we imagine there were one or two harpsichordists per performance, the total complement was 24 or 25. What this suggests is that even where the scoring of two passages from two operas of comparable date, one heroic and the other comic, appears similar, the original sound of the two may well have been different. The difference in fact relates to the quality of sound produced by a large orchestra with many stringed instruments on the one hand and a chamber orchestra on the other.

The first of the orchestral items to be discussed has least to do with the operatic score, yet is important if we regard 'opera' as the sum total of the evening's entertainment in the opera house. This item is ballet. Anyone studying Italian opera of the late seventeenth century will realize there was no great effort on the Italians' part to learn from and copy the close

[3] *The present state*, p. 353.
[4] A. della Corte, *Piccinni*, 1927, p. 7, says that the Fiorentini orchestra consisted of 12 violins, 2 violas, 2 cellos, 2 basses, 2 oboes, 2 trumpets, 1 harpsichord, though he gives neither his source nor the date when the orchestra had that number of players.
[5] *La grande orchestra*, p. 53.   [6] Naples Archives, Casa reale teatri (1799–1801), f. 1517, *bis*.

integration of dance and song within Lully's French operas. A few dances will be found here and there interpolated into the course of an act of a Venetian opera; most occur at the ends of acts, a position that became standard once the literary reform movement of the approximate 1690 period got under way. At the end of that century impresarios in Italy seem to have been undecided which of the cast-offs, sung comedy or dance, would better serve as a type of entr'acte to the new emerging heroic opera. In some cases the two were amalgamated, comic servants in the opera coming on to engage in some prank, for example the spurious conjuring up of spirits, or in some grotesque dance or mime, and then finding themselves the centre of often very unwelcome attention from a larger, dancing group.[7] In the early 1700s the management of the S. Bartolomeo theatre in Naples came down clearly on the side of those who preferred sung comedy, hence the appearance in Neapolitan scores of comic scenes as end pieces or entr'actes about which more will be said in the next chapter. Charles III however preferred dancing to comedy, so after 1735 all operas produced at the S. Bartolomeo, and afterward at the S. Carlo, had ballets and not comic scenes as entr'actes.[8]

An idea of the comparative standing of opera and ballet within an opera production may be gained from examination of opera librettos and the amount of information contained in them about the dances. The average Italian libretto of the first years of the eighteenth century gives very little such information, announcing just the subject matter of the dances in a short phrase or sentence. This is quite different from the situation after *c.* 1755 when more and more theatre managements began to order the publication within the libretto of full synopses of major ballets. By this time too it was common practice to print the names of the dancers and choreographer.[9] The name of the composer of the dance music also appeared on occasion—and his name was rarely that of the composer of the opera. The synopses make it clear that the first two ballets (that is, the entr'actes) had become very elaborate affairs, and the third, if there was one to round off the evening, could be elaborate too. Bigger ballets no longer used the stage scenery of the preceding opera act; they had their own. They were in every respect quite independent creations.

---

[7] See Dent, *Alessandro Scarlatti*, pp. 41, 50.

[8] Prota-Giurleo, *Breve storia*, p. 106.

[9] At Naples the names of *singers* began to appear in opera librettos from the start of Medinaceli's viceroyship in 1696.

There are sufficient references to dances in scores and librettos of early comic opera at the Fiorentini and Nuovo to prove that dances were not foreign to this type of entertainment either. Lalande after his Neapolitan visit of the mid-60's maintained the ballets performed at the Nuovo were 'often very well regulated'.[10] Indeed the ballets at the Nuovo may have been getting too good, for Sharp in his *Letters from Italy*, published in 1766, declared that ballets were banned from productions at the smaller theatres in Naples, save under special licence, 'lest they should divert the public from the King's Theatre'.[11] Burney also commented on this ban and its effect on comic opera in the city.[12] Not till the '80s does the court seem to have relaxed its ruling. The management of the del Fondo theatre (founded 1779) seems to have been allowed to promote large ballets in some of its productions. The managements of the other small theatres then began to get permission too. In 1801 the impresario of the S. Carlo was sufficiently alarmed to object to the del Fondo's promotion of ballet saying that only his theatre had the right. The royal deputation then in charge of the city's theatres observed that the king had sometimes granted permission over the previous decade to the del Fondo to stage *balli formali*, that the other theatres had obtained the same, and that they (the deputation) would have to seek royal advice on the matter.[13]

Conclusions about the music of operatic dances and ballets must remain tenuous at present because of the few dances or suites contained in Italian opera scores. Other evidence that might be used to help, such as Handelian opera suites, is circumstantial in view of the fact these were performed in North European locations. One reason for the lack of preservation of most eighteenth-century operatic dances is that the operatic and dance composers were usually two different people; and since the dance composer seldom had the international reputation that the other could, or did, enjoy, his music was not preserved with such care. Only when French and Gluckian influences began to leave their mark on Italian opera was ballet incorporated into the opera itself, and the opera composer considered it his duty to write the ballet as well as the rest of the music. So the dances within works like Jommelli's *Armida abbandonata* (a *ciaccona*) and Paisiello's *Fedra* (2 major groups of dances) are preserved in the scores concerned. Because of

[10] *Voyage d'un françois*, vi. 360.
[11] p. 92.
[12] *The present state*, p. 310.
[13] Naples Archives, Casa reale teatri (1799–1801). f. 1517, *bis*.

lack of any collection of Neapolitan opera ballets so far discovered, we turn to a MS. collection of ballets performed in opera at Turin between 1748 and 1762 to gain some idea of musical developments. These MSS. are housed at the S. Cecilia Academy in Rome.[14] The first point about the Rome MSS. is that the number of dances per ballet is much larger than that within a Handel opera, or other score, of the 1730s or earlier. The ballets of *Ezio* (opera music by Lampugnani, ballet music by Alessio Rasetti), first of the Turin works concerned, have fifteen, nineteen, and nineteen items respectively. The number of items in major ballets of later date rises to twenty or more. As for the length of individual dances, this varies from one to eight pairs of staves, two to four being the most common. The Turin ballets are more organized than earlier examples in that they tend to commence with a formal introduction, a march perhaps or a *sinfonia* in one movement. These are followed by dances which, as in earlier opera suites, fall into four main categories: action pieces such as combats and parades; traditional and aristocratic dances such as the sarabande, minuet, and chaconne; characteristic dances for Hungarians, Chinese, Hebrews, Harlequins, Gamesters, etc; and finally dances of not too well defined character. It is noticeable that where ballets have a coherent and dramatic scenario, the last two mentioned categories of dance increase at the expense of the traditional dances such as the sarabande. In this respect the music shows an advance over suites of earlier opera with a large majority of dances based on traditional dance steps. The ballet shows the waning influence of the old suite also in its more frequent use of different keys for different dances—the old suite had tended to stick to one and the same. A conservative element of the Rome MSS. though is the limited range of key. G, D, A, C, and F major are the strong favourites, which is more selective even than the range within contemporary arias.

One wonders whether this preference for sharp keys was designed to make things easy for the string players. Not all the best orchestral players, it seems, played in the ballets. In Naples a royal decree of August 1778 ordered that only the leaders of the first and second violins at the S. Carlo were to be exempt from duties during ballets in future[15]—so several players must previously that season, or during previous seasons, have considered ballet time as time out. One or two librettos of operas produced

---

[14] *Raccolta d'arie e balli di 10 opere*, G.MSS. 12–4. The ballets are contained in the first and third of these volumes.

[15] Prota-Giurleo, *La grande orchestra*, p. 10.

elsewhere in Italy during the '80s distinguish between the *capo d'orchestra* or *primo violino dell'opera* on the one hand and the *primo violino de' balli* on the other.[16] So here too the first violin yielded his position during ballets to a substitute. This is not the sort of thing to inspire confidence that the ballets were particularly well played. It is impossible to tell from the Rome MSS. what the orchestration was in full, since the music is in short score (on two staves) and often only the two outside parts are written down. There are a few indications for wind solos, but no signs that the instrumentation was as carefully worked out as, for example, that in Gluck's ballet *Don Juan*.

The object of the music was of course to set the dance in motion. Neat, crisp rhythms were desirable; which may explain why in the Rome MSS. as well as in later Italian ballets like those in Paisiello's *Fedra* there was a predominant use of short time signatures, $\frac{2}{4}$ rather than $\frac{4}{4}$, $\frac{3}{8}$ and $\frac{6}{8}$ rather than $\frac{12}{8}$, etc. The *Fedra* ballets contain few items, for they come in the middle of acts and are designed to be short enough not to impede the action of the opera. The longer dance items here show clearly how the Italian dance form tended to expand by becoming an agglomerate of more and more musical sentences or periods of similar style and even length and periodization. No very elaborate structure was attempted by Paisiello. Modulations were restricted. Double bars and repeat signs were put round parts of the music or not as the case might be. Often no musical reason is apparent why one section has such signs and another not, so reasons connected with the dance must be held responsible. The music of the *giaccona* [*sic*] in particular tends to spin itself out like the closing bars of a comic opera finale. In general the musical material is as light and easy to assimilate as anything in the score, partly because of the swinging rhythms and even periodization. And this in turn leads one to wonder whether the popularity of ballet over opera among late-century Italian audiences owed something to its relatively unsophisticated music as well as to the visual effect.

Should the question be asked why the opera composer rarely composed the ballet music, the first answer may be that ballet was not a field in which the musician was king. The great ballet master, Noverre, once put music and ballet in the same relationship as Algarotti put poetry and music. Algarotti stressed how the poet should determine the over-all shape of the drama, and how music should be poetry's 'handmaid'.[17] Noverre must

[16] This author has noted instances in *Idalide*, Turin, 1786 (operatic music by S. Rispoli), and in *Catone in Utica*, Florence, 1787 (operatic music by G. Andreozzi).

[17] Cf. *Essay on the opera*, p. 31.

have been mindful of Algarotti in the following passage from his *Lettres sur la danse, et sur les ballets* (1760): 'Music is to dance what the words are to music. This parallel means simply that music for dancing is not or should not be other than the written poem that fixes and determines the movements and action of the dancer . . .'[18] So, according to this, music was the check and discipline on the dancer that poetry was on the musician. Such statements arguing a close liasion between arts were fashionable at that time especially because of Algarotti's *Saggio*. They however obscured the other fact, that poetry in the case of opera, and music in that of ballet, were not merely the check but paradoxically the precondition for the free expression of the musician and the dancer. The second reason why the opera composer did not interest himself in ballet may be related to the observation made in chapter three of this book about the belief of some Italians in the supremacy of vocal music. If the music had to relate to the text, did it also have to relate to visual stage effect and to action on stage unaccompanied by words? To judge from the scores, we might be inclined to say that some Italian composers thought not. Dent correctly observed about A. Scarlatti's earlier operas in Naples that

there are many places . . . where the recitative is interrupted for an appreciable time by some sort of action, such as the wrestling match and the lottery extraction in 'Olimpia Vendicata', and numberless duels and battles, or by an elaborate change of scene such as takes place in 'Massimo Puppieno'. But Scarlatti never seems to think it necessary to fill up this gap with descriptive instrumental music, unless we suppose that he extemporized it himself at the *cembalo*. That is conceivable, for we do sometimes find a battle scene accompanied by a direction for a trumpet fanfare, which is very rarely written out in full.[19]

Scarlatti's successors at Naples hardly made greater effort than he did to fill in moments of action. They sometimes composed marches for the entry of the hero or sovereign; but battles, though a common feature of heroic opera productions, were either rarely set or else just not inserted into the score. The few musical battles to be traced, noisy unisons and rushes up and down the scale for the most part, seem rather short for the purpose. In this regard it is interesting to find Cimarosa writing the words *Da capo se occorre*—'back to the beginning if necessary'—after the battle music in his *Oreste*, 1783. So here music and action were certainly not timed so that they exactly coincided. Some battles must have been elaborately

[18] J. G. Noverre, *Lettres sur la danse*, Lyons, 1760, p. 142.
[19] *Alessandro Scarlatti*, p. 43.

produced. This is proven by several eye witness accounts. Sara Goudar says that in contrast to the situation in Paris or London where 'poor wretches' taken off the streets were engaged as extras, at the Naples' S. Carlo the military was called in and performed battle sequences with perfect precision.[20] The part played by the military is confirmed by the S. Carlo accounts for the 1785–6 season preserved in the Naples Archives and containing the following entries:[21]

To D. Rosario Pietrasanta Adjutant Major of the Royal Italian Guards 91.20 [ducats to be] distributed to 19 sergeants, at the rate of 60 granas each, 28 corporals, 20 granas, and 722 men, 10 granas each, for having performed as extras in the drama entitled Ifigenia in Aulide,	91.20
To the Lieutenant of the Royal Swiss Guards D. Gio. Dreutzer 214.20 [ducats] as above for [service in] Lucio Vero for 42 sergeants, 84 corporals, and 1722 men at the same rates,	214.20
To the said D. Rosario Pietrasanta 234.60 [ducats] as above for [service in] Enea e Lavinia for 46 sergeants, 92 corporals, and 1886 men, at the above [rates],	234.60
To the said D. Gio. Dreutzer 182.40 [ducats] as above for [service in] Olimpiade for 38 sergeants, 76 corporals, and 1414 men,	182.40

These figures do not necessarily mean that up to 2,000 men appeared all at once on the boards of the S. Carlo or that there were massed spectacles equalling anything seen nowadays in open air performances at the Baths of Caraculla or the Verona amphitheatre. It is possible that different detachments of the guards were called upon to perform their arms drill in the opera in turn. The accounts disclose that the first opera *Ifigenia in Aulide* (music by I. Pleyel) was performed 19 times between 30 May and 30 July 1785; the second, *Lucio Vero* (music by Sacchini), 21 times between 13 August and 17 October 1785; the third, *Enea e Lavinia* (music by G. A. Guglielmi), 23 times between 4 November 1785, and 12 January 1786; and the last, *Olimpiade* (music by Paisiello), 19 times between 12(?) January and 27 February 1786. If we divide the total number of soldiers per opera by the number of performances we find that both in *Lucio Vero* and in *Enea e Lavinia* the result is 88, which might represent the size of the nightly detachment. The figures for the other two operas do not work out so neatly.

The one non-vocal piece of music in both heroic and comic opera that

[20] *Rélation historique des divertissements du carnaval de Naples*, p. 10.
[21] Naples Archives, Casa reale antica, f. 1269, *bis*.

always remained the responsibility of the opera composer was the overture.[22] It is well known that the Italian overture came to have three standard sections (fast-slow-fast), that this standardization occurred around the 1690s, and that one of the composers responsible was Alessandro Scarlatti.[23] For the moment let us confine the term 'Italian overture' to those with this particular tripartite form so as not to confuse them with other, earlier overtures by Italian composers. One of the things that may well have struck the average opera goer of the 1690s about the new overture was its allegro opening, for many previous overtures had started with a few bars or more of slow music.[24] Those in favour of the new form may have argued that the music, which had to arrest the audience's attention while it was settling itself down, could best serve its function by having a rumbustious beginning. The festive spirit of the occasion furthermore demanded flourishes suitable for, if not always played by, the trumpet—the sort of thing we find at the opening of this Sarri overture:

EXAMPLE 17
Sarri, *Le gare generose fra Cesare e Pompeo*, Overture, movement 1
(Performed at the Teatro S. Bartolomeo, Naples, 1706)

The fact that this instrument was used in, or was associated with, such openings meant that composers often wrote overtures in D major, a key suited to most baroque trumpets. D major remained a common choice for overtures throughout the eighteenth century. We might indeed call it a traditional choice, for the trumpet had ceased to dictate the style of the overture's opening well before the mid-century and more and more sizes of trumpet became available so more keys might be essayed.

It is impossible to say exactly which type of instrumental music was the direct ancestor of the Italian overture. Consideration would have to be

[22] The earliest Neapolitan comic opera known to survive intact is A. Scarlatti's *Il trionfo dell'onore*, 1718; and from this date the comic opera overture has to be taken into account as well as the heroic opera overture. The present author has never noted any major musical distinction between the two. So it is unwise to assume that throughout the eighteenth century the comic opera overture shows the more progressive tendencies, as F. Tutenberg does in 'Die Opera buffa-Sinfonie und ihre Beziehung zur klassischen Sinfonie', *AM*, 1926, viii, 452 ff.

[23] Lorenz, *Alessandro Scarlattis Jugendopern*, i. 227–8, gives details of the first of Scarlatti's overtures in the form of an 'Italian overture'. This piece appears in a version of *Tutto il male non vien per nuocere* which Lorenz dates 1686/7 or earlier.

[24] Cf. H. Hess, *Die Opern Alessandro Stradella's* Leipzig, 1906, p. 57.

given to trumpet and violin sonatas of the Bologna and Rome schools as well as to the overtures of earlier opera. Following the line of thought basic to the conception of many early *canzone* and *sonate da chiesa*, composers considered the three sections of the Italian overture to be interrelated, not self-sufficient items. Only the last of the three, in the style and form of a dance and usually in triple time, could normally be considered an item that could stand by itself. The slow section, in complete contrast, varied in scope and size but was often short and reminiscent of those tiny adagio or *grave* passages in some of Corelli's sonatas[25] that form a bridge between faster sections of greater import. There is a curious analogy with the *da capo* aria here in that the overture's slow section, like the aria's second, commonly moved furthest from the main tonality and, perhaps as a result, had the thinnest instrumentation. The section exhibiting the most modern tendencies was usually the first, for here the influence of the concerto was most evident. The fugal opening, handed down from older prototypes, became more and more a formality, then was dropped completely. As contrapuntal device disappeared, so the new continuo homophony came in, the music moved forward with more compelling thrust, and the musical periods became elongated and moved more securely to the cadence. Harmonic sequences and circle of fifths progressions became part of the overture's musical language as they already were in the case of other, modern instrumental pieces. What however prevented the overture from becoming truly like the concerto or sonata was its function. While the concerto style suggested musical expansion, the overture's function demanded conciseness. Far too often we find an overture getting under way with characteristic drive and energy. Its composer then seems to realize that the music is assuming too big proportions for his purpose, so he stops it short with a lame cadence or else on a discord such as a dominant or diminished 7th demanding resolution. This is followed by a pause and, usually, a double bar line; the second section then starts, which will resolve the discord. Should this section prove to be merely a short interlude, then the final dance has the function of tidying up the overture as a whole.

It may not have escaped notice that the Italian overture became fashionable at about the same time as the *da capo* aria. By stabilizing the external shape of the overture composers were now in a position to concentrate on the organization of material within it. But while the internal organization of the aria was standardized by *c.* 1720, no equivalent articulation yet

[25] Especially within Opus I (Rome, 1683) and Opus IV (Bologna, 1694).

occurred in the first two movements of the overture. Composers of the '20s and '30s were the ones in fact to give each of the three movements a coherent design and sufficient content so that we can talk of overture 'movements' and not 'sections' in each case. Some early first movements/ sections of course contradict the above generalization. One striking example is in Mancini's overture to *Alessandro il grande in Sidone* of 1706 (Example 18, pp. 171–3). We would hesitate to say that this movement had any influence over the design of future ones in sonatas and symphonies. It contains nonetheless all the main, external features of first-movement sonata form of the 1740s or even later. These features include a first section leading to the dominant key, a double bar and repeat signs in the middle, and a second section in two parts, the first in related keys and the second (beginning bar 31) primarily in the tonic. The musical material at the start and end of the two sections matches. There is an obvious recapitulation of most of the opening material in the second of the two parts of the second half.

The appearance of double bars and repeat signs here and in a small minority of other early first movements[26] is interesting because it suggests the influence of some kind of binary, probably dance, form. The reader should note that repeat signs finally disappeared from the overture's first movement around the time, during the '30s and '40s, that they came into the first movement of the concert symphony. So the repeat of a section, as in a dance, was never a tradition that 'took' in the overture's opening movement as it did elsewhere. The connection between the Italian overture (called by Italians *sinfonia*) and the classical symphony needs no elaboration here. Suffice it to say that the overture's first movement developed as the concert symphony's did into a piece with the main features of what we call classical sonata or symphonic form (complete or abridged). The chief structural distinction between them was that one had no repeats of the two halves, but the other very often did. Whether much needs to be made of this point is an open question.[27] The overture

[26] The present author has so far seen just three early first movements by Neapolitans in binary form (either simple or extended) with repeat signs. One is Example 18 above. The others are in the overtures to Scarlatti's *La fede riconosciuta*, 1710, and Mancini's *Trajano*, 1723.

[27] Cf. H. C. Robbins Landon, *The Symphonies of Joseph Haydn*, London, 1955, p. 21, who suggests that with Haydn's *Acide e Galatea* overture 'we reach a point where there is no difference between the symphony and the overture forms'. Robbins Landon's own edition of this overture, Doblinger, Vienna, 1959, shows it to contain no repeat signs. A symphony like Haydn's no. 9, which Robbins Landon maintains is an overture in origin, has the conventional repeats and double bars in its first movement. So were they inserted in order to turn the movement into a symphonic one?

EXAMPLE 18

Mancini, *Alessandro il grande in Sidone*, Overture, movement 1
(Performed at the Teatro S. Bartolomeo, Naples, 1706)

probably did without repeats because its function required it to be short. The aesthetic question whether a piece in sonata form is or is not improved by repeats of exposition, then of development-recapitulation, involves the exercise of value judgements that each hearer must make for himself.

Less need be said about the main changes made in the second and third movements during the '30s and '40s. Slow movements were now markedly lyrical, being fully fledged and shapely melodies in many instances. They were no longer links between the first movement and the last; no longer mere exercises in harmonic progression either. Composers of the period still retained the traditional, binary structure for the last movement, but they now started to cut out the repeat signs in the middle of it—once again the need to limit the performance time may have been responsible. The speed of this movement tended to become moderate-paced, and the minuet style replaced the fast *giga* style that had once prevailed.

Many details about the organization and style of material within overture movements—whether for heroic or comic opera—have in fact been mentioned with reference to the vocal aria in the previous chapter. The later the music, the more likelihood of an extended piece (especially if it is a first movement), of extensive use of balanced phrasing, of diversity of melodic material and orchestral colour. One difference between aria and overture relates to the fact that, perhaps because of associations between 'vocal line' and 'pleasing melody', there was less mere spinning out of melodic material in the first than in the second. We sometimes find in overtures written before *c.* 1750 that the composer, having to get from one point of structural importance to another, and not having anything special to say in between, will utilize a melodic particle for the transition and work it over during an indefinite number of bars until the harmonic progression employed happens to reach the right key, cadence, or whatever. On the different question of the expanding length of music, it is worth while looking for a moment at a phrase like

EXAMPLE 19
Sarri, *Didone abbandonata*, Overture, movement 1
(As performed at the Teatro S. Giovanni Grisostomo, Venice, 1730)

which in its original context served as a *piano* contrast to the *forte* opening of an overture movement, and imagine that we could alter it and lengthen it thus:

EXAMPLE 20

This process of distending the melody was an important one in the evolution of certain types of Italian music during the approximate 1730s–'50s period. By this process composers tended to lengthen the distance between the melodic segments and thus the period of time between one harmony and another. The distance between each segment or particle became so wide in some instances as to lead to splits in the melody, and each particle became a separate unit—as we have contrived to do in the case of the ♫. fragments in the above example. In order to fill in the breaks in the melody, more busyness was required of the supporting instruments, so these were called upon to produce light, repetitive patter accompaniments. A slow harmonic rate, considerable use of short motives, patter in the middle and lower strings—here are some of the hallmarks of, especially, comic opera styles of the second half of the eighteenth century.

The suggestion that overtures rarely possessed those moments of musical distinction found within certain concert symphonies of comparable date is well taken.[28] There was no point in trying, within the overture, to enchant an audience that would not listen anyway; and many an overture leaves the impression that its composer was not aiming for anything striking or memorable but for the smoothest possible piece that could be forgotten immediately after. In many opening movements by Jommelli and later Neapolitans more attention seems to be given to the variety of texture and dynamics than to the quality of material. Following on from the forte, flourishy opening comes a contrasting, piano passage serving as a kind of 'second subject'. A thunderous forte usually follows that. If there is a middle section, then it tends to use limited orchestral resources and episodic material. Then another thunderous entry proclaims the start of the recapitulation. In the case of second and third movements of the post-mid-century period, the signs are that these were influenced by the

[28] Cf. Robbins Landon, *The symphonies of Joseph Haydn*, pp. 225–6.

principles of classical sonata writing that composers had worked out in the
concert symphony and also in the overture's first movement. But they
were never designed on such a big scale as the first movement. In some
cases a simple rondo plan was adopted. We note that middle movements
were usually medium- rather than slow-paced, the style graceful and
legato by comparison with that of allegro movements in which much
staccato playing had become *de règle*. Last movements were usually the
shortest and varied the most in pace. In cases where the time signature was
$\frac{3}{8}$ or $\frac{6}{8}$, the speed was a quick one, and the strings had an incessant quaver
patter, this patter even seems to point in the general direction of the
Beethoven scherzo style as exemplified by the Eroica third movement.

The increasing length of the overture's movement one must have been
among the reasons for the final phasing out of movements two and three.
At Naples, so it seems, these movements were dropped *c.* 1780. Burney
however declared that the overture to one of the comic operas he saw
there in 1770, Paisiello's *Le trame per amore*, had one movement only,[29] and
that another, the one in Piccinni's *Gelosia per gelosia*, had two.[30] The
present author has not been able to check on the 1770 version of *Le trame*,
but he can vouch for the presence in the Piccinni score of the conventional
three movements—these are marked allegro spiritoso, andante, allegro. So
this raises the question as to whether comic opera productions of the time
included all the overture as written. The suggestion that second and third
movements be cut must have been aired in Italy by 1770. Gluck at Vienna
helped lead the way toward one-movement overtures with examples in
his *Il re pastore* (1756) and *Orfeo* (1762). The overture's structure could be
reformed or curtailed in a number of ways of course, and several were
tried. We find Leo re-using the last part of movement one as movement
three in his *Olimpiade* overture heard in Naples in 1743.[31] Jommelli cut
short the first movement of his *Armida abbandonata* overture just before the
recapitulation for which the second and third movements acted as a kind
of substitute. There was also a method of curtailing the overture by overlapping the third movement, and even the second, with the start of the

[29] *The present state*, p. 306.

[30] Ibid., p. 321.

[31] A refinement of Leo's technique is found in Paisiello's overture to *Demofoonte*, Venice, 1775,
which is in effect a single sonata-form movement with a slow section (analogous with the old second
movement) inserted prior to the recapitulation. See H. Abert, 'Paisiello's Buffokunst und ihre
Beziehung zu Mozart', *Gesammelte Schriften und Vorträge*, Halle, 1929, p. 393, for comments on
Paisiello comic overtures with thematic links between first movement and last.

action.[32] Piccinni in his *I viaggiatori* overture, Naples, 1775, let the curtain rise at the beginning of the third movement, an andante vivace in $\frac{3}{8}$, which turns out to be the opening of the first vocal item, a quartet. This last-mentioned experiment of course connects the overture with the opera itself in a very real sense. The idea that overture and opera should be related in other than a purely casual way was gradually gaining ground over the '60s–'70s period, owing to the promptings of Algarotti and other theorists favouring the meaningful interrelationship of all elements in opera and to the example of a few composers with radical leanings like Jommelli and Gluck.[33] Few cases of meaningful relationship between overture and opera exist in Neapolitan scores prior to 1780 however, and the link up between the two, especially by the practice of quoting themes from the opera in the overture,[34] is something consolidated after the period in question.

[32] This technique was employed by Jommelli in his overture to *Fetonte*, Stuttgart, 1768. See *Denkmäler Deutscher Tonkunst*, 1907, xxxii. 1 ff.

[33] The example of French opera before Gluck's incursion into this field should not be overlooked either. Rameau's overture to *Zoroastre*, 1749, is supposed to be a short tone poem descriptive of the scenario of the opera.

[34] H. Goldschmidt, 'Traettas Leben', *Denkmäler der Tonkunst in Bayern*, xiv. (1), pp. xxxviii–ix, points out that the middle movement of the overture to Traetta's *Farnace* (Naples, 1751) is based on Tomiris' aria in Act II, also that the middle movement of the overture to Traetta's *Sofonisba* (Mannheim, 1762) is based on the final quintet of that work.

Comic Opera—the Texts

THOUGH the S. Carlo was a Neapolitan theatre, no evidence exists to suggest that its management thought itself under an obligation to support local, Neapolitan talent at all times. The heroic opera performed there was a manifestation of an all-Italian and even international art whose musical features were coincidentally influenced by a prominent group of composers from the Neapolitan locality. S. Carlo managements could and did promote the work of outsiders when it suited them. On the list of S. Carlo productions therefore appear works not only by Neapolitans but by others, for example B. Galuppi, Gluck, J. C. Bach, J. Misliweczek, J. Schuster, and V. Martin y Soler, who already possessed good reputations or who were in Naples and so were given a commission for the novelty value. No one will deny that there were some distinctions between heroic opera in one centre and another—especially after Gluck's reform began to have its impact. But if anyone had to point to one branch of Italian opera that possessed strongly defined local features, his choice would surely fall on the short comic scenes sometimes inserted into heroic opera and also on full-length comic opera. Eighteenth-century Italians used several terms with which to describe comic opera: *opera buffa, intermezzo, intermezzo comico (giocoso), dramma giocoso (comico, semiserio, eroicomico), commedia per musica, farsa,* and others.[1] This should not confuse the reader. All categories can basically be reduced to the two mentioned: the short comic scene or group of scenes (sometimes called an intermezzo or group of intermezzos) designed primarily as an interlude or companion piece to another work such as an opera or spoken play, and the full-length comic opera designed as the main or only event on the theatrical bill. The usual locales for these types of opera at Naples have already been defined: the S. Bartolomeo, till 1735, for the one; and the small theatres like the Fiorentini, from 1709, for the other.

It is well known that the short comic opera consisting of a few scenes only, sometimes called an intermezzo, grew out of the humorous scenes of

---

[1] See A. della Corte, *L'opera comica italiana nel '700*, Bari, 1923, p. 10.

seventeenth-century Venetian opera in which the servant characters, the pages, nurses, and hunchbacks, passed comment among themselves on their masters and the court customs of the day, and played tricks on each other or made amorous advances. Such scenes became removed from the main opera as the characters mentioned gradually disappeared from it. Operas produced in Venice at the end of the seventeenth century possessed little or no comedy—we have already seen how Zeno tended to ignore it (see pp. 41–2 above). But if the Venetian literati were in favour of abandoning the comedy, other Venetians were not, and their desire for humorous scenes in opera periodically reasserted itself. When G. C. Bonlini compiled his list of operatic productions at Venice between 1637 and 1730, he noted that comic *intermedi* (*sic*) were introduced into some Venetian operas from around 1706 'with the sole object of tempering seriousness with humour'.[2] These *intermedi* were groups of comic scenes that accompanied a larger opera, and differed from previous groups seen at Venice in an important particular: their texts were printed in a separate booklet. Whether intentional or no, the separate comic libretto was a sign of the distinctiveness of the scenes from the heroic opera they accompanied. Separate publication also encouraged a closer relationship between the scenes themselves, that is, each group of comic scenes (or *intermedi* or *intermezzi*) was on the way to becoming a little art form on its own.

Intermezzo is by and large an eighteenth-century term replacing the earlier terms *intermedio* and *intramezzo* to describe a dramatic entr'acte. Very often it has the specific connotation of comic scenes sung or spoken by two or more characters.[3] By contrast the term *intermedio* or *intramezzo*, when used in seventeenth-century librettos of full-length opera, was rarely applied to the comic scenes specifically. A few early librettos indicate the presence of *intermedii* (*intramezzi*, etc.) with a short description of the action but without publication of dialogue.[4] This author knows of at least

---

[2] *Le glorie della poesia e della musica contenute nell'esatta notitia de'teatri della città de Venezia*, Venice, 1730, p. 149. On p. 150 Bonlini states such *intermedi* were never promoted by the management of the Venetian S. Gio: Grisostomo theatre.

[3] In the early eighteenth century the singular word, *intermezzo*, was used to describe a single scene or entr'acte inserted into another work. It was not used to describe a group of such entr'actes, which group was a group of *intermezzi* (plural). By the mid-century however the singular, *intermezzo*, was employed to mean just such a group.

[4] See the descriptions of Turkish dances forming four *intramezzi* in the libretto to *Irene*, Venice, 1695, words by G. F. Roberti, music by C. F. Pollaroli. The libretto to *Il pastore d'Anfriso*, Venice, 1695, words by Roberti, music by Pollaroli, is another with indications for *intramezzi*. These involve appearances and dances for gods, satyrs, nymphs, etc.

one other set of *intermedii* with dialogue for allegorical figures.[5] The latter set is serious in intent. A hint of later, eighteenth-century practice is contained in a small libretto including arias and two *intermezzi* (*sic*) for *Il re infante*, an opera with words by M. Noris and music by G. A. Perti performed at the Malvezzi theatre, Bologna, in 1694. It seems these arias and intermezzos were inserted into the production after the opening night, so it was too late to incorporate them in the full libretto and a separate one was printed. The argument put forward in the preface of the small libretto supporting the insertion of the intermezzos emphasized how they enhanced the value of the main work: 'Two *intermezzi* have also been added to it, so that when you see the farcical side mixed with the serious, the latter will appear all the more welcome.' The intermezzos have a simple plot. The one character appearing in both scenes is Gildo, a servant who also appears in the opera. In the first scene he feigns wooing a lady, Dircea, and wins from her a ring. In the second he is tricked in turn and loses it to another lady, Despina, and her male accomplice. The story seems designed to point the moral that no one can be deceitful and get away with it.

The first groups of Venetian intermezzos printed in separate booklets were probably *Lesbina e Milo* and *Bleso e Lesba*, *Lesbina* accompanying the opera *Paride in Ida*[6] and *Bleso* perhaps accompanying *La regina creduta re*.[7] These operas were performed at the S. Angelo theatre, Venice, in 1706. Each set of intermezzos consists of three scenes, a common if not standard number in intermezzos of the first twenty years of the century. The libretto of *Bleso e Lesba* states that the first two scenes come at the ends of Acts I and II of the main opera while the third follows the aria 'E la corte vo vivo inferno'.[8] So if this last-mentioned had to follow an aria, it had to come in the middle, not at the end, of Act III. In both groups of intermezzos the dialogue is between two comic characters, a man and a woman, who engage in much unsubtle argument and verbal sparring. One of the two falls for the other and hints or proposes that they should marry. This is followed by a refusal, insults, quarrels leading almost to blows, then a final acceptance of the proposal. The chief alternative to this general

[5] In the libretto to *Argiope*, Venice, 1649, words by N. and G. B. Fusconi, music by A. Leardini. For a description of operatic entr'actes *c.* 1680, see E. J. Dent, 'A Jesuit at the opera in 1680', *Riemann-Festschrift, Gesammelte Studien*, Tutzing, reprint 1965, pp. 386 ff.

[6] Words by F. Mazzari, music by C. Manza and A. B. Coletti.

[7] Words by M. Noris, music by M. A. Bononcini.

[8] The libretto of *Regina creduta re* in the Marciana library, Venice, contains no reference to an aria beginning 'E la corte'. This may put in doubt Wiel's linking *Bleso e Lesba* to it, see T. Wiel, *I teatri musicali veneziani del settecento*, Venice, 1897, p. 12.

dramatic plan was for the librettist to marry the two off earlier and then show the disadvantages of their union. This was adopted in the case of another group of intermezzos performed in Venice in 1706. *Frappolone e Florinetta* is different from the two previously mentioned in that it is preserved in manuscript form.[9] In the first scene Frappolone, a roguish agent, explains how he is defrauding his master by altering the accounts. Florinetta makes comments on the latest cosmetics. The two decide to marry. In the second the by now married couple start to quarrel. The woman complains that she wants more freedom and that her clothes are unsuitable. Frappolone, desperate, decides his only hope of salvation is to leave home. In the third he appears dressed as a soldier about to depart for the wars and after a bit of burlesque exits, warning his wife to be chaste in his absence.

Here then are two types of dramatic plan which, with variants, appear over and over again in early eighteenth-century intermezzos. In nearly all these cases the characters engage in a game of 'one-upmanship'. They dress in disguise or change their style of behaviour, as Frappolone does, to fool or terrify their partner. They show off, display their (incomplete) knowledge of the classics, the theatre, court customs, compete in little singing matches, poetry writing, or dancing. All this is to put them in a position where they can advance their cause or pour scorn on the other. The shrewder of the two characters is usually the female. This had not always been the case. In mid-seventeenth-century Venetian opera the female was represented as lecherous and long in the tooth. Any attempt of hers to impress the younger man was usually nullified by her ugliness and uncouth behaviour, so that he did his best to be rid of her. But around 1700 there was a change about, the lady becoming younger and more sprightly and the man older by comparison. And as it was part of the theatrical tradition for youth to appear cleverer and less ridiculous than old age, the girl now had her turn to outpoint her husband or lover.

The dialogue of these first Venetian intermezzos is of interest too. It is quite different from anything uttered by the kings and queens of Zeno's work because it contains fewer restraints of language, more references to everyday affairs, and as a consequence a wider range of vocabulary. This freedom of dialogue is noticeable throughout eighteenth-century comic

---

[9] MS. in the Marciana library, Venice. Its title page reads: 'Frappolone e Florinetta / Intermezzi / rappresentato l'anno 1706 nel teatro di San Cassiano / nel Carnovale con il Dramma intitolato: Statira.'

opera if compared with heroic opera of comparable date. The comic aria does not always condense thought into a few lines—which was Zeno's or Metastasio's practice. It is longer, more verbose. Frappolone, for example, enters scene three dressed in his military uniform and sings this aria:

> Per seguir più bel mestiero,
> Diventato
> Io son soldato.
> E già detto hò al mio Barbiero
> Che vò baffi pennacchiati
> Ciglia grosse, e peli irsuti;
> Per poter col guardo turbido,
> A nimici imprimer spasimo,
> Dar spavento, e far terror.
> Ecco ormai senza timore
> D'aver sopra il mio revisore,
> Porta meco il mio essercizio
> Che il rubbar non è più vizio,
> Anzi à dargli il titol vero
> Chiamarollo ardir guerriero
> Che fà gloria, e porta onor.

(To make a better career, I have become a soldier; and I have already told my barber I want pointed moustaches, huge eyebrows, and shaggy hair, so that I can shock, frighten, and terrorize enemies with my wild look. Not afraid from now on of wearing my visor[?] I act on the assumption that robbery is no longer a crime. Rather, to give it its true name, let me call it the warlike zeal that brings glory and honour with it.)

The position and number of lyrical items in intermezzos is another interesting point. Each scene, or intermezzo, of *Lesbina e Milo*, *Frappolone*, and later works of the same type, has two or more arias/ensembles. Arias in the middle of an intermezzo are rarely the signal for the exit of the singer, so the convention about exits after arias does not apply here. Perhaps it was argued that the departure of either of the two characters in the middle of an intermezzo held up the action. At the end of each intermezzo came a duet, followed this time by the exit of both singers. Because this duet was often a point of friction between the couple, it served the same function as the act finale to larger comic operas of later date, and may reasonably be considered a miniature prototype of the other.

What has been said so far about the Venetian intermezzo may be applied to its artistic equivalent at Naples—except that (*a*) the comic entr'acte was not referred to as *intermezzo* in Neapolitan librettos printed before the

1720s, and (b) the Neapolitans showed greater reluctance than certain Venetians in getting rid of comic scenes altogether. In fact the consistent growth of the intermezzo out of the comic scene of old Venetian opera occurred in centres like Naples rather than in Venice itself. In the late 1690s when there were few traces of comedy in opera at Venice, operas at the Naples' S. Bartolomeo had plenty. Scarlatti's *La caduta dei decemviri* (1697), *Il prigionier fortunato* (1698), and *Eraclea* (1700), for example, each had no fewer than five comic scenes. None of these scenes occurred at the end of an act. Though Neapolitans had previously ventured to put comic scenes at act endings when it suited them,[10] not till the early eighteenth century did they regularly choose just three of them per opera and start to shift the first two out of the acts and into the entr'acte position. By so doing they related them more closely to Venetian intermezzos. It might be useful at this point to put side by side some of the contrasting features of Venetian intermezzos of 1706 and after and Neapolitan comic scenes of the same period. Features of the Venetian intermezzos are set on the left, Neapolitan scenes on the right.

	VENICE	NAPLES
1	The text of so-called *intermezzi* was printed separately from the text of the main opera.	Comic scenes were printed in the libretto of the main opera. They were first called *intermezzi* in the 1720s.
2	The intermezzo booklet took its title from the names of the protagonists.	Separate titles for groups of comic scenes first appeared in librettos *c.* 1720.
3	The intermezzo booklet might or might not contain information about the date and place of performance. The name of the main opera was often not mentioned, and the position of the third comic scene was rarely clarified.	The exact position of each comic scene was indicated in the libretto.
4	Intermezzo characters rarely appeared in the main opera.	At first one or both comic characters had supporting roles in the main opera. They lost these roles in the 1720s.

[10] A good example is Provenzale's opera *Lo schiavo di sua moglie* (1671) whose Acts I and II terminate with three and two scenes respectively for the comic servants.

Final emancipation of the Neapolitan intermezzo came when not merely the comic characters disappeared from the main opera but all references in the one to the other also disappeared. In J. Hasse's first opera to be produced at the S. Bartolomeo, *Sesostrate* (1726), we still find such cross-references. The two comedians, though confined to their own scenes, yet act the role of servants or friends of characters in the main opera. Their social positions alternatively rise and fall according to the fortunes of their masters or friends and their treatment of each other changes accordingly. This means that the intermezzos cannot be properly understood without reference to the heroic text. Full emancipation was aided too by the reduction of the scenes from three to two—which meant each scene henceforth was a true entr'acte. This phasing out of the third scene, which occurred *c.* 1730, may have had beneficial effect also on the coherence of the art form. It must be remembered that a complete act intervened between the performance of one comic scene and the next, which may have discouraged the librettist from relating the scenes as closely as he could. Two scenes were a neater package. The most famous of all Neapolitan intermezzos, Pergolesi's *La serva padrona* (words by G. A. Federico) which originally went with the same composer's *Il prigioniero superbo* (1733), has the two scenes only.

There was one case where a highly popular theme first appeared in a group of intermezzos and was then transferred to larger comic opera. Metastasio's *Didone abbandonata*, as produced at the S. Bartolomeo in 1724, had two successful intermezzos portraying an impresario, Nibbio, engaging Dorinda, a singer, for his company.[11] The inspiration for this may have come from Marcello's well-known book *Il teatro alla moda*, which lampooned the various professionals, workmen, and patrons, of the opera of the day. Besides satirizing the personal eccentricities of the characters, the writer of the intermezzos also poked fun at the conventions of heroic opera by making the characters sing arias, and Dorinda an accompanied recitative, in a mock heroic style. There are some sly hints at the absurdities of heroic opera, as when Nibbio encourages the lady to complete her accompanied recitative with an aria and expresses astonishment that she will not do so, for, he says, it is the modern practice to sing one at this juncture. He thereupon decides to finish Dorinda's recitative with an aria of his own. The required song, he explains, should contain mention of

[11] See M. Scherillo, *L'opera buffa napoletana*, Naples, 1916, pp. 146–50, for further remarks on these intermezzos. It is not known whether Metastasio wrote the intermezzos' text.

some *farfalletta* or *navicella*, a satirical reference to the many allusions in aria poetry to pastoral scenes, the sea, and other aspects of nature. The poetic allusions in his own song get so mixed that near nonsense results. Librettists were constantly prepared to satirize heroic opera in this way:

> La farfalla, che allo scuro
> Va rondando intorno al muro
> Sai che dice a chi l'intende?
> Chi una fiaccola m'accenda,
> Chi mi scotta per pietà.
> Il Vascello, e la Tartana
> Fra scirocco, e tramontana
> Con le tavole schiodate
> Va sbalzando,
> Va sparando
> Cannonate
> In quantità.

(The butterfly that flits around the wall in the dark, do you know what it is saying to whoever hears it? Who's putting a torch to me? Who's burning me, in heaven's name?

The merchantman and tartan, caught between south and north winds, lurches about with its tables unfastened, firing cannonades in plenty)

The decision of Charles III to order ballets in place of intermezzos during heroic opera performances cut short the development of the Neapolitan intermezzo just when it had reached an interesting phase. It left the development of the intermezzo almost entirely in the hands of opera writers in Rome and cities farther north. Between the '30s and '60s the Central and North Italian intermezzo involved more and more characters and grew in size to the point where it could be compared more with full-length comic opera than with the miniature entr'actes of old. The term itself became synonymous with *farsa/farsetta* which had no entr'acte connotations. Whoever wants to discover how close full-length comic opera and the intermezzo/farsa became might examine any of Goldoni's full-length librettos in three acts—his *Il filosofo di campagna* is a good one to take[12]—that afterward was turned into an intermezzo or farsa in two 'parts' (i.e., acts), and then compare the two versions. The full-length work was easily shortened into the other without any impairment of its essentials. From this it is fair to conclude that the intermezzo generally acquired the

[12] Compare *Il filosofo di campagna*, set by B. Galuppi, S. Samuele theatre, Venice, 1754, with either *La serva astuta, farsetta per musica*, Valle theatre, Rome, 1757, or *La serva astuta o sia il filosofo in campagna*, *intermezzo in due parti*, S. Angelo theatre, Venice, 1761.

variety of plot, characterization, and stage scenery of full-length opera without suffering from some of its redundant elements.

Before leaving Naples's part in the development of the intermezzo into an independent, self-contained work, we should mention the case of *La locandiera*, a short comic opera produced at the S. Carlo in 1738 to celebrate the arrival in Naples of Charles III's wife, Maria Amalia. The words were by G. A. Federico, the music by P. Auletta. The work, called a *scherzo comico per musica* in the libretto, is distinctive for being one of the only two comic operas produced at the S. Carlo in the eighteenth century.[13] It is in two parts and is of relatively small proportions, which facts are explained by the work's function. Among the now lost sections of the Naples Archives were documents relating to the commissioning of this opera. According to U. Prota-Giurleo, who collected the information, Charles's original idea was to order an entertainment for his queen consisting of intermezzos[14] and ballets. It was pointed out to him, however, that recent intermezzos went in pairs and were short, that the time of performance was in the region of three-quarters of an hour only, and that even if ballets were added before, in the middle, and after, the total performance would still barely last an hour and a half. The librettist was therefore told to prepare a libretto longer than a traditional pair of intermezzos, with the condition that he was not to arrange 'for more than six characters, nor [write] more than two acts or *intermezzi* [sic], with a maximum of twelve arias among which number a duet or two may be included if necessary'.[15] He was also permitted to interweave some mute persons into the comedy.[16] The use of the term *intermezzi* in this context shows how its connotations were beginning to broaden. As for the question of the dances that went with *La locandiera*, little information is at present available about them. The only clue in the libretto that there were dances at all is the remark 'Inventor and director of the dances Sig. Francesco Aquilanti'.

The text of *La locandiera* is written in a mixture of Neapolitan and Tuscan dialects, but the Neapolitan is 'Tuscanized' and far from broad, and the majority of the characters uses Tuscan only—Tuscan being of course

---

[13] The other was *Una cosa rara* by Martin y Soler, performed in 1789. See U. Prota-Giurleo, *Breve storia*, pp. 112–13.

[14] The idea of ordering intermezzos may have been to please the queen. Later the same year she expressed interest in seeing intermezzo performances at the royal palace, see ibid., pp. 114–15.

[15] There are in fact 13 lyrical items, plus a short final chorus and some additional short lyrical strophes or fragments, in the score of the opera.

[16] From the directives issued by the Marchese di Salas, president of the council of ministers, Naples Archives, Teatri, f. 1 (archive destroyed).

the literary and aristocratic language of Italy. The action of the opera takes place in Leghorn, Tuscany, to match the language. Early comic operas written for the Fiorentini, Della Pace, and Nuovo theatres contain much dialect in Neapolitan, and the action usually matches the language by taking place in or around the city of Naples. Prominent use of local dialect was the first, and by no means the least, difference between full-length comic opera at Naples on the one hand and heroic opera and intermezzo at Naples on the other[17] during the eighteenth-century period. It also distinguished comic opera at Naples from comic opera elsewhere in Italy. For Italians in other cities put less value on dialect in opera than Neapolitans did. This peculiarity of the Neapolitan brand was the main reason in our view why its best examples never gained the international reputation acquired by certain other comic operas by Neapolitan composers that used Tuscan only. The comparative isolation of the Neapolitan type was recognized at the time and occasionally regretted. The Abbé Galiani, for one, tried desperately to convince Madame d'Epinay by letter in 1771 that marvellous new comic operas were being created at Naples. But how to do this when their charm evaporated, removed from their home atmosphere? 'I repeat to you that you can appreciate nothing of the peak of perfection to which Piccinni has raised our comic opera. Have no fear that Neapolitan comic operas will come to France. That has never happened; they do not get even to Rome. You will have Italian comic operas like *La buona figliola*[18] but no Neapolitan ones.' He said he would send her some pieces with translations, so she could see for herself it was necessary to come to Naples to savour the local product.[19] In March 1773 he was writing again, this time praising Paisiello's most recent comic compositions. But he had not sent her any of Paisiello's work, he declared, for it was 'too Neapolitan'.[20]

It would be an exaggeration to claim that Neapolitan comic opera never reached farther north, especially in the last quarter of the century, but it is true that impresarios in other major centres preferred their own or else

---

[17] A few of the earliest operas at Naples contain dialect for one, or at the most two, characters. Spellecchia in *Orontea* (words by G. A. Ciccognini, music by M. A. Cesti and others) Naples, 1674, sings in Neapolitan. Giampetro in *Stellidaura vendicata* (A. Perrucci—F. Provenzale) Naples, 1674, uses Calabrian dialect. Dialect is also found in a few of the earliest sacred operas performed by the conservatories, see p. 15 above. It is hard to find dialect in eighteenth-century comic entr'actes or intermezzos at Naples; but note III.xiv of *Tigrane* (D. Lalli—A. Scarlatti), 1715, in which the two comedians use Bolognese while disguised as 'Dottor Graziano' and 'Zaccagnia'.

[18] This libretto by Carlo Goldoni was first set by Egidio Duni and performed at Parma in 1757. Piccinni's more famous setting was staged at the Delle Dame theatre, Rome, in 1760.

[19] *Correspondance inédite*, i. 336–7.   [20] *Correspondance inédite*, ii. 162.

other non-Neapolitan material.[21] In all cases where Neapolitan works were produced farther north, the Neapolitan dialect was removed. The converse, that non-Neapolitan comic opera rarely reached Naples, is also true. Nor were librettos by non-Neapolitans commonly used there, not even those of the famous Carlo Goldoni (1707–93) whose full-length comic opera texts were set and reset in Venice, Rome, Milan, etc., from the end of the 1740s. When one of his librettos was taken as basis for a Neapolitan production, it was substantially modified—as anyone can check who compares his *Il mondo della luna* (first set by Galuppi, Venice, 1750) with the Neapolitan version set by Paisiello under the title of *Il credulo deluso* (1774). The implication of all this is that Neapolitan impresarios relied on local libretto writers. M. Scherillo in his book *L'opera buffa napoletana* has already provided much information on the work of these librettists. In spite of subsequent research, we remain uncertain about the biographical data of several of them. Judging from the quality and/or quantity of their work, commentators deem the following among the most important. The earliest included: Francesco A. Tullio (1660–1737), who wrote several works including *La Cilla* (1706 or 7),[22] the first recorded comic libretto in Neapolitan dialect; 'Agasippo Mercotellis', writer of three librettos including the first opera in dialect at the Fiorentini, *Patrò Calienno de la Costa* (1709), *nom de plume* perhaps for Nicolò Corvo; and Aniello Piscopo, who wrote three surviving librettos dated 1717, 1719, and 1719. Among librettists commencing in the '20s–'30s period were Bernardo Saddumene, Gennaro Federico (d. between 1743 and '48), Pietro Trinchera (1702–55), and Antonio Palomba (1705–69). A group whose activities in the libretto field started in the 60's included Francesco Cerlone (*c.* 1730–*c.* 1812), Giuseppe Palomba, and perhaps the best of all Neapolitan comic librettists, Giambattista Lorenzi (1721–1807).[23]

---

[21] When *Il falegname*, words by G. Palomba and music by Cimarosa, first staged at the Fiorentini in 1780, was produced at the S. Moisè theatre in Venice, in 1784, the Venetian impresario thought it wise to warn his 'respectable public': 'This opera is certainly not one of the best planned or adapted to the taste of an intelligent public like the one in this city, for the work is by a Neapolitan poet and written for the Neapolitan theatre where they take no notice either of the way characters are drawn or the manner of performance.'
  See Wiel, *I teatri musicali veneziani*, pp. 382–3.

[22] *La Cilla* was performed at the house of the Prince of Chiusano in December–January, 1707–8. Sartori, 'Gli Scarlatti a Napoli', *RMI*, xlvi. 380–1, points to a reference in the libretto's dedication to a performance 'the year past', which might mean there was a performance in 1706.

[23] Biographical information on these librettists here drawn from *Enciclopedia dello spettacolo*, Le Maschere, Rome, 9 vols., 1954–62.

The immediate predecessors of the dialect operas at the Fiorentini were certainly not the short comic scenes (later the intermezzos) of the S. Bartolomeo. Not only the language was different. The full-length comic opera was a three-act work with a cast of seven or eight characters on average, as opposed to the three or four scenes and two characters (with possibly an additional mute or two) of the other. The scope and size of the two types were in fact too diverse for anyone now to talk of an evolution of the Neapolitan comic opera out of the Neapolitan intermezzo. In very general terms, a line of ancestry for *La Cilla* and *Patrò* might be sought back to those rather rare seventeenth-century operas such as *Il potestà di Colognole* (Florence, 1657)[24] whose chief characters are of the lower orders of nobility and bourgeoisie rather than of high rank and whose texts contain a certain amount of dialect. In general terms, too, some parallels may be drawn between these works and spoken comedy at Naples, for example those of Nicolò Amenta (1659–1719) which attempt to revive the quality and spirit of sixteenth-century Italian comedy and are in Tuscan for the most part. There may be parallels, too, with a few comedies either entirely or largely in dialect. We know of one comedy in Neapolitan, *Mezzotte*, performed at the Castel dell'Ovo, Naples, in 1701. Another dialect play, *La Deana o Lo Lavenaro* by Nicola Maresca, was published and performed in Naples in 1706.[25] The *commedia dell'arte* cannot be forgotten as one possible progenitor of *Patrò*, and more will be said on this in a moment. One commentator has made the interesting suggestion that the line of dialect operas at the Fiorentini (from 1709) was encouraged by the arrival of the Austrians in 1707 and the subsequent easing of censorship regulations.[26]

The question of the immediate artistic ancestry of *Patrò*[27] is perhaps less important than the fact that it follows, and creates the precedent for other Neapolitan comic operas to follow, the basic conventions of Italian

[24] Words by G. A. Moniglia, music by J. Melani. Text in A. della Corte, *Drammi per musica del Rinuccini allo Zeno*, ii. 7 ff.

[25] V. Viviani, *Storia del teatro napoletano*, Naples, 1969, pp. 251 ff.

[26] E. Battisti, 'Per una indagine sociologica sui librettisti napoletani buffi del settecento', *Letteratura*, Rome, 1960, viii. 120–1.

[27] Croce, 'I teatri di Napoli', 1890, xv. n. 4, 282–3, has discovered a close similarity between the texts of *Patrò* by Agasippo Mercotellis and *La Perna* by Nicolò Corvo. It is on this evidence that he and others have assumed Mercotellis and Corvo to be one and the same. What has not been made clear is that *La Perna* (known through a nineteenth-century MS. copy now in the National Library, Naples) is itself an operatic libretto (in Neapolitan dialect). There is no conclusive evidence which of the two texts came first and no evidence that *La Perna* was ever set.

comic theatre—this term here being used in its broadest sense. Take the characters first of all. There is Patrò himself, known to everyone as Ciommo, living with his wife Renza and with two young people, Fortonato and Lella. Lella is thought to be his daughter. There is Sciarillo Caporale with his servant Meniello and his female slave Perna. Finally there is Luccio, friendly with Fortonato and in love with Lella. Nothing particularly original will be discovered in their qualities, which may be classified as both regional and universal. Their regionalism is brought out in the language they speak and their tendency to involve themselves in scuffles, arguments, etc., that have little to do with the plot, but present a picture of Neapolitan life and the volatile and extrovert nature of some of the city's inhabitants. Their universal side comes out in the way they conform to certain bourgeois and lower-class 'types', represented time and time again in Italian comedy since the sixteenth century. Standard is their grouping in households, each headed by a middle-aged man who is ineffectual in his efforts to control it, or with some laughable eccentricity. Standard are the children and servants attempting to work the dramatic situation their way under the noses of their parents and patrons. Standard too are the love affairs and marriage proposals. In the early part of this opera Luccio's love for Lella is not returned; Patrò betrothes Lella to Sciarillo—this is equally unwelcome to her—on condition that Sciarillo gets rid of Perna; Perna is in love with Fortonato and he with her; but Patrò also has his roving eye on Perna, which arouses the suspicions of Renza. The librettist's way of untangling all these complexities is to allow it to be discovered at the end that several of the youngsters are in fact living in the wrong families. Fortonato and Lella are really Sciarillo's children; Perna is really Patrò's daughter. So Lella's engagement to Sciarillo is automatically dissolved, and Patrò's inclinations toward Perna may be explained as an instinctive affection for a close relative.[28]

The appearance of traditional and standard types of character in so many Neapolitan and Italian comic operas has led before now to the making of comparisons between them and *commedie dell' arte*.[29] The elderly gentleman of opera may, like Pantalone, be a miser or a flirt with the ladies; may, like Dottor Graziano, parade his bogus knowledge; or perhaps, like Tartaglia or Pasquariello, be a mere simpleton. The servants may be divided into those who are dull-witted, like Pulcinella in some of his manifestations,

---

[28] Synopsis of *Patrò* in Scherillo, *L'opera buffa napoletana*, pp. 62–74.
[29] E.g. in H. Abert, *W. A. Mozart*, 7th edn., Leipzig, 1955, i. 332–3.

and those like Coviello, for example, who are shrewd, quick-witted, and capable of turning any situation to good account. There are the pairs of young lovers, more sentimental and serious than the rest perhaps. And there are various 'professionals', the swaggering soldier (Capitano Spavento), the medical doctor, the notary and lawyer. Seldom do these characters appear in comic opera at Naples under the traditional *commedia* names that everyone has heard of; but just occasionally they do in operas of the second half of the century whose third act is totally or largely replaced by a separate *burletta* or *farsetta* (so-called). We will cite two examples. In Act III of *Il finto sordo*, produced at the Fiorentini in 1771 with words by P. Mililotto and music by Pasquale Tarantino, the characters act *La serva scaltra*, a type of play within the play and described in the libretto as a *burletta*. Within this *burletta* are eight character parts including Tartaglia, Pulcinella, and Arlecchino. *Il medico*, the comic opera which as we said earlier (see pp. 16–17 above) was performed by the boys of the S. Onofrio in 1767, also has a separate piece in its third act, *Li burlanti*, containing, among other parts, two for Pulcinella and Coviello.

The theoretical support for this standardization of characters was based on certain neo-classical concepts of theatre. Theatre had morally to instruct, and the best way of letting comedy do so was through the inverse procedure of the one followed in tragedy. To put the matter at its simplest— tragedy was supposed to cause sympathy toward the noble hero in his trials and tribulations; comedy was supposed to cause disrespect of the human foibles being caricatured. At the same time playwrights were warned to be careful in their comedies not to lampoon some of the more serious vices, in case the humorous demonstration of these actually led to imitation and hence damaged public morals.[30] Characters had therefore to be selected whose faults were ridiculous yet basically innocuous. Alternatively they had to uncover ridiculous traits in others. Some theorists gave lists of the types suitable and safe for comedy. This was Muratori's: 'a chatterbox, miser, jealous man, coward, flatterer, boaster, vain woman, stupid servant, partial judge, ignorant attorney, shrewd artisan, and many other varieties of type.'[31] This list is none too different from the *commedia* list above and suggests that theorists and the general public both wanted the same sort of thing, even if their reasons were different. Incidentally, ridicule of harmless mannerisms steered comedy away from certain types

[30] See Muratori, *Della perfetta poesia*, ii. 69 ff., and Planelli, *Dell'opera in musica*, pp. 267–9.
[31] *Della perfetta poesia*, ii. 73. Note a similar though shorter list in Planelli, op. cit., p. 269.

of satire, for example political, that in a city like Naples would probably have brought quick reaction from the authorities.[32] Those who are looking at the matter from a literary standpoint will quickly conclude that eighteenth-century theorists must have had a narrow view of comedy if, by their definition, it had to deride human fault and deride it in and through these characters. In this connection it is worth reading what Perrucci had to say in his *Dell'arte rappresentativa* of 1699 on ways of raising a laugh in the theatre. His remarks referred specifically to the problem of humour in improvised comedy, yet they were not irrelevant to other forms of spoken and sung comedy as well. There is no need to comment on them except to say that he seems not to have realized how likable qualities in a character may play their part in creating humour.

Concerning the subject of raising mirth there are six methods: the first is through [depicting] mental vices, mocking the vainglorious, the parasites, and misers, and through [depicting] physical vices . . .

The second method is that of imitation, by which a hunchback, a man with a limp, or certain defects of the voice or body, are rendered contemptible . . .

The third method is that of simulation, acting the part of a Frenchman, German, Turk, or Spaniard, or the part of madmen or drunkards.

The fourth method is acting with contempt, which one does making a wry mouth, opening it, putting out the tongue, laughing inanely, romping, hissing, or crying immoderately or crudely.

The fifth is in the use of indecent words . . . [which] we have from the beginning inveighed against.

The sixth is in the use of insulting words, suitable only for servants, clowns, and parasites.

And the seventh is to speak servilely and like a rustic, and there are other methods.[33]

While the very nature of comic opera placed it low in the theatrical order of things, there was no denying that it had high entertainment value. And no dramatic technique contributed more to its liveliness than that long-established device: disguise. Disguise was an essential technique of comic opera to an extent that was not so in Metastasian opera—though it occurred there also. We have already seen cases of unwitting disguise in

---

[32] Note the Neapolitan court's ban on *Il Socrate immaginario*, words by Lorenzi, music by Paisiello, near the start of what looked like a successful run at the Nuovo theatre in 1775, on the grounds that it was 'indiscreet'. It is generally considered by scholars that the work contained satire directed at Saverio Mattei, the poet and theorist, who was favoured at court. *Il Socrate* returned to the Neapolitan public stage in 1780.

[33] Ed. A. G. Bragaglia, Florence, 1961, pp. 231–2.

Patrò where the characters are unaware of their true identity till the end of the drama. In other instances characters deliberately fabricate new identities. They might, for example, be fleeing from the wrath or vengeance of another individual or from the law. They might be discreetly enquiring into the whereabouts of a missing relative, betrothed, or a criminal. They might be trying to gain admittance to somewhere not open to them or be imitating someone to enjoy his privileges. A sub-category is the disguise of a character in the clothes of the other sex. The casting of male singers in female roles and female singers in male, with the chance that they could 'disguise' themselves in their proper clothes, added greatly to the opportunity for intrigue and *double entendre*. Eighteenth-century librettists were not able to seize this to the extent some of their seventeenth-century predecessors had done, for the reason that plots were less complex. But the technique of confusing the sexes yet remained popular and became a feature of some comic operas at the Fiorentini and Nuovo. Up to *c.* 1780 the managements of these theatres often cast female singers in the roles of young men. The reasons were that music for high voices was fashionable and comic opera at Naples did without castratos.[34] The casting of women in male roles allowed the librettist, if he desired, to make the most of the bisexual nature of their part. An instance is *Inganno per inganno*, words by Federico and music by N. Logroscino, heard at the Fiorentini in 1738. Here two young men gain admission to their sweet-hearts, jealously guarded by their brother, by dressing up as women. The disguise, as so often happens in comic opera when it is purposeful, gets them into more trouble. Their ladies believe they are women and strongly reject their advances. Various other people react unfavourably to their (feminine) presence out of suspicion or jealousy.[35]

What saved comic opera in its early years from becoming stereotyped was the willingness of its authors to absorb new artistic and literary influences and fuse new refinements with the old-fashioned clownery. Many factors were involved here, including one element of opera we have referred to already and must refer to again: language. In 1718 the management of the Fiorentini reversed its previous policy of presenting operas either entirely or largely in Neapolitan and promoted operas in Tuscan

[34] Occasionally a minor part was taken by a male singer with soprano range. The part of Ridolfo in *L'amor vuol sofferenza* (1739), words by Federico, music by Leo, was acted by one Signor Giacomo Ricci whose top note in the score is B above the treble stave. The libretto says Ridolfo is a 'young Genovese', suggesting perhaps that the singer was still an adolescent.

[35] A fuller synopsis of *Inganno* is in Scherillo, *L'opera buffa napoletana*, pp. 217–19.

instead. During 1718–19 three such 'Tuscan' operas were staged, all with texts by Tullio: *Il gemino amore* (music by A. Orefice), *Il trionfo dell'onore* (music by A. Scarlatti), and *La forza della virtù* (music by Feo). The dedication in the libretto of *Gemino* explains the management's motive. 'This year there has been a change from Neapolitan to the Tuscan idiom in the comedies appearing at the small Fiorentini theatre. Their action is not heroic or royal but is concerned with domestic and household events. It is hoped that such events, being acted by both grave and ridiculous characters, will please equally for their gravity and facetiousness.' The experiment of all-Tuscan operas was not repeated. What we find emerging from 1719 however is a bilingual opera in which some characters (among them the most serious) use Tuscan and others (including the more ridiculous) use Neapolitan. Some may interpret this simply as a return to older dramatic practice, as for instance in the *commedia dell'arte*.[36] There is also another and quite different point that Neapolitan impresarios had the problem of finding singers and had wider choice if their shows permitted non-Neapolitan performers. This is suggested in the preface of one of Saddumene's earliest librettos, *La noce de Veneviento*, opera staged at the Fiorentini in April 1722[37] as follows:

In writing this comedy, I have had to obey the person giving the orders and not let my fancy direct me. Therefore I have not created the usual sort of work with low-class persons only, but have also included civilised people in it, just as if it were a 'cloak and dagger' comedy (as the expression is). The object is to make a new work, not so much for the sake of the changes of situation as for the Neapolitan speech which is of two types, the one civilised and the other coarse, to suit the characters concerned, and in order not to make our language too difficult for certain foreigners in the cast.

Here therefore was an opera all of whose characters sang in Neapolitan, but some used a much Tuscanized version of it. Saddumene was among the librettists who during the '20s popularized the use of both dialects in one and the same libretto. The Tuscanization process reached a stage in his *La Rosmene*, set to music by Leo and performed at the Nuovo in 1730, where six of the eight characters sang throughout in Tuscan and only two in Neapolitan. This seems the farthest the process went. Thereafter the proportion of singers using the one dialect or the other varied from libret-

---

[36] Perrucci, *Dell'arte rappresentativa*, ed. Bragaglia, pp. 162 ff. and 194 ff., recommended that Tuscan be used by all young lovers and local dialect by fathers and old men.

[37] The composer's name is not mentioned in the libretto.

tist to librettist and from libretto to libretto. The only consistent thing about the language of all these works was the use of Neapolitan by at least a minority of the cast.

Two manners of speech were a useful aid to dividing one group of characters from another—in the case of comic opera the serious or semi-serious (called *parti serie*) from the comic (called *parti buffe*). Language will often give a clue to the degree of seriousness to be found in the qualities of any character—that is, the more serious he is, the more likelihood of his using Tuscan. It is easy to assume, as Scherillo tends to do, that the appearance of serious characters in comic opera from *c.* 1718–20 was the result of the influence of heroic opera and the propensity of comic opera to parody the other. Heroic opera's influence was marked when it came to such matters as the exit of characters after arias. Librettists quickly learned to parody Metastasio's aria poetry. It is interesting to note, however, how the lovers of the more serious works by Saddumene and Federico are not to be compared with Metastasio's so much as with those of earlier opera, for example Stampiglia's, for the reason that they are volatile in the extreme, plot the downfall of rivals by every devious means, and act boorishly while using flamboyant and often very baroque language. A quite different source of inspiration for the insertion of serious characters may have been Spanish seventeenth-century drama. Saddumene referred to it in his *La noce* preface, note the expression 'cloak and dagger' comedy (spelt in Neapolitan *commedia da cappa e spata*, that is *comedia de capa y espada*). Scherillo mentions one Saddumene libretto, *La Carlotta* of 1726, based directly or indirectly on a drama of Tirso de Molina.[38] Spanish sources of inspiration might also help explain why comic opera thereafter began to incorporate more sensational themes—for example, the protection of, or attack upon, the virtue of the female by the male, epitomized later by Mozart's *Don Giovanni*—that added spice to its subject matter.

The appearance of this type of theme was one sign that librettists gradually moved away from the concept that comic opera had merely to ridicule. The sentimental strain appearing in certain librettos of the second half of the century was another. Here we see the influence of new literary genres, especially the French and English sentimental novel, and the *comédie larmoyante* of Nivelle de la Chaussée, none of which can be considered comic in the old-fashioned sense. As the variety of subject increased,

[38] Molina's *Villana de Vallecas*. Scherillo, *L'opera buffa napoletana*, p. 158, here bases his information on another source.

so did that of its background scenery. All that librettists demanded in the earliest comic operas at the Fiorentini and Nuovo were simple sets depicting a location, for example a street or square, in the Neapolitan area. But as comic opera began to develop out of its first phase in the '20s–'30s, they began to demand indoor as well as outdoor scenes, also more changes of scenery per opera. They then asked for sets depicting distant places, and, after the mid century, romantic and fantastic ones like ruined castles with rusty gates, grottoes and caverns, deserts, fantastic seascapes, and oriental temples. In some later operas there were also occasions for magical transformations of scene—reminiscent not of Metastasian works but of French and of seventeenth-century Venetian opera. Witness the following stage direction in the libretto of *L'osteria di Marechiaro*, III.vii, words by Cerlone and music by Insanguine, produced at the Fiorentini in 1768:

A room of medium size in the middle of which a table stands set ready for dinner. Lesbina, the Abate, the Marchese, and Dorina have taken their places round it. Then at a sign from the Count the said table shall be transformed into a gruesome rock in the middle of a tempestuous sea with four marine monsters each pretending it wishes to devour one of them. At the same time the above-mentioned room shall be changed into a broad sea beach with outsize waves that try to submerge the said rock.

This work revives memories of the Arabian Nights,[39] its chief character, one Count Zampano, finding a genie in a bottle which on release protects him with magic. It flies through the air, petrifies his opponents into stone, and gives him power to produce his own tricks like changing a dining room into a seascape. How popular this material was at Naples can be gauged from the fact that it was used for two productions at the Fiorentini in 1768 (the first with music by Insanguine and the second, with altered text for its Act III, with music by Paisiello) which together ran for over a hundred performances.

The mixing of serious and comic characters in a libretto created problems for librettists both from the point of view of the plot and from that of the arrangement of musical items. The conventional modes of behaviour of the two groups were so different that some modification to one or other was necessary if they were properly to be integrated in one plot and sing the same musical ensembles. If we look first at the matter of the plots we note that in some of the earlier Neapolitan librettos of the '20s–'40s this

---

[39] According to Scherillo, *L'opera buffa napoletana*, p. 309, the story is reminiscent of an episode in Lesage's *Diable boiteux*.

integration is hardly attempted and two sets of characters carry forward two separate plots in alternate sections. A case is *Lisa pontegliosa* (Fiorentini, 1719) with text by Piscopo and music by G. di Domenico, in which four of the cast, Rita and Lisa (female cousins) and Tonillo and Cianniello (young shepherds), pursue their own serious and erotic affair. Set against a pastoral background, the plot is one of amorous intrigue in which Rita is jealous of her cousin and finally drives her to attempt suicide. As she jumps from a cliff, she is caught on the branch of a tree and so saved from destruction (shades here of Tasso's *Aminta*). The other four characters share the same stage but play practically no part in the action described. They have their own action, which has a humorous aspect. The humour is to be found partly in the different ages of the four, all of whom are in love. Pascale, the old shepherd, is enamoured of Nannella, whose widowed mother, Colonna, would like Pascale for herself. Nannella is in love with Pascale's son, Sosca. And the central figure of the group is Sosca who plays the double game of making his own advances to Nannella while forced to present his father's case to her. The librettist follows one of the golden rules of Neapolitan comic operas of the eighteenth century in arranging for a vocal ensemble of sorts at the end of each act. Sosca, Nannella, and Pascale sing the finale of Act I; the same three plus Colonna sing together at the end of Act II; and the whole cast joins in for the last finale of all. The principle emerging here is one generally applicable to comic operas of the first half of the century in which serious and comic characters tend to go their own ways. The comedians sing the first two finales, and put the stamp of their particular personality on them.[40] The majority, or all, of the cast sings in the last ensemble which, because of the participation of the serious characters, is itself 'serious'—with various dramatic and musical implications which must be discussed.

In a previous chapter it was pointed out how the good manners of the serious characters in heroic opera prevented any disorderly conduct or confrontation during an ensemble. By putting a serious item at the end of Act III, the librettist ensured that it became little more than a formal close or epilogue in which the cast closed its ranks and sang in sweet and unruffled accord. In a comic ensemble, by contrast, a certain amount of conflict, jumble in the vocal part-writing, even incoherent babble, was in

---

[40] This means that seldom more than half the cast is involved in either of the first two finales. An exception is the finale to Act II of *Ottavio*, words by Federico, music by Latilla (Fiorentini, 1733), which is an octet sung by all characters in the cast.

order. When handled by a capable librettist, such an ensemble at the end of an act could represent a point of maximum turmoil, a sort of climactic moment toward which the plot of the previous scenes builds up. We can see straight away that one of the librettist's problems was to get his serious characters off the stage and his comedians on to it before such a finale. The smoothness of this manipulation was some measure of his skill just as Metastasio's ability to arrange characters' exits in heroic operas was some measure of his. In certain comic operas of the '20s–'40s a logical sequence of events leading up to and including the Acts I and II finales is not attempted, the librettist finding perhaps that the dramatic situation that looks like shaping up within the act involves a character who cannot appear in the ensemble at the end of it, so dramatic climax and final ensemble cannot coincide. In such a case the final scene of the act (with the ensemble) becomes rather like a comic 'intermezzo',[41] since it is not closely connected with the penultimate one. The need to make the first two finales fitting climaxes to the preceding action became imperative in the mid-century period because of two further developments. The first, and most important, was the increasing length and complexity of the music of the comic finale, making this the undoubted musical climax of the act. The second was the gradual breakdown of the old distinctions between comic and serious characters to the extent that there were now in opera certain middle-of-the-way characters (*mezzi caratteri*) who were sufficiently colourless to be able to combine with either group and could sing in the comic finales. This meant in practice that the average number of participants in the finales increased, and the dramatic situation at these moments became more varied. A certain technical problem now came very much to the fore. While the first two finales provided dramatic and musical climaxes, the third was still a comparatively short musical item and a mere epilogue to the action. How could sufficient stimulus be provided for Act III when the biggest musical items (points of maximum conflict between the characters) were already over? The lack of vitality in the action of so many third acts suggests that librettists had no easy solution. In fact some of these acts are so weak that we begin to wonder what reason, other than tradition, could be behind the retention of the act.

By the early '70s the distinctions between character types had further relaxed to the point where serious characters could join in comic ensembles.

---

[41] Cf. E. Dent, 'Leonardo Leo', *SIM*, 1906–7, viii. 558.

From now on all characters could sing in all finales, and the tendency was to make more and more of them do so—so the librettist's task was now to bring the maximum number on for the act endings. Now at last there was no technical reason why the finale ending Act III should be any different from those ending the previous acts. The interesting thing is that no attempt seems to have been made radically to improve its status or quality. As concomitant of this the third act of many operas remained as weak as before. A work particularly affected by its uninspired finish, and one that might be cited because it is among the most famous of Neapolitan comic operas, is *Il Socrate immaginario* (1775) with words by Lorenzi[42] and music by Paisiello. None of Lorenzi's third acts is in fact weaker. The libretto has as chief personality one D. Tammaro Promontorio, crazily involved in the study of ancient philosophy, who believes that he is a second Socrates and that his none too intelligent barber friend, Mastro Antonio, is Plato. As Socrates he feels he is no longer bound by the conventions and insists he can enjoy two wives and marry his daughter to two husbands. The other characters play upon his fond imaginings, produce a Laertes from among his neighbours (this is really his daughter's young admirer, Ippolito), suggest he gets advice from demons in a grotto (which allows for a marvellous parody of the scene in Gluck's *Orfeo*—seen in Naples the previous year—where Orpheus enters Hades), and finally, to cure him, arrange for the arrival of a message ordering his suicide. Tammaro's rather unwilling drinking of his poison (really a somniferous drug) and his falling asleep are the central themes of the musical finale to Act II—up to which point the plot has shown great invention. But Tammaro's 'death' is in fact the librettist's final trump and leaves him with little more to play with. The choice is deliberate but results in a dull third act. The librettist cannot make Tammaro keep up his Socratean pretence after the death episode, and his problem is that when Tammaro awakens in Act III with his delusions cured, all the humour attached to an imaginary Socrates disappears. Both Lorenzi and Paisiello try to keep the work alive still by arranging some musical ensembles in the last act; but nothing properly revives our interest when it is so clear that the librettist is marking time till the end, with its sorting out of the various couples.

Was the time therefore ripe for the contraction of the full-length opera into a two-act one? In one or two isolated cases where the third act was a

---

[42] For the latest comments on the Abate Galiani's part in the creation of the libretto, see V. Monaco, *Giambattista Lorenzi e la commedia per musica*, Naples, 1968, pp. 89 ff.

separate *farsetta* or *burletta*, with new characters and new title,[43] then the preceding acts constituted in effect a complete work by themselves. In the Paisiello version of *L'osteria di Marechiaro*, the Act II finale is both the climax of the action and its resolution. The characters here become amenable to Count Zampano's suggestion he marry the girl of his choosing; the Count in return undoes the mischief he has managed with his magic; the cast sings 'Viva' and the works ends happily. Act III is a quite separate piece. The notion of two-act operas was therefore in the air at Naples in the 60s–'70s period,[44] but what was not possible yet in that city was a two-act work that represented the entire operatic bill for the evening. Instead Act III was in the process of being gradually phased out. When examining the matter of the size of acts, this author compared the numbers of scenes per act of a few early and late Neapolitan comic operas and made the list that is set on p. 201. He makes no claim to having made a 'scientific' sample. The figures are nonetheless suggestive, especially as regards the dwindling size of Act III in relation to the others. Since size of act does not depend solely on scene changes (based, as in heroic opera, on characters' entries and exits) but also on the number of lyrical items, the latter figure is also recorded in the list in so far as it was found possible to ascertain it (from the libretto alone in several instances). The third act of many early Neapolitan comic operas was as large or nearly as large as either of the two previous. By comparison, the third act in Neapolitan comic operas of the 1770s was appreciably shorter than either of the others. We should emphasize that, because the Acts I and II finales of later operas are often spread over two or more 'scenes', each 'scene' of these finales is listed as a separate lyrical item. This is to give a better idea of the comparative length of the lyrical music.

The decrease in the number of scenes of the last act continued to the point where, *c.* 1790, the act consisted of a maximum of two scenes with a single

---

[43] Cf. p. 191 above.

[44] The idea of detaching the whole or part of Act III from the remainder of the action had already been put into practice on at least one occasion during the 1750s. See Napoli-Signorelli, *Vicende della coltura*, v. 565–6:

The plays of Signor Goldoni were then enjoying much favour, and [Antonio] Palomba wanted to try an imitation of them in an opera that he called *La Commediante* . . . This opera seemed to have little chance of success . . . So it was thought to strengthen the work by appending in Act III a *favoletta* called *La Canterina* which was to be acted like a run-through of a musical intermezzo. Fortunately, the music added to it by Nicola Conforto, guided by Domenico Macchia who was its director, was not inappropriate to the characters . . .

La Commediante and *La Canterina*, both with Conforto's music, were performed together at the Fiorentini theatre in 1754.

TITLE OF OPERA	NO. OF SCENES AND (IN BRACKETS) LYRICAL ITEMS PER ACT		
	ACT I	ACT II	ACT III
Patrò Calienno de la Costa (Words by Agasippo Mercotellis, music by A. Orefice. Performed Fiorentini, 1709)	16 (17)	23 (18)	19 (14)
Il trionfo dell'onore (Words by F. A. Tullio, music by A. Scarlatti. Performed Fiorentini, 1718)	26 (14)	31 (18)	16 (9)
La mpeca scoperta (Words by F. Oliva, music by? Performed Fiorentini, 1723)	18 (14)	19 (15)	23 (14)
Le zitelle de lo Vommaro (Words by B. Saddumene, music by P. Pulli. Performed Fiorentini, 1731)	16 (10)	17 (11)	11 (9)
Inganno per inganno (Words by G. Federico, music by N. Logroscino. Performed Fiorentini, 1738)	15 (13)	17 (12)	15 (10)
Il barone di Zampano (Words by P. Trinchera, music by N. Porpora. Performed Nuovo, 1739)	16 (13)	14 (11)	12 (9)
L'idolo cinese (Words by G. B. Lorenzi, music by G. Paisiello. Performed Nuovo, 1767)	14 (12)	18 (13)	14 (5)
La somiglianza de' nomi (Words by P. Mililotti, music by Paisiello. Performed Nuovo, 1771)	13 (10)	20 (16)	8 (6)
I furbi burlati (Words by P. de Napoli, music by N. Piccinni. Version of 1773, performed Fiorentini)	11 (14)	17 (13)	4 (4)
Il Socrate immaginario (Words by Lorenzi, music by Paisiello. Performed Nuovo, 1775)	13 (13)	16 (10)	8 (4)
Dal finto il vero (Words by S. Zini, music by Paisiello. Performed Nuovo, 1776)	12 (9)	10 (8)	4 (3)
Il fanatico per gli antichi romani (Words by G. Palomba, music by D. Cimarosa. Performed Fiorentini, 1777)	15 (12)	16 (13)	7 (7)

lyrical item. This item was not a short chorus or ensemble for the majority of characters, as the terminal item always had been in the past, but a love duet for the two leading comedians. So the affairs of the other characters had to be rounded off before the last scene of all, either during the Act II finale or in recitative at the start of Act III. During the 1790s the third act was at last phased out.

Prior to the final disappearance of this act there was a period during the '80s and early '90s at Naples when some comic operas were written without one and others with. It is possible to conjecture that this diversity was because some operas shared the theatrical bill with other pieces, for example with a one-act *farsa* or with ballets, so could be relatively short, while others had to be long enough to fill an entire evening's entertainment. Many two-act operas of this period had companion pieces. Those performed at the del Fondo in the second half of the '80s, for example, were supported by ballets, as was heroic opera. The effect of the court's general ban on ballet at the small theatres seems to have been to make comic opera longer than it might otherwise have been. Burney made this point during his Neapolitan visit of 1770 when he attended performances of Paisiello's *Le trame per amore* and criticized it, saying 'there was no dancing, which made it necessary to spin the acts out to rather a tiresome length . . . The performance began about a quarter before eight, and continued till past eleven o'clock'.[45] Clearly the Neapolitan public, having paid for admission, expected to be entertained for what it considered a worthwhile period. The desire of managements of the small theatres in the last years of the century to obtain permission to produce ballet (see page 163 above) may well have been connected with the matter of the presence or absence of a third act and with the problem of filling up time once this act had become so superfluous that no one could bear to perform it any more.

If great emphasis has been put on the comic finales and the dramatic consequences of these items, we should not forget that the librettist had to plan his work bearing in mind other things too. Everyone knows how singers affected the plan of heroic opera. More research is required on the extent to which they influenced the development of comic opera, but some influence they certainly held. While comic singers were not so internationally known as the great stars of heroic opera, the best among them acquired fame in their own localities. Naples had several locally-renowned

---

[45] *The present state*, p. 310.

comic singers, male ones especially.[46] The employment by Neapolitan theatre managements of certain singers time and time again must have helped perpetuate certain character 'types'—on which we have already passed comment—and also stimulated the popularity of certain types of dramatic situation and of musical aria/ensemble. To illustrate the point that Neapolitan comic opera came to have certain stereotyped dramatic situations in addition to the comic finales, we refer to a criticism of comic opera found in the second volume (published in Naples in 1813) of an edition of Lorenzi's librettos. The passage comes from the preface which describes part of Lorenzi's career, and it refers to the time before 1766 when he produced his first comic libretto, *Tra i due litiganti il terzo gode*, performed at the Fiorentini with music by G. Astarita. The argument runs that Lorenzi was at first unwilling to write librettos because he objected to the way librettists had to subordinate their interests to those of so many other people, and also because of

the barbarous system introduced into the ordering of such dramas, with, namely, a noisy operatic opening for several voices, a cavatina at the first entry of the prima buffa or a duet at the first meeting between her and the primo buffo; a terzet or quartet or quintet in the fourth or fifth scene of the opera, which often puts the poet in great embarrassment because the climax of the scenario is not yet sufficiently developed, so the item is often lacking in interest; the last aria but one of Act I then being for the primo buffo, the last aria of all for the prima buffa, and the act finishing with a finale of seven or eight scenes which must terminate with a ripieno in which all the actors say the same words, whether these be suitable to their characters or no, and in which a noisy sinfonia is made by voices and instruments with imitations, canons, fugues, and strettos, leading with much shouting and noise to the end of the act. At this point the curtain falls, as though everything were over, then after a quarter of an hour it rises again and Act II commences. After a brief scene the minor character [*ultima parte*] must sing something called the aria del sorbetto;[47] afterwards there usually comes a duet between the two buffi, then

---

[46] Among singers at Naples we might mention: (1) Gioacchino Corrado, prominent as the male singer in comic scenes (intermezzos), first at the Fiorentini and then at the S. Bartolomeo from 1706 to 1735, and who afterwards sang in comic opera (till *c.* 1744); (2) Simone de Falco, the tenor who acted the aged female roles in comic opera from *c.* 1717 to *c.* 1738; (3) Antonio Catalano, a leading bass-baritone in comic opera from *c.* 1743 to *c.* 1763; (4) the two Casaccias, Giuseppe and Antonio, both bass-baritones, the one active in comic opera from *c.* 1749 to *c.* 1783, and the other from *c.* 1758 to *c.* 1793. See the operatic lists in Florimo, *La scuola musicale di Napoli*, iv., for further information on casting.

[47] The earliest reference this author has found to the selling of sorbets during arias sung by the *ultima parte* is in Mattei, *Elogio del Jomelli*, 1785, p. 91. How far back this practice went is conjecture, but there is no evidence at present that it obtained during the Scarlatti-Pergolesi period.

an aria for the tenor with his recitativo strumentato; finally another concerted item between the leading characters, followed by a finale similar to the first. In the last act, which must be very short (that is if the opera has not to finish after Act II, as is now sometimes the case to lessen the annoyance of those who come to the theatre not for the opera but to observe the boxes with their glasses, take tobacco, yawn, and doze), the action finishes with a duet between the prima buffa and the primo buffo, who, so custom dictates, must get married.[48]

This passage gives an incomplete picture in the sense that it does not account for all lyrical items, including most arias for the serious characters. Furthermore it seems to be describing Neapolitan comic opera of the wrong historical period. The presence of an ensemble opening Act I and of ensembles during the course of acts is characteristic more of opera of the '70s onwards than of the '60s. The reference to a final duet for the leading comedians points to opera of about 1790. Any truth that it contains is therefore in the nature of a general rather than precise one, just as Goldoni's account of what he was told to write in a heroic libretto (see above, p. 54) must be taken as indicative of general trends only. It is nonetheless valuable for correcting any notion that if the librettist was tied by convention in heroic opera he was somehow freer to use comic opera as a vehicle for his own expression.

[48] G. B. Lorenzi, *Opere teatrali*, Flautina, Naples, 1813, ii. pp. iv–v.

Comic Opera—the Music

EIGHTEENTH-CENTURY composers did not necessarily have to re-think their styles when switching from the composition of serious to comic music. Styles with serious associations were suitable for most 'serious' moments in comic opera, and even when the dramatic situation was comical, a composer could often get satisfactory results by distorting the right 'serious' style for the context. For this reason there is no need to enquire into the music of comic opera with quite that eye for detail that went into the examination of heroic opera in Chapter 3. What is necessary now is comment on where and how comic opera differed from heroic opera. The matter of grotesque distortion of a serious technique for humorous ends is one that can be dealt with first of all and quickly. There is a good choice of possible illustrations from opera to prove that a device like a vocalization, superfluously elongated, placed on the wrong vowel, with misapplied accents or with grotesque intervals, may have a comic effect. Mention was made in the last chapter of an aria for the male character, Nibbio, in the second intermezzo to *Didone abbandonata* (1724) by Metastasio and Sarri (see p. 185 for the aria text), and part of the music is printed on pp. 206–7. Each of its vocalizations contains some exaggerated feature, the first on *farfalla* possessing most ungraceful, 'butterfly' leaps, the one on *pietà* its own inelegant plunge on to the final A, the third on *scotta* being obviously descriptive of a man taking evasive action to avoid a singeing. The use of vocalization in this context as a humorous parody of heroic opera is too obvious to need comment.

Big leaps, like those found in Nibbio's part below, were common to many an aria for bass or baritone singers in comic roles, and served to do one, or both, of two things. In the first instance they emphasized the character's excitable and volatile nature; in the second they imitated certain mannerisms of his speech delivery. There were certain other mannerisms that were easy to parody for the sake of creating ridicule and/ or laughter, and composers, in the eighteenth century as before, fastened on to some of them to distort them in music. Stuttering was one; uneven speech giving the effect of panting was another; over-rapid speech was a third. The comparatively long texts of some seventeenth- and eighteenth-century arias had particular purpose when the composer wanted the singer to rattle words off at a fast rate. Passages of high-speed jabber varied in length and difficulty, but some were both fast and long. Especially noteworthy is a passage for the male comic in the middle section of the duet 'Non ti voglio' from A. Scarlatti's *Tiberio imperatore d'oriente* (Naples,

EXAMPLE 21
Sarri, *Dorinda e Nibbio*
(Performed at the Teatro S. Bartolomeo, Naples, 1724)

1702). Here is a string of semiquavers (each to a separate word syllable) proceeding through 15 bars of $\frac{4}{4}$, non-stop save for one cadence and pause near the middle.[1]

Another obvious manner of distorting a musical phrase for comic purposes was to involve the use of extra-musical sounds like animal noises. In the Act II finale to *L'amor vuol sofferenza* (Naples, 1739) with words by Federico and music by Leo,[2] a character named Mosca—which literally means 'fly'—is teased by two companions who imitate the croaks of a frog and bleats of a sheep and goad him into responding with 'zu' noises appropriate to a large insect. The use of onomatopoeia is not limited to farmyard imitations. For example, the swish of a sword is rendered by one D. Cola, the Neapolitan character in Auletta's *La locandiera* performed at the S. Carlo in 1738, by the words 'zaffa zuffa' a number of times while his notes proceed in pairs up E, A, C sharp, E. Nibbio in the aria from the *Didone* intermezzo mentioned illustrates the cannonlike noises of the tables bounding about the ship's deck with 'bu' noises alternatively up and down the octave. There were in addition other extraneous noises made by comic characters not in the onomatopoeic class yet belonging to the extra-musical. These were the various 'eh's', 'ah's,' and 'uh's', signs of anguish or doubt that appeared in the parts of the eccentric characters and were sung probably with certain inflections of voice suitable to the meaning. Note, for example, the phrase 'Ma che ti pare, ah?' in the well-known 'Sempre in contrasti' from Pergolesi's *La serva padrona*. This phrase ends with an octave leap upwards to the 'ah', an invitation for an upward curving inflection certainly but not necessarily for a carefully placed top note. Music like this is too allied to gesture to be considered merely an exercise in pure singing.

A matter of a different kind from the preceding, since it concerns not distortion of musical styles or sounds but a musical style itself, is the influence on comic opera of popular song. There are many short songs both in seventeenth-century Venetian opera and in eighteenth-century comic opera that seem imitative of popular-style ditties. But whether they actually imitate popular models from outside the theatre is difficult to judge. The catchiness of these operatic songs may be explained by such features as simple intervals, one type of rhythm, clear form, and, usually,

[1] Dent quotes a short section in *Alessandro Scarlatti*, p. 52.

[2] This opera is published with many editorial markings in the series *Musiche e musicisti pugliesi*, Bari, 1962, ii. The editor is G. Pastore.

major key. Several short items in Provenzale's operas for Naples are of this type. Most are allocated to the comic characters, but a few are given to the high-ranking ones too. For example, Theseus, one of the heroes of *Lo schiavo di sua moglie* (1671), breaks unexpectedly into this tune in II.xiv:

EXAMPLE 22
Provenzale, *Lo schiavo di sua moglie*, II, xiv
(Written 1671)

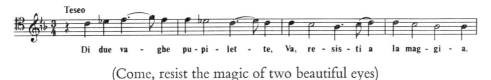

Di due va - ghe pu - pi - let - te, Va, re - sis - ti a la mag - gi - a.

(Come, resist the magic of two beautiful eyes)

The whole of this phrase is repeated piano, after which the music drops a fourth on to the dominant and goes through the same process of phrase, then phrase repeated piano, to new words. By expressing himself so, Theseus reveals a rather boyish and unsophisticated side to his nature alien to the typical hero of Metastasian opera of sixty or seventy years later. The Metastasian hero does not express himself like this because well before the 1720s the popular-style canzonet had been confined to the comic scenes only.

Scherillo was the first to point out certain dialect song texts in eighteenth-century comic opera at Naples that seem to have a popular or traditional source, or at least are imitative of popular song.[3] We notice three things about them. Many have topical or historical allusions. A few are versions of children's games. Most seem casually interpolated into the drama in the sense that characters sing them to while away the time rather than interpret or comment upon a dramatic situation, as they do in the more conventional arias. Scherillo rarely states a concordance proving that the operatic stanzas he quotes stem from popular or traditional songs.[4] Among the few stanzas for which he provides a concordance is one from the opening ensemble of *La fuga*, Naples, 1777, words by Lorenzi and music by Gaetano Monti.[5] The tune in Monti's score proceeds so:

[3] The texts were first published by Scherillo in 'I canti popolari nell'opera buffa', *Giambattista Basile*, Naples anno I, editions of 15 January, 15 February, and 15 March 1883, and later inserted into *L'opera buffa napoletana*, 1916, pp. 464 ff.

[4] A few concordances between operatic stanzas quoted by Scherillo and much older song material are mentioned in G. M. Monti, *Le villanelle alla napoletana e l'antica lirica dialettale a Napoli*, Città di Castello, 1925, pp. 152–4, 158.

[5] *L'opera buffa napoletana*, p. 483.

EXAMPLE 23
G. Monti, *La Fuga*, i, i
(Performed at the Teatro Nuovo, Naples, 1777)

(And the Turkish girl who went by sea came to Naples and seized me)

The concordance is with two lines of verse in one of Nicolò Amenta's spoken comedies, *La Carlotta*. In II.ix of the edition of this work published in 1708 (Raillard, Venice?), one Capitano Marcantonio sings 'to himself while he walks'

> E la bella che ghieva pe maro
> (And the beautiful girl who went by sea)

and then later on in the same scene

> E li Turche se la pegliaro
> (And the Turks seized her).

A much closer concordance with the Amenta verse however is to be found in Auletta's opera *La locandiera* (1738). The song in the score of this opera is called a *canzonetta affettuosa*, and most of it is reproduced below— the remainder being mere repetition or variation of the final cadence formula.

EXAMPLE 24
Auletta, *La locandiera*, ii, xi
(Performed at the Teatro S. Carlo, Naples, 1738)

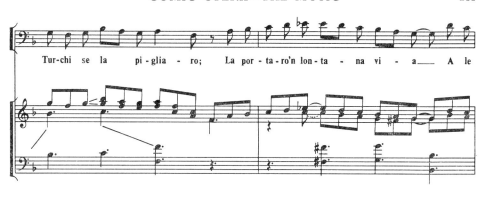

Tur-chi se la pi-glia - ro; La por-ta-ro'n lon-ta - na vi - a___ A le

par-te de la Tor-chi - a,___ a le par-te de la Tor-chi - a;

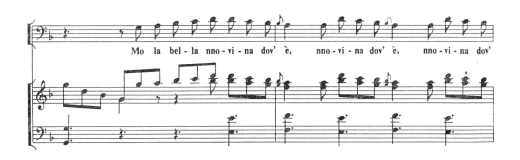

Mo la bel - la nno-vi-na dov' è, nno-vi-na dov' è, nno-vi-na dov'

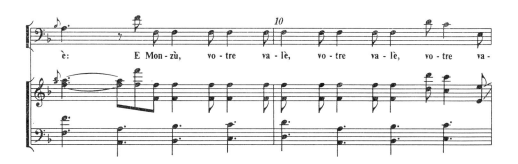

è: E Mon-zù, vo - tre va - lè, vo-tre va - lè, vo - tre va-

(And the beautiful girl went by sea, and the Turks seized her. They carried her a long way off to a part of Turkey. Now guess where the beautiful girl is. Monsieur, I remain your servant)

There is a further concordance between an old Neapolitan song text, that may go back to the sixteenth century, and an item in Piccinni's *Gelosia per gelosia*. The latter was one of the two comic operas Burney saw and praised for their tunefulness during his visit to Naples in 1770. As quoted by L. Molinaro del Chiaro, the song text goes:

> Nu me chiammate chiù Donna Sabella,
> Chiammàteme Sabella sbenturata;
> Patrone i'era 'e trentasè castelle,
> La Puglia bella e la Basilicata.[6]

(Don't call me Lady Isabella any longer, call me unfortunate Isabella. I was owner of thirty-six castles, of beautiful Puglia and Basilicata.)

Towards the close of *Gelosia* the leading comic pair sings a duet of reconciliation in three main musical sections the first of which concerns us here. The text of this section contains what appears to be a series of

---

[6] *Canti del popolo napoletano*, Naples, Argenio, 1880, p. 236. The Abbé Galiani recorded a slight variant of this same verse in his collection of Neapolitan poetry (Library of the Società di Storia Patria, Naples, *F. Galiani varia*, xxxi, A.9, p. 311 *bis*). For views on the identity of Isabella mentioned in the song, see F. Galiani, *Del dialetto napoletano*, modern edn. annotated by F. Nicolini, Naples, 1923, pp. 293–4.

EXAMPLE 25
Piccinni, *Gelosia per gelosia*, III, ix
(Performed at the Teatro Fiorentini, Naples, 1770)

(I am Aurora no longer, I am not she. I am an unfortunate pilgrim.
Don't call me Lady Isabella any longer, ah menicò, call me unfortunate Isabella.
Look how he snatches my quinces from me[?]. What does this shepherd want from me?
Sing, my Cecilia, for I have tuned my bagpipe with the llero llero llè.)

disconnected statements until it is realized that lines 3 and 5 are a quote from the above song stanza. Because these lines are a quote, the question arises whether others are too, and the text is a type of song medley. Piccinni's music (the start of it is recorded in Example 25 above) leaves us guessing about the extent to which he has used the music either of the Isabella song— if indeed it had its special melody—or of any other. From bar 27 the music is continuous and one line of verse passes straight on to the next as though they were all of a piece. The nonsense refrains add to the popular character of the music as a whole.

The use of $\frac{6}{8}$ or $\frac{12}{8}$ time in the last three music examples, and the slight melancholy flavour of some of them, is common to certain other dialect songs in comic operas by Pergolesi, Piccinni, and others. So the question arises whether these features form part of what might be called a native, Neapolitan style.[7] The question has relevance partly because of a suggestion made in the past that changes in the musical style of the Neapolitans at the start of the eighteenth century were due to the influence of styles specifically connected with their home area.[8] Unfortunately no one has cared to define what such styles might be, and if the hypothesis is that they were both indigenous and popular, then the hypothesis may remain hard to prove. Eighteenth-century Italians did not regard popular song tunes as of more than passing value, and so did not publish or record them as part of a national heritage, as late nineteenth-century Italians did. Nor did eighteenth-century commentators at large provide many helpful clues to the type of popular music originating outside the theatre then enjoying a vogue in Southern Italy. Mattheson gives as clear an indication as any in his *Das neu-eröffnete Orchestre* (1713):

The Neapolitan and Sicilian style depends chiefly on a quite distinct and artless manner of singing. Their principal species [of music] is either a slow English jig or a simple measure, making for unaffected *tendresse*. The other species, in an allegro

[7] *Michelemmà*, which may be the oldest surviving, traditional song tune associated with the Neapolitan area, is also notated in $\frac{6}{8}$ time.
[8] See. H. Kretzschmar, *Geschichte der Oper*, p. 168.

or frolicking time, usually consists of a song *à la barquerole*.[9] There remains in this type of composition an element closely reflecting common taste, both because the average man in these lands uses the guitar for his pleasure while singing, and because so much depends there upon the approbation of the crowd.[10]

In his later *Der vollkommene Capellmeister* Mattheson stated that a characteristic of Neapolitan and Sicilian music was the iambic rhythm, and he provided as illustration of it the following musical phrase from a piece by R. Cesare:[11]

EXAMPLE 26

Non mi di - te che m'a - ma - te, oc - chi non vi cre - de - rò, non cre - de - rò etc.

(Don't tell me you love me; eyes, I shall not believe you)

In point of fact several supposedly old songs of Neapolitan or southern Italian origin possess the accented short—unaccented long at the end of phrases.[12] Note the same feature also in bars 16 and 19 of the above Piccinni music (Example 25), and in the Vinci music example below. It is not so clear whether an unvaried series of such rhythms within the phrase— as Mattheson has them—was a characteristic of Neapolitan music.

Burney's comments on Neapolitan street song suggest that it was then highly idiosyncratic. His observations on the subject may be summarized as follows: (1) the street singing was noisy and vulgar; (2) the songs were

---

[9] It is worth recording that four arias designated *barcarola* appear in Leo's comic operas. These arias are 'Feruta la cervetta' (*La semmeglianza di chi l'ha fatta* (1726), II.xiii), 'Mò che libero lo core' and 'E bizejo delle femmene' (*Lo matremonio annascuso* (1727?), II.ix and III.xiii), and 'Pensa ch'io t'amo' (*Amor vuol sofferenza* (1739), III.vii). The present author is obliged to Mr Graham Hardie for pointing out to him the cases in *Matremonio annascuso*. 'Pensa ch'io t'amo' is in $\frac{6}{8}$ time; the others are in $\frac{4}{4}$. 'E bizejo' has no tempo indication; the others have 'allegro'. All three arias in $\frac{4}{4}$ possess the same basic type of melodic rhythm. Compare for example the start of 'Mò che libero': ♫♫♫♫ ♫♫
♫♫♫♫♫ etc., with that of 'Feruta': ♫♫♫♫♫ ♫♫♫♫♫ ♫♫ ♫♫ etc. It would appear that the term *barcarola* as used by Leo has musical rather than dramatic significance.

[10] p. 204.

[11] p. 165.

[12] Some very general idea of popular Neapolitan idioms will be gained from a glance at nineteenth-century Neapolitan song collections composed and/or edited by Guglielmo Cottrau (1797–1847), Teodoro Cottrau (1827–1879), Vincenzo de Meglio (1825–1883), etc. These collections contain a proportion of songs with old texts. Whether the music of these same songs is also old remains a matter for debate, since some editors may have altered their material without acknowledgment. For more on this matter, see E. de Mura, *Enciclopedia della canzone napoletana*, Naples, 1970, i. 234 ff.

accompanied throughout by violin and colascione, a Neapolitan guitar usually with two strings; (3) the voice part moved slowly; (4) the music went through a series of surprising modulations, for instance from A major to F or C, then from F to E flat, followed by a return to A, managed in such an imperceptible manner as not to shock the ear. Sometimes there were transitions to B flat or D flat 'returning, or rather sliding' always into the original key of A.[13] Finally, as summary, Burney adds: 'I heard these musicians play a great number of Neapolitan airs, but all were different from other music'.[14] His point about the colascione seems to back Mattheson's observations on the guitar. A colascione was occasionally brought on to the opera stage at Naples by a comic singer who used it for accompaniment.[15] Burney's point about the strange modulations is more problematical. Any strange sliding from B flat or D flat to A, 'imperceptibly', might be difficult to notate anyway, and all we can say so far is that there is little evidence of this sort of thing in operatic song.

While on the subject of idiosyncratic music, however, we must mention one very strange song from opera that seems to catch the flavour or a performance by some untutored or street singer. The item concerned comes at the very start of the earliest comic opera in Neapolitan dialect whose music has survived intact, Vinci's *Li zite n'galera* (1722). The character, Ciccariello, enters singing what is basically an unaccompanied song but with intervening passages for the strings. The music of these passages is so primitive that it could be an imitation of some style of self-accompaniment by a street performer. Ciccariello's own line of music is odd because many phrases are at variance with the time signature, and the composer has obviously had difficulty fitting them in. The notation ignores convention, especially toward cadences. In the Example on pp. 222–4 the notation of the vocal part is exactly as in the MS., which is claimed to be autograph. The writing cannot be considered a mistake, for the remainder of the MS. is perfectly straightforward and Vinci was no pupil at the date of composition of this work. The adjacent notes G sharp—A—B flat may or may not suggest some kind of vocal slide.

There should be no confusion at this or any stage between popular song of local and of foreign origin. The insertion of foreign, that is not South Italian, song into opera at Naples was not regular, and its appearance there

[13] *The present state*, pp. 297–8, 311.
[14] Ibid., p. 312.
[15] Cf. Dent, *Alessandro Scarlatti*, p. 51.

EXAMPLE 27
Vinci, *Li Zite n'galera*, i, i
(Performed at the Teatro Fiorentini, Naples, 1722)

Le vor - ria da no muor-zo a lo pe-dil-lo,_____ E strac-cià la po-

- dea de la gon-nel-la._____

pò pec-chè sò tan - to pec-ce-ril-lo,_____
ve - do ngo-ra chi-sto e nzo-ra chil-lo,_____

Mme vor-ri - a ab - bus-cà na pec-ce-rel - la, na
E pe mme no nce stà na mo-glie-rel - la, na

(If only I could become a little mouse to give Sister Annella a shock, and nibble her foot and pull the hem off her skirt. Being so small, could I but then find a little lady, for I see Mister this and Missis that, but for me there is no little wife. Come these stones [?] you carry in your breast, you carry them to wound me. And for me there is no little wife.)

was a calculated, chic and exotic touch. So Madama Perlina, the *scuffiara* (milliner) in *La modista raggiratrice* (Naples, 1787 and 91), words by Lorenzi and Paisiello, regards it important to her profession to speak a few words of French and sings two verses of 'Malbroug [sic] s'en vat'en guerra [sic]' at a particularly humorous moment during the first act finale.[16] The insertion of local Neapolitan song may or may not have affected the music of local opera more fundamentally. In view however of the still in-conclusive evidence about eighteenth-century popular song at Naples, one cannot say for sure what influence it generally had on the operatic music of the city, and what influence opera had upon it. A case might be made out for saying that music in $\frac{12}{8}$, and to some extent also music in $\frac{6}{8}$ time tended to become associated with popular song, and so was for this reason confined more and more to the more popular kind of opera, comic opera, as the century continued. Anything like a jig or a tarantella rhythm in fast time also seems to have acquired similar associations and contemporaneously became rarer in heroic opera scores. The desire of composers to write the sort of tune the public would appreciate may have contributed to the number of simple melodies, easy to memorize, found in comic opera. None of this however ties the matter down to the influence of Neapolitan popular song specifically.

In truth the simplicity of much vocal music in comic opera at Naples may also have been due to the limited vocal techniques of some singers engaged by managements of the small theatres. Algarotti stated that Italian comic operas and intermezzos of his day had more 'expression' than other modern compositions because the limited abilities of the singers prevented composers from indulging their fancy 'in a wanton display of all the secrets of their art'.[17] It is not difficult to discover some vocal parts in comic opera that would tax the powers of the best singers anywhere. The enormous leaps and range of, for example, D. Pietro's aria, 'Si stordisce', from Pergolesi's *Lo frate 'nnamorato* (Naples, 1732)—its range lies between F below the bass stave and C two and a half octaves higher—is not some-thing any bass singer undertakes lightly. One notices, nonetheless, a certain restraint in the over-all amount of virtuoso writing. This is most obvious in the parts for the serious characters in the sense that these were modelled the most closely on those of heroic opera so it is easiest to compare their

[16] See Abert, *Gesammelte Schriften*, p. 375, for mention of 'foreign' musical touches in other comic operas by Paisiello.
[17] *Essay on the opera*, p. 49.

music with that sung by the great virtuosi on the S. Carlo stage. The vocalization or other embellishment in an aria by a serious character was rarely a satirical parody of heroic opera. It served to show off the technique of the singer, or alternatively—and this was its more common function in the second half of the century—to prove that he was acting a serious role. Its presence, rather than its length or difficulty, helped to show who he was.[18] The trouble with a vocalization in a serious context is that it tends to sound frigid and conventional. Neither it nor any other device in this context is capable of reflecting those subtleties of speech, variations in the singer's thought, imitations of tone of speech, that the best comic music can express. Although a distinguishing mark of a serious character, it does not bring that character alive; and in comic opera that otherwise contains music that is full of life, humour, and of light and shade, it sounds out of place. This criticism applies specially in those many serious arias put unconvincingly into the drama because the librettist has been unable to assimilate the serious characters into his story. Such items give the impression they are there to provide the singer, not the character, with his due. This was a defect of Italian comic opera everywhere. There is a dreadful aria of the sort for Elisetta ('Se son vendicata') near the end of certain MSS. of Cimarosa's *Il matrimonio segreto* (originally of 1792), and even Mozart could not disguise the essentially non-dramatic nature of an item like D. Anna's 'Non mi dir' from *Don Giovanni*.

A generalized distinction between heroic and comic opera is that the music of the former was conceived in terms of its broad effect while the latter's reflected minute changes in the action and sense of the words. The type of music becoming fashionable during the 1720s–40s period and containing contrasting motives, variety of texture between phrases, and many changes of dynamics, gave particular opportunity to the composer working in the comic opera field. Once again it seems worth while taking a particular piece of music as illustration, and no piece is more suitable for the purpose than the duet 'Lo conosco' from Pergolesi's *La serva padrona*, a work readily available in modern editions. There should be general agreement that the music of the first vocal paragraph, for Serpina, is substantially the same as Uberto's reply, beginning 'Signorina

---

[18] Piccinni's *La buona figliola* (Rome, 1760) is a good opera to study from the point of view of the relationship of vocalizations to serious characters. Three out of four items in which vocalizations appear with any degree of prominence are arias for one or other of the *parti serie*, the Cavaliere Armidoro and the Marchesa Lucinda. See Benevenuti's edn. of this work, *I classici musicali italiani*, vii (1942), 72 ff., 115 ff., 205 ff.

v'ingannate' (bar 17). The differences are that his part starts in the dominant key, while hers began in the tonic, and contains an additional comic vocalization to illustrate the word *volate*. In spite of the general similarity between their notes, the music does not sound the same each time. Serpina, who is trying to secure Uberto's affections, begins by declaring his looks betray his interest in her. Her pertness is complemented by the staccato playing of the strings, her boldness by her own repeated notes. Uberto's reply is most unenthusiastic. Perhaps his words are alone responsible for the impression that he is not bent on marriage. Or it may be that the music supports this impression by dropping in pitch and so losing some of its edge. Whatever the reason Uberto's entry causes a change in the dramatic tone. It changes again when Serpina sings next (bar 28). The music has now reached A major, the dominant of the dominant, and Pergolesi, to bring it back to D, uses a standard modulatory formula of the period: chromatic supertonic chord followed by dominant, then the same chord sequence a tone lower. The sudden halt in the quaver movement at this point and the use of white notes replacing black is again far from unusual in music of that era. But used at the moment Serpina re-enters with her 'Ma perchè?', it denotes a change in her tactics and so is far from conventional. Instead of being outspoken as she was before, she tries in her new passage to wheedle her way into his affections by using the most seductive and attractive melody possible. Uberto, in turn, will have none of this. In bar 40 he gives vent to his smouldering anger—the orchestral parts here coming into unison—in a slow, rising chromatic scale beginning on low A. The analysis of this music could proceed further, but is sufficient to show the presence, within a single tempo, of a variety of textures and types of melodic phrase—similar to the variety beginning to appear also in heroic opera of that era and discussed earlier in Chapter III. Not enough evidence is yet assembled for anyone to say which genre was the more innovatory from the point of view of musical style. But what is clear is that more rapid fluctuations of dramatic situation and expression were permitted within an item in a single tempo in the comic context than in the other.

The comic ensemble is a fascinating topic, and an important one since it exhibited the most forward looking developments in the art of allying music to swiftly moving action. The type of ensemble written in the late seventeenth and early eighteenth centuries was, like the serious one, a point of momentary interaction between characters during which nothing was resolved. And since the order of words within it did not affect the way the story went afterwards, it could be set in some preconceived and arbitrary musical structure. Because of the fashion, most duets (as well as arias) in comic scenes and intermezzos at the S. Bartolomeo were set in *da capo* form. What happened to the majority of ensembles in comic opera at the small Neapolitan theatres in the first half-century cannot be ascertained because relatively few scores of that type and date have survived. The scores left suggest that composers of comic opera wrote most arias and some ensembles in *da capo* form, but that they treated other ensembles including, from the 1720s at least, the act finales in a freer manner. Two points about early finales are worth making at once. The first concerns time length. The earliest finales that abandon *da capo* form and therefore a gratuitous repeat of a large section of music tend to be very short, far too short, in fact, to provide the sort of climax one expects from a finale of later date. Dent quoted the start of the second finale from Leo's *La semmeglianza di chi l'ha fatta* in an article published some sixty years ago,[19] but the whole deserves quoting to give an idea of its size (see Example 28, pp. 229-33). The second point concerns simultaneous singing. An early-eighteenth-century comic ensemble is rarely an anarchical slanging match in which each character interrupts the others all the time and sings different words simultaneously with everyone else's.[20] Leo's music below shows the more normal treatment. The vocal line is tossed rapidly from part to part, but there is a certain reluctance to let all voices pitch in at once. Rather, the lines of division between the two groups of characters—the old pair, Virgilia and Franco, and the young pair, Lisetta and Cicotto—are carefully maintained so that the contrast between them is clear.

In drawing attention to the pairing of characters, we are reminded that of all multi-voiced entries in comic ensembles of the first half-century the two-voiced were by far the most common. For one reason or another, composers were fairly reluctant to use the full ensemble when they had more than two characters to manipulate. Perhaps this was due to school-room teaching that words would not be heard in a scramble. Perhaps they were not yet certain that parts could be simultaneously differentiated. Or perhaps they had the idea that the effectiveness of a multi-voiced entry depended on its fastidious use. Whatever the reason, Pergolesi, Auletta, and

---

[19] 'Ensembles and finales in eighteenth-century Italian opera', *SIM*, 1910–11, xii. 116–17.

[20] Something like an allout brawl develops though in 'Penza ben', the quartet in III. xii of Scarlatti's *Il trionfo dell'onore*. This is quoted in Dent, 'Ensembles and finales', *SIM*, 1909–10, xi. 557–69.

EXAMPLE 28
Leo, *La semmeglianza di chi l'ha fatta*, II, xvi
(Performed at the Teatro Fiorentini, Naples, 1726)

(Franco	Why do you despise me?
Lisetta	Eh, because you are going mad, sir.
Virgilia	I'm good enough to knock you to bits!
Cicotto	There now, don't lose control!
Franco	You wish to pull my leg!
Virgilia	You're asking me to rough you up!
Lisetta ⎫ Cicotto ⎭	Look what the sillies want!
Franco ⎫ Virgilia ⎭	Get out of here!
Lisetta ⎫ Cicotto ⎭	O these stupid old people!
Franco ⎫ Virgilia ⎭	You say this to me? Off, or I'll throttle you!
Lisetta ⎫ Cicotto ⎭	Now who's talking, te, te, te!
Franco ⎫ Virgilia ⎭	I'll show you!

Leo were reluctant to employ all voices together except at moments of peak intensity. One can but guess at the normal procedure adopted by Nicola Logroscino,[21] one of the most popular composers of comic opera at Naples between the late '30s and early '60s, because so little of his music remains. The finales to Acts I and II of his *Il governatore*, performed at the Nuovo in 1747, suggest his methods were none too different from those of the previously mentioned. The Act I finale for three voices contains 99 bars in all. There are only about four bars worth of orchestral solo. The characters therefore go hard at it, but only some thirteen bars contain simultaneous singing (always for two voices). The second finale, a quintet, does make use of the fullest possible vocal texture, but only for some 21 bars near the end of a piece that is eight times longer.

Many humorous ensembles therefore consisted of a series of solo phrases tossed from character to character and interspersed with a few multi-voiced entries. But what else was required to make these pieces effective? One point then realized by composers was that there were uses for an additional, continuous melodic line to bridge the gaps between

---

[21] Logroscino's posthumous fame is in fact built up on very little. One of the earliest commentators to praise him was J. B. de Laborde, *Essai sur la musique*, iii. 198: 'Logrorgino [*sic*], contemporary of Pergolesi, Leo, Feo, etc., is the god of the comic genre, and has served as model for almost all composers of this type of work'.

voice entries and maintain momentum. The means lay in the orchestra. What Vinci provided in the Acts I and II finales to *Li zite n'galera* was a perpetual patter of violin quavers (and some semiquavers in the second finale) that provided continuity and also a light, slightly jittery style excellent for a comic piece.[22] The same technique was used by other composers, their staccato string patter almost becoming the chief melodic contour, and the voice parts seeming to interlock like jigsaw pieces within the orchestral framework. This matter is connected with another, namely structure. Each composer had to decide whether to write his finales in a recognizable form, binary or ternary for example, or let the music 'run on', creating a free form of its own. With a continuous or nearly continuous string patter in the orchestra and with a humorous mix-up on stage, the temptation was more and more to let the music run on. For this reason comic finales showed consistent signs of being freely shaped to suit the action earlier than other ensembles. A structural detail that soon emerged in certain finales was the recurring motive—recognizable especially when allied to change in vocal texture, that is to the multi-voiced entry. It is easy to see how the joint entries for Vannella and Cardella in the quintet ending Act II of Pergolesi's *Lo frate* stand out as a type of refrain throughout the ensemble.[23] Another instance of the recurring phrase appears in the Act I finale to Leo's *L'amor vuol sofferenza*, mentioned earlier for its animal imitations (see above, p. 208). As usual the vocal work in this ensemble is mainly solo. As soon as one character starts making animal noises, however, the others start theirs. The onomatopoeic phrases begin to take over the music, then slide together and create an old-fashioned cacophony. The last vocal phrase of all is nonetheless a solo. Dent pointed out that several early finales end this way and suggested it was because some characters left the stage before the finish.[24] There can be no question that singers always departed in turn, since some finales terminate with a section for full ensemble. Dent's suggestion might however help to explain why composers did not aim for a terminal build-up of textures as a regular course.

Hermann Abert has put the Italian eighteenth-century opera finale into four main categories according to structure. These are the aria-, through-composed-, rondo,- and chain-finale types.[25] By 'aria-finale' he apparently

---

[22] N. d'Arienzo, 'Origini dell'opera comica', *RMI*, 1899, vi. 487–8, quotes a section from the first finale.

[23] Quoted in Dent, 'Ensembles and finales', *SIM*, xii. 122–8.

[24] 'Ensembles and finales', *SIM*, xii. 129–30.

[25] *Gesammelte Schriften und Vorträge*, p. 388.

meant a lyrical piece with one or more sections, each possessing a recognizable 'song or aria' shape. Both this and the through-composed kinds have been mentioned already, the latter sometimes containing rondo or recurring elements. The chain-finale, however, is new to our discussion. This particular type was built up of a chain of musical sections, each possessing its individual style, its own speed and its own time signature. The evolving drama contributed to its over-all coherence. Its music was held together by a firm tonal structure, the main key firmly anchored at either end and various modulations and key shifts occurring in the middle. Precisely where the moments of change from one section to the next came, and how many sections there were, depended on the composer. Because it was an action piece, much more depended on his sense of timing and his stage-craft than was the case in simpler and shorter ensembles. In those instances where he decided to unify a chain-finale with a recurring musical motive, then a hybrid resulted, a kind of rondo-cum-chain-finale in fact.

The idea of a chain of sections was not far from composers' minds in the early eighteenth century. There is, for example, a remarkable duet (not finale this time) in II.xviii of Scarlatti's *Il trionfo dell'onore* with eight sections few of which are melodically connected, with seven changes of time signature (always $\frac{3}{4}$ or $\frac{4}{4}$) and fluctuating speeds varying from adagio, allegro, to presto.[26] It was not till the fifties and sixties, though, that the chain-finale became prominent and fashionable. At this time many changes were taking place in the structures of lyrical items within comic opera—for example the *da capo* was finally being abandoned in arias and replaced by other structures, notably the abridged-sonata or two-part form. The finale was not less prone to change, and some might say it exhibited the most changes of all. The 'chain' method of construction now came in, in part because the size of the piece had grown so much—proportionately faster than other items—that it naturally tended to fragment. There is no evidence yet that the Neapolitans in particular contributed to the introduction of the chain-finale. Baldassare Galuppi, the Venetian composer, was experimenting with rather lyrically orientated finales of this sort by the early 1750s. Whether Logroscino at Naples was contemporaneously attempting the same thing, no one can tell at present. The finales to Insanguine's first comic opera, *Lo funnaco revotato* produced at the Fiorentini in 1756, are each in one tempo. This is suggestive, for one imagines that the composer would have provided chain-finales in this his first attempt at

---

[26] Mentioned in Dent, 'Ensembles and finales', *SIM*, xi. 546.

a commercial success had they then been popular at Naples. As late as the winter of 1758 Piccinni was writing one-movement finales for his *La scaltra letterata* (produced at the Nuovo), the first of these finales being a particularly orthodox binary piece with two run-throughs of the text and of the basic musical material.[27] However in his first comic opera for Rome, *La buona figliola*, performed there in February 1760, appear finales of a more progressive kind, with sections in different tempi and time signatures, with recurring musical phrases after the rondo pattern, with a continuing action and with characters able to move on and off during the course of the piece.[28] For the Fiorentini theatre at Naples later that year Piccinni wrote the finales of *La furba burlata*, an opera so successful that it ran for about eighty performances, more like the run of two operas, and was staged again the next year at the Nuovo. According to Napoli-Signorelli its finales were a great success.[29] Napoli-Signorelli went further, however, and attributed to these finales historical importance for being the first of their kind at Naples.

This opera introduced a novelty into our comic musical theatre. At Naples the act finales had been limited to a few lines at the moment of maximum action; but in the rest of Italy they were long and contained within many lines various incidents giving rise to variety of musical tempi and motives, as can be seen in Goldoni's *Buona figliola* and *Filosofo di campagna*. [Domenico] Macchia proposed to the anonymous writer[30] to introduce this varied and lengthy finale into Neapolitan comic opera. And the anonymous writer and Piccinni, who was to compose the music, consented . . . [31]

Discussion of *La furba* must remain limited since its score is difficult to put together. It was not the work of a single composer but, like so many eighteenth-century operas, an assortment of new items and old. The libretto, which survives, informs us that the opera had a new text designed to incorporate certain musical items by Logroscino that he had written for

---

[27] H. Abert's examination of Piccinni's comic operas prior to *c.* 1760 leads him to claim that the finales in them were of two types, the first being in a freely treated aria-form, the second consisting of several sections, each however treated as a separate and lyrical song unit. See *Gesammelte Schriften*, pp. 359–60.

[28] Ensembles during which characters come and go occur in several of Goldoni's comic librettos written in the 1750s. The method was either to make characters go off and then return during the course of the piece or bring on additional characters after the start. The first finale to *Il mondo della luna* (music by Galuppi, Venice, 1750) is an early instance of both methods in operation.

[29] *Vicende della coltura nelle due Sicilie*, v. 567–8.

[30] i.e. the librettist, P. de Napoli.

[31] *Vicende*, v. 567.

an earlier work.[32] It had been impossible to revive the latter since it did not suit the present cast. The 'greater part' of the music of the new work was by Logroscino and Piccinni. The libretto then states which items were by Logroscino (three) and which by Piccinni (seven including the three finales). It therefore leaves the majority of arias (somewhat under twenty) unaccounted for.[33] There is no way of resolving this paradox in the libretto's wording unless and until individual items can be identified in miscellaneous aria collections of the period that state the names of the composers. Comment on *La furba burlata* might end here were it not for the fact that Piccinni set a revised version of the libretto in 1773 under the title *I furbi burlati*. The music this time is extant. A comparison of the librettos shows that the words of most arias and ensembles do not match, so presumably Piccinni set these afresh in 1773. Just one of the original aria texts is retained in a shortened form. The two finales ending Acts I and II are also retained, but have been revised and substantially enlarged. They may have been preserved because they were action pieces and to reject them was to change the story fundamentally. At the same time the similarity of the two finales' texts leads us to wonder whether Piccinni retained some of his original music preferring to reconstruct it rather than write an absolutely new piece. There are times within the score when it is possible to see how he may have reconverted his old music inserting new and/or extra passages where necessary. Parts of the Act I finale to *I furbi* are printed on pp. 240–56, the original 1760 words or their replacements being in standard type, those that are additions being in *italics*. Should this music prove not to be a reconstruction after all, a study of it and of the two texts is still valuable as a means of examining certain trends in the comic ensemble at Naples, and Piccinni's personal development as an ensemble writer in particular, over the period 1760–73.

   To understand the dramatic situation during the first finale, it is necessary to know that a cunning servant girl, Aurora, and her brother, Tommasino, are trying to improve their circumstances by marrying Alessandro and Bettina respectively. To do this they have, among other things, to obtain the goodwill of Aurora's employer and Bettina's patron, D. Flaminio, described in the libretto as 'credulous and stupid'. Minicuccio, D. Flaminio's manservant and Bettina's old lover, is highly suspicious of the scheming

---

[32] *Fante di buon gusto*, words by A. Palomba.

[33] G. Tintori, *L'opera napolitana*, Milan, 1958, p. 201, believes Insanguine also had a hand in the composition of the work.

pair, and does all he can to thwart them. Alessandro loves Giustina, D. Flaminio's niece. Prior to the start of the finale, D. Flaminio and Minicuccio have caught Aurora and Tommasino plotting to give Alessandro a love token in the form of a letter and ring. On being questioned, Aurora turns the tables by insisting that Alessandro sent the tokens to her and asking D. Flaminio to hand him back the ring and letter unopened. Alessandro appears (bar 1) and is surprised to be told off by D. Flaminio for being forward with the ladies. After D. Flaminio, Aurora, and Tommasino have left, Alessandro opens and reads his 'returned' letter (bar 56) in front of Minicuccio. The latter at once realizes that the letter was a message for Alessandro after all and dashes out to inform his master of this new evidence. Giustina and Bettina now appear (bar 90). Giustina assumes that the letter is from some other lover of Alessandro, and in a fit of rage snatches the letter and flounces off, followed shortly after by Bettina. D. Flaminio, Minicuccio, Aurora, and her brother, return (bar 148) to examine the letter which, of course, Alessandro no longer holds, so nothing can be proved. Alessandro is miserable at the thought of having offended Giustina and leaves. Aurora exits. D. Flaminio, always ready to believe the pretty Aurora rather than Minicuccio, now rounds on his servant (bar 216) and gives him a verbal lashing, Tommasino in the meantime adding sweet and reasonable comments to further his own ends.

There are several differences between the general plan of this finale and that of 1760. One detail is that the original has but one person trying to worm her way into the confidence of D. Flaminio, not a brother and sister as here. The words of that character, Cannatella (who sings in Neapolitan), are now shared between Aurora and Tommasino (who are declared to hail from Frascati and sing in Tuscan). A more important point is that five out of the seven members of the cast of *La furba* appear in its first finale; the total cast of seven appears in the first finale of *I furbi*. The adapter of the text has not changed the story by adding the extra parts, those of Tommasino and Bettina. Bettina's entry is unnecessary, since all she does is look on while Giustina snatches the letter and add remarks to reinforce Giustina's. Her entry is clearly arranged because of the strengthening convention that as many characters as possible should appear on the stage during a finale. While this gave extra scope for characters with serious traits who previously had been denied entry into ensembles of this sort, their share of responsibility within these pieces tended to remain smaller than that of the others. The relatively minor parts for Giustina and

EXAMPLE 29
Piccinni, *I furbi Burlati*, ɪ, xiii
(Performed at the Teatro Fiorentini, Naples, 1773)

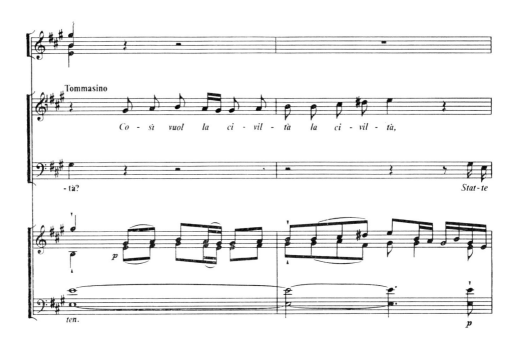

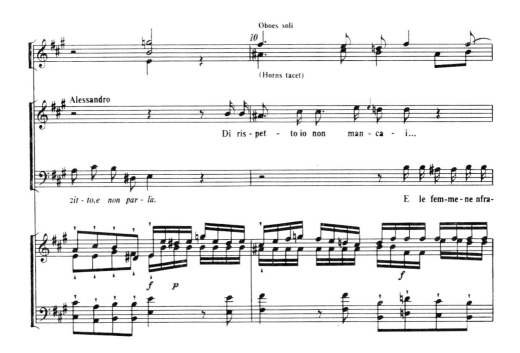

*In the libretto the words "Son tua" are consigned to Alessandro

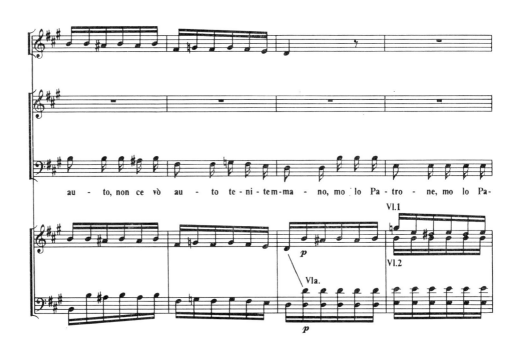

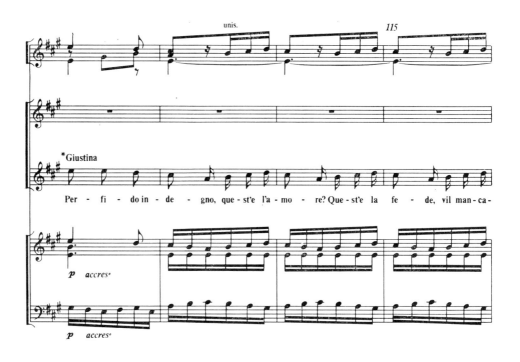

*"Qui Giust. si fà avanti e le strappa la lettera."

(D. Flaminio	My Master, I tell you, Sir, you are imagining things. Do you know whose house this is?
Alessandro	I know it's yours.
D. Flaminio	And if you know it, you know too you have to respect it?
Tommasino	*Civility requires it.*
D. Flaminio	*You keep quiet!*
Alessandro	I was not lacking in respect . . .
D. Flaminio	And why don't you meanwhile leave the ladies alone, Sir?
Tommasino	*An honourable man doesn't behave like this.*
D. Flaminio	*Shut up you, leave the talking to me!*
Alessandro	I never thought to do wrong . . .
D. Flaminio	Sir, you've done wrong enough. (I'm ready to lose my temper.)
Tommasino	(*Please don't get involved.*)
D. Flaminio	(*Observe in silence and don't meddle!*) Here is your ring . . .

Alessandro	'Dear Alessandro'.
Minicuccio	What, who's writing?
Alessandro	'Aurora Palo'.
Minicuccio	That's rich!
Alessandro	'I'm yours. You see the adour that enflames my heart by the jewel *I send you.*'
Minicuccio	That's enough for me. Hold it in your hand, I'm going to fetch my Master now. (exit)
	(Giustina and Bettina enter)
Giustina	(*That's my lover.*)
Bettina	(*How handsome he is! But he's reading; let's listen.*)
Giustina	(*You say well, let's stop here.*)
Alessandro	'Donn' Alessandro, my adored one.'
Giustina	(Oh dear, what do I hear!)
Bettina	(*You don't write, Madam!*)
Alessandro	'Have pity on my passion.'
	(At this point Giustina comes forward and snatches the letter)
Giustina	Vile, perfidious one! So this is your love, this is your troth, you wretch! Don't show yourself to me again! (exit carrying the letter)

Minicuccio	Believe your own eyes, not me.
Aurora Tommasino	} Oh dear, we're ruined . . .

D. Flaminio   Now I'm not going to chatter . . .
Minicuccio   Sir, listen to me . . .
Tommasino   *Please stop it . . .*
Minicuccio   What I've said . . .
D. Flaminio   March, vanish, scram . . .)

Bettina in the first finale to *I furbi* provide illustration. There is also the point that while the number of characters involved in large ensembles increased there was not necessarily more real ensemble singing. For most of the first finale to *I furbi* the vocal line is still a single one consisting of statements and ripostes, and only during the last section for D. Flaminio, Minicuccio, and Tommasino (beginning at bar 216) does the composer attempt to mix the voices in a humorous fashion.

The fact that this last section is for three voices only has ramifications of its own. At the end of the corresponding passage of the 1760 version only two characters are on stage. By the '70s, though, the more normal procedure was to bring on the maximum number of characters for the ending. The act finales of *La buona figliola* had already shown the modern technique of a build-up of characters for the last bars when they sing as a group, or in two opposing groups, in four or more real parts. The ensemble furthermore is a true S.A.T.B. one, since comic opera always had its complement of one or more bass soloists which heroic opera did not have. Should anyone examine the texts of *La furba* and *I furbi* and turn to the second finales, he will find that the earlier one includes parts for four characters of whom three are singing towards the close while the later (a sextet for all bar Giustina) ends with a mix-up for the full complement.

The first thing that perhaps strikes the observer about Example 29 is the comparative busyness of the orchestra and of the strings especially. No one could accuse Piccinni of spreading his orchestral forces thinly[34]— though the size of the Fiorentini orchestra was probably not large. The fussier notes and thicker harmonies, when compared with Pergolesi's or Logroscino's work, mean that more of the musical substance passes into the orchestra generally. Much of the vocal writing, especially the comic, patter phrases, is now incorporated into the harmony of the music and no longer into its melody. There is a relatively new technique of letting instruments play the tune while the voices enter at irregular and some-

---

[34] Burney, *The present state*, p. 306, declared that Piccinni's copyists demanded extra wages because of the excessive number of instrumental notes in his scores.

times distant intervals during the course of it—see the section beginning bar 56. Perhaps here is an embryonic *parlante* technique—developed slightly in the last decades of the eighteenth century and more fully in the nineteenth—which uses the orchestra as the main bearer of the music while the characters add random comments in a kind of monotone. The tune from bar 56 onwards is extremely insipid, being no better or worse than most melodic work in Piccinni's finales. It could be that here melody *per se* was of secondary importance, since his primary object was to keep the music in motion. No jerky or dotted rhythms appear in this Example— again a factor aiding the musical flow.

What contributes to the impression that the sections with the old words (in standard type) are reconstructed from an older composition is the constantly fluctuating tonality of those sections. Generally speaking, the later and the bigger the ensemble, the longer the passages keep to one key without any sign of modulating to another. The sections in Example 29 with new words do tend to be non-modulatory. We also note that some of the 'new' phrases are stylistically distinctive from the surrounding music—this is especially true during the first fifty bars or so. The over-all result is again symptomatic of general trends, the finales of late comic operas acquiring greater variety of style and texture within each main section of the chain as well as between the sections themselves. Whether the moments of change of speed and time signature are the same as in the 1760 version remains conjectural, as is a lot else to do with that earlier version. The three important time changes in the score of 1773 occur when (1) Alessandro turns to read his letter, (2) Minicuccio leads D. Flaminio, Aurora, and Tommasino back to examine this letter, and (3) D. Flaminio turns on his servant after the letter has disappeared. Each change in the music reinforces the point that the dramatic situation has altered funda- mentally. An analysis of these moments of change suggests that they occur because, as in (1), new material evidence is provided which requires the attention of all characters present—hence the attention-catching trick of a new time-speed, or, as in (2), a new group of characters enters bent on a different course of action to the preceding, or, as in (3), certain feelings built up during a section break out and become uncontrollable. New evidence, new characters, a new outburst of emotion—here are three common motivations for changes of style and time signature within late eighteenth-century finales. It is worth noting that in Example 29, as in most other large comic ensembles, the final section has a fast tempo, which provides a most satisfying culmination to the music as music, but may well disguise the lack of resolution in the dramatic situation at that moment.

Get hold of a formula that seems to work each time, and one's natural inclination is to exploit and expand it. The success of the finale was as responsible as any factor for the gradual increase in the number of other ensembles observable within comic opera of the 1770s and early '80s. Previously the large majority of lyrical items per work had been solos: arias, canzonettas, and cavatinas. The finale itself expanded, spreading backwards from the end of the act to engulf more words and scenes. Whereas some 200 to 300 bars had been considered an adequate length for a finale in the 1760s, 400 to 800 bars were more of the order of things by the mid-'80s. This did not necessarily result in more and more sections in different styles. Ten or eleven seem to have been the maximum, and usually there were fewer. What happened though was that the music embraced certain additional styles within the conventional number of sections. Even accompanied recitative appeared in certain finales, notably Paisiello's.[35] Techniques enabling the composer to write at greater and greater length included: a slowing down of the average rate of harmonic movement, the use of longer and longer pedals, more crescendos over static chords, and constant repetition of common chord progressions without necessary recourse to modulation. Melodies were distended (something was said on this on p. 175 above), and short accompanimental motives were used to fill up large tracts of score like a decorative, wallpaper pattern. Finally, a large slice of music could be, and in certain late instances was, repeated *en bloc*—which meant the words were reused as well. The repeat was useful especially in the last section, whenever the music was required to last a certain psychological time-span longer than the time required to enact the words. Other points might be mentioned to the music's credit. The imaginative use of wind instruments by composers like Paisiello and Cimarosa did much to add variety to the sound colour. In particular, these instruments were required to provide short motives alternating with and overlapping other motives for the strings—so the two instrumental groups were interlinked yet offset—as well as provide the more old-fashioned solos and the harmonic filling-in common to Piccinni's scoring. The texture of the music was gradually made to sound lighter, even though the number of types of instrument employed in the orchestra might be higher than

[35] The earliest finale with accompanied recitative that the present author has seen is in Act II of Paisiello's *L'osteria di Marechiaro* (1768). This does not of course preclude earlier instances.

before, because of a more imaginative mixture of legato and staccato and because of the use of accompanimental rhythms for the strings that avoided the main beat, for example ♩ or ♩, both reminiscent of all too common accompaniments in nineteenth-century arias. The debit side was expressed by Napoli-Signorelli in volume five of his *Vicende* published in 1786. Looking back at the progress of the finale since the time of *La furba burlata*, he shrugged the subject off with the remark: 'We need but add that comic finales must be long, and that since then they have become very long and very tedious'.[36] This is the earliest adverse criticism of the finale so far discovered in a Neapolitan source. The trouble with this musical item was not that it possessed no moments of exhilaration or humour, but that it appeared as a matter of course in every comic opera in the city. It was simply another example of how the creators of opera at Naples were swayed, even ruled, by the prevailing fashion. The regular visitor to the Neapolitan comic theatre might therefore be forgiven if after witnessing a score of finales he presumed he would find little remarkable in the next one.

[36] v. 568.

Manuscript sources of the musical examples

Bibliography

This list comprises the chief printed sources consulted. Librettos and music scores are omitted.

1. NAPLES AND NEAPOLITAN MUSIC: SEVENTEENTH- AND EIGHTEENTH-CENTURY SOURCES

ADDISON, J., *Remarks on several parts of Italy, &c, in the years 1701, 1702, 1703*, London, 1705.

ALLACCI, L., *Drammaturgia di Lione Allacci accresciuta e continuata fino all'anno mdcclv*, Venice, 1755.

ARCHENHOLTZ, J. W. VON, *England und Italien*, 5 vols., Leipzig, 1787.

ARTEAGA, S., *Delle rivoluzioni del teatro musicale italiano*, 1st edn., 3 vols., Bologna, 1783–5; 2nd edn., 2 vols., Venice, 1785.

BARETTI, J., *An account of the manners and customs of Italy, with observations on the mistakes of some travellers with regard to that country*, 2nd edn., London, 1769.

BURNEY, C., *The present state of music in France and Italy*, London, 1771.

—— *A general history of music*, 4 vols., London, 1776–89.

CELANO, C., *Notitie del bello, dell'antico, e del curioso della città di Napoli*, 10 vols., Naples, 1692.

CONFUORTO, D., *Giornali di Napoli dal mdclxxix al mdcic*, Naples, *CSIM*, 1930, i–ii.

CONTANT D'ORVILLE, A. G., *Histoire de l'opéra bouffon*, Amsterdam, 1768.

COYER, G. F., *Voyages d'Italie et de Hollande*, 2 vols., Paris, 1775.

DE BROSSES, C., *Lettres familières écrites d'Italie en 1739 et 1740*. 2nd edn., 2 vols., Paris, 1858.

DE LABORDE, J. B., *Essai sur la musique ancienne et moderne*, 4 vols., Paris, 1780.

DE LALANDE, J., *Voyage d'un françois en Italie, fait dans les années 1765 & 1766*. 8 vols., Venice, 1769.

D'ENGENIO, C., *Napoli sacra*, Naples, 1624.

DE SAINT-NON, J-C. R., *Voyage pittoresque ou description des royaumes de Naples et de Sicile*. 5 vols., Paris, 1781–6.

DE VILLENEUVE, J., *Lettre sur le méchanisme de l'opéra italien*, Naples, 1756.

DU BOCCAGE, A-M., *Recueil des oeuvres de Madame Du Boccage*, 3 vols., Lyon, 1770.

FUIDORO, I., *Successi del governo del Conte d'Onatte*, Naples, *CSIM*, 1932, iii.

—— *Giornali di Napoli dal mdclx al mdclxxx*, Naples, *CSIM*, 1934–9, v–vii.

GALIANI, F., *Correspondance inédite de l'Abbé Ferdinand Galiani*, 2 vols., (Treuttel et Würtz,) Paris, 1818.

GOUDAR, S., *Relation historique des divertissements du carnaval de Naples*, Lucca, 1774.

GRÉTRY, M., *Mémoires ou essai sur la musique*, Paris, 1789.

GRIMM, F. M., *et al.*, *Correspondance littéraire, philosophique et critique*, 16 vols., ed. Tourneux, Paris, 1877–82.

GROSLEY, P. J., *New observations on Italy*, English edn., 2 vols., London, 1769.

HAWKINS, J., *A general history of the science and practice of music*, 4 vols., London, 1776.

MARPURG, F. W., *Historisch-kritische Beyträge zur Aufnahme der Musik*, 5 vols., Berlin, 1754–78.

MATTEI, S., *Elogio del Jomelli, o sia il progresso della poesia e musica teatrale*, Colle, 1785.

MATTHESON, J., *Das neu-eröffnete Orchestre*. Hamburg, 1713.

—— *Der vollkommene Capellmeister*. Facs. edn., *DM*, I. v, Kassel, 1954.

MEYER, F. J. L., *Darstellungen aus Italien*, Berlin, 1792.

MILIZIA, F., *Del teatro*, Venice, 1774.

NAPOLI-SIGNORELLI, P., *Storia critica de'teatri antichi e moderni*, 1st edn., Naples, 1777; 2nd edn., 6 vols., Naples, 1787–90.

—— *Vicende della coltura nelle due Sicilie*. 5 vols., Naples, 1784–6.

Neapolitan journals, *La Gazzetta di Napoli* (1675, 1677–8, 1681, 1685–8, 1692–1700, 1702–5, 1708–17, 1719–25, 1734–40, 1746, 1753–4, 1759–60).

PARRINO, D. A., *Teatro eroico, e politico de'governi de'vicerè del regno di Napoli dal tempo del re Ferdinando il cattolico fino al presente*, 3 vols., Naples, 1692–4.

—— *Napoli città nobilissima, antica, e fedelissima*, 2 vols., Naples, 1700.

PÖLLNITZ, K. N., *Lettres et mémoires du Baron du Pöllnitz, contenant les observations qu'il a faites dans ses voyages*, 3rd edn., 5 vols., Amsterdam, 1744.

QUADRIO, F. S., *Della storia, e della ragione d'ogni poesia*, 7 vols., Bologna-Milan, 1739–52.

RAGUENET, F., *A comparison between the French and Italian music*, Modernized version of the 1709 English edn., *MQ*, 1946, xxxii.

ROUSSEAU, J-J., *Dictionnaire de musique*, Paris, 1768.

SALA, N., *Regole del contrappunto pratico*, Naples, 1794.

SHARP, S., *Letters from Italy, describing the customs and manners of that country*, London, 1766.

SIGISMONDO, G., *Descrizione della città di Napoli e suoi borghi*, 3 vols., Naples, 1788–9.

2. OTHER RELEVANT SOURCES OF THE SEVENTEENTH AND EIGHTEENTH CENTURIES.

ALGAROTTI, F., *An essay on the opera*, English edn., Glasgow, 1768.

BACH, C. P. E., *Essay on the true art of playing keyboard instruments*, Modern English edn., trans. Mitchell, New York, 1949.

BIANCHI, G. A., *Dei vizi e dei difetti del moderno teatro*, Rome, 1753.

BONLINI, G. C., *Le glorie della poesia, e della musica contenute nell'esatta notitia de'teatri della città di Venezia*, Venice, 1730.

BROWN, J., *Letters upon the poetry and music of the Italian opera*, Edinburgh, 1789.

BURNEY, C., *The present state of music in Germany, the Netherlands and United Provinces*, 2 vols., London, 1773.

—— *Memoirs of the life and writings of the Abate Metastasio*, 3 vols., London, 1796.

CRESCIMBENI, G. M., *La bellezza della volgar poesia, spiegata in otto dialoghi . . . con varie notizie, e col catalogo degli Arcadi*, Rome, 1700.

DA CALZABIGI, R., 'Dissertazione su le poesie drammatiche del Signor Abate Pietro
   Metastasio'. *Poesie del Signor Abate Pietro Metastasio*, Paris, 1755, i.

EXIMENO, A., *Dell'origine e delle regole della musica colla storia del suo progresso,
   decadenza, e rinnovazione*, Rome, 1774.

GALIANI, F., *Del dialetto napoletano*, Modern edn. ed. Nicolini, Naples, 1923.

GASPARINI, F., *L'armonico pratico al cimbalo*, 3rd impression, Venice, 1729.

GEMINIANI, F., *The art of playing the violin*, Modern edn., ed. Boyden, London,
   1952.

GOLDONI, C., *Commedie*. 16 vols. in 8, containing autobiographical notes, Venice,
   Pasquali, 1761.

—— *Mémoires*, 3 vols., Paris, 1787.

GOUDAR, S., *De Venise rémarques sur la musique et la danse ou lettres de Mr. G à Milord
   Pembroke*, Venice, 1773.

HEINSE, W., *Musikalische Dialogen, oder Philosophische Unterredungen berühmter
   Gelehrten, Dichter und Tonkünstler über der Kunstgeschmack in der Musik*,
   Altenburg, 1805.

HILLER, J. A., *Anweisung zum musikalisch-richtigen Gesange*, Leipzig, 1774.

KRAUSE, C. G., *Von der musikalischen Poesie*, Berlin, 1752.

LAMBRANZI, G., *Neue und curieuse theatralische Tantz-Schul*, 2 parts, Nürnberg, 1716.

MAFFEI, F. S., *De'teatri antichi e moderni*, 2nd edn., Verona, 1754.

MARCELLO, B., *Il teatro alla moda*, Modern edn,. ed. d'Angeli, Milan, 1956.

MARPURG, F. W., *Kritische Briefe über die Tonkunst*, 2 vols., Berlin, 1759–63.

—— *Anleitung zur Musik überhaupt und zur Singkunst besonders*, Berlin, 1763.

MATTEI, S., 'La filosofia della musica o sia la riforma del teatro', *Opere del Signor
   Abate Pietro Metastasio*, Naples, de Bonis, 1781, iii.

MATTHESON, J., *Die neueste Untersuchung der Singspiele*, Hamburg, 1744.

METASTASIO, P., *Lettere del Signor Abate Pietro Metastasio*, 5 vols., Nice, presso la
   società tipografica, 1786–7.

—— *Lettere ed opere postume del Signor Abate Pietro Metastasio*, ed. d'Ayala, 3 vols.,
   Venice, 1808.

MOZART, W. A., *The letters of Mozart and his family*, ed. Anderson, 3 vols., London,
   1938.

MURATORI, L. A., *Della perfetta poesia italiana spiegata e dimostrata con varie osservazioni*,
   2 vols., Modena, 1706.

NOVERRE, J. G., *Lettres sur la danse, et sur les ballets*, Lyon, 1760.

ORTES, G. A., *Riflessioni sopra i drammi per musica*, Venice, 1757.

PERRUCCI, A., *Dell'arte rappresentativa premeditata ed all'improvviso*, Modern edn., ed.
   Bragaglia, Florence, 1961.

PLANELLI, A., *Dell'opera in musica*, Naples, 1772.

QUANTZ, J. J., *On playing the flute*, Modern English edn., trans. Reilly, London,
   1966.

ST. EVREMOND, *Oeuvres meslées*, London, 1705.

SALVADORI, G. G., *Poetica toscana all'uso dove con brevità, e chiarezza s'insegna il modo
   di comporre ogni poesia*, Naples, 1691.

SULZER, J. G., *Allgemeine Theorie der schönen Künste*, 2 parts, Leipzig, 1771–4.

TARTINI, G., *Traité des agréments de la musique*, Modern edn., ed. Jacobi, Celle, 1961.

TOSI, P. F., *Observations on the florid song*. English edn., ed. Galliard, London, 1743; German edn., ed. J. F. Agricola, with the title *Anleitung zur Singkunst*, Berlin, 1757.

WALTHER, J. G., *Musikalisches Lexicon*, Facs. edn., *DM*, I, iii. Kassell, 1953.

ZENO, A., *Lettere di Apostolo Zeno*. 2nd edn., 6 vols., Venice, Sansoni, 1785.

3. NINETEENTH-CENTURY SOURCES

CELANO, C., and CHIARINI, G. B., *Notizie del bello, dell'antico e del curioso della città di Napoli . . . con aggiunzioni de' più notabili miglioramenti posteriori fino al presente per cura di Cav. Giovanni Battista Chiarini*. 5 vols., Naples, 1856–60.

CROCE, B., 'I teatri di Napoli', *Archivio storico per le province napoletane*, Naples, 1889–91, xiv–xvi; in shortened book form, Bari, 1947.

D'ARIENZO, N., 'Origini dell'opera comica', *RMI*, 1895, 1897, 1899–1900, ii. iv. vi–vii.

DE ROSA, C. A. (MARCHESE DI VILLAROSA), *Memorie dei compositori di musica del regno di Napoli*, Naples, 1840.

DE SANCTIS, F., *History of Italian literature*. English edn., trans. Redfern, 2 vols., London. 1931.

FLORIMO, F., *La scuola musicale di Napoli e i suoi conservatori*, 4 vols., Naples, 1880–2.

GAGLIARDO, G. B., *et al.*, *Onori funebri renduti alla memoria di Giovanni Paisiello*, Naples, 1816.

GALVANI, L. N. (SAVIOLI, G.), *I teatri musicali di Venezia nel secolo xvii*, Milan, 1878.

GERBER, E. L., *Neues historisch-biographisches Lexicon der Tonkünstler*, Modern edn., 2 vols., Graz, 1966.

JAHN, O., *Life of Mozart*, English edn., trans. Townsend, 3 vols., London, 1891.

KELLY, M., *Reminiscences of Michael Kelly of the King's Theatre, and Theatre Royal, Drury Lane*, 2 vols., London, 1826.

KOCH, H. C., *Musikalisches Lexicon*, Offenbach-am-Main, 1802.

VON KOTZEBUE, A., *Travels through Italy in the years 1804 and 1805*, English edn., 4 vols., London, 1806.

KRETZSCHMAR, H., 'Die venetianische Oper und die Werke Cavallis und Cestis', *VM*, 1892, viii.

LORENZI, G. B., *Opere teatrali*, 4 vols., containing prefaces with biographical information, Naples, Flautina, 1806–20.

MARTUSCELLI, D., (ed.) *Biografia degli uomini illustri del regno di Napoli*, 10 vols., Naples, 1813–25.

MOLINARO DEL CHIARO, L., *Canti del popolo napoletano*, Naples, 1880.

MOUNT EDGECUMBE, EARL OF, *Musical reminiscences of an old amateur chiefly respecting the Italian opera in England for fifty years from 1773 to 1823*. 2nd edn., London, 1827.

NAPOLI-SIGNORELLI, P., *Elementi di poesia drammatica*, Milan, 1801.

ORLOFF, G., *Essai sur l'histoire de la musique en Italie*, 2 vols., Paris, 1822.

PEROTTI, G. A., *Dissertation sur l'état actuel de la musique en Italie*, French edn., Genoa, 1812.

ROLLAND, R., *Histoire de l'opéra en Europe avant Lulli et Scarlatti*, New edn., Paris, 1931.

SCHERILLO, M., 'I canti popolari nell'opera buffa.' *Giambattista Basile*, first 3 issues, Naples, 1883.

—— *L'opera buffa napoletana durante il settecento. Storia letteraria*, 2nd (enlarged) edn., Naples, 1916.

SCHLETTERER, H. M., 'Die Opernhäuser Neapels', *MM*, 1882–3, xiv–xv.

SPOHR, L., *Autobiography*. English edn., London, 1865.

TADDEI, E., *Del real teatro di S. Carlo*, Naples, 1817.

WIEL, T., *I teatri musicali veneziani del settecento*, Venice, 1897.

4. NAPLES AND NEAPOLITAN MUSIC: TWENTIETH-CENTURY SOURCES

ABERT, H., *Niccolo Jommelli als Opernkomponist*, Halle, 1908.

—— *Gesammelte Schriften und Vorträge*, ed. Blume, Halle, 1929.

—— *W. A. Mozart*. 7th edn., 2 vols., Leipzig, 1955.

ACTON, H., *The Bourbons of Naples*, 2nd edn., London, 1957.

ADLER, G., (ed). *Handbuch der Musikgeschichte*, Reprint, 2 vols., Tutzing, 1961.

BATTISTI, E., 'Per una indagine sociologica sui librettisti napoletani buffi del settecento', *Letteratura*, Rome, viii (1960), nos. 46–8.

BORREN, C. VAN DEN, *Alessandro Scarlatti et l'esthétique de l'opéra napolitain*, Paris, 1921.

BÜCKEN, E., *Die Musik des Rokokos und der Klassik*, Potsdam, 1931.

BUKOFZER, M., *Music in the baroque era*, New York, 1947.

CANTRELL, B., *Tommaso Traetta and his opera Sofonisba*, Dissertation, University of California, Los Angeles, 1957.

CARAVAGLIOS, C., *Il folklore musicale in Italia*, Naples, 1936.

DELLA CORTE, A., *Paisiello*, Turin, 1922.

—— *L'opera comica italiana nel'700*, Bari, 1923.

—— *Piccinni*, Bari, 1928.

—— *Gluck e i suoi tempi*, Florence, 1948.

DE MURA, E., *Enciclopedia della canzone napoletana*, 3 vols., Naples, 1970.

DENT, E. J., 'Leonardo Leo', *SIM*, 1906–7, viii.

—— 'Ensembles and finales in 18th century Italian opera', *SIM*, 1909–11, xi–xii.

—— *Alessandro Scarlatti: his life and works*, New impression, ed. Walker, London, 1960.

DI GIACOMO, S., *Maestri di cappella, musici e istromenti al tesoro di San Gennaro nei secoli xvii & xviii*, Naples, 1920.

—— *I quattro antichi conservatorii musicali di Napoli*, 2 vols., Palermo, 1924–8.

18*

DOWNES, E. O. D., 'The Neapolitan tradition in opera.' *IMS*, 8th congress, New York-Kassel, 1961, i.

—— *The operas of Johann Christian Bach as a reflection of the dominant trends in opera seria 1750–80.* Dissertation, Harvard University, 1958.

GERBER, R., *Der Operntypus Johann Adolf Hasses und seine textlichen Grundlagen*, Leipzig, 1925.

GOLDSCHMIDT, H., 'Traettas Leben', *Denkmäler der Tonkunst in Bayern*, 1913, xiv. (1).

GROUT, D. J., *A short history of opera*, 2nd revised edn., New York, 1965.

HAAS, R., *Die Musik des Barocks*, Potsdam, 1929.

HANSELL, S. H., 'The cadence in eighteenth-century recitative', *MQ*, 1968, liv.

HUCKE, H., 'La Didone abbandonata di Domenico Sarri nella stesura del 1724 e nella revisione del 1730.' *GMN*, 1956, ii.

—— 'Die neapolitanische Tradition in der Oper,' *IMS*, eighth congress, New York-Kassel, 1961, i.

—— 'Verfassung und Entwicklung der alten neapolitanischen Konservatorien', *Festschrift Helmuth Osthoff zum 65 Gebürtstage*, Tutzing, 1961.

KRETZSCHMAR, H., 'Zwei Opern Nicolo Logroscinos', *JMP*, 1908, xv.

—— H., *Geschichte der Oper*, Leipzig, 1919.

LAZZERI, G., *La vita e l'opera letteraria di Ranieri Calzabigi*, Città di Castello, 1907.

LOEWENBERG, A., *Annals of opera, 1597–1940*, 2nd revised edn., 2 vols., Geneva, 1955.

LORENZ, A., *Alessandro Scarlattis Jugendopern*, 2 vols., Augsburg, 1927.

MANCINI, F., *Scenografia napoletana dell'età barocca*, Naples, 1965.

MONACO, V., *Giambattista Lorenzi e la commedia per musica*, Naples, 1968.

MONDOLFI BOSSARELLI, A., 'Vita e stile di Francesco Provenzale. La questione dell' "Alessandro Bala".' *Annuario del Conservatorio di Musica S. Pietro a Maiella*, 1962–3, x.

—— 'Ancora intorno al codice napoletano della "Incoronazione di Poppea"', *RIM*, 1967, ii.

MONTI, G. M., *Le villanelle alla napoletana e l'antica lirica dialettale a Napoli*, Città di Castello, 1925.

PANNAIN, G., *Le origini della scuola musicale napoletana*, Naples, 1914.

PASTORE, G. A., *Leonardo Leo*, Gelatina, 1957.

PROTA-GIURLEO, U., *Alessandro Scarlatti 'il Palermitano'*, Naples, 1926.

—— *Nicola Logroscino 'il dio dell'opera buffa'*, Naples, 1927.

—— *La grande orchestra del R. Teatro San Carlo nel settecento*, Naples, 1927.

—— *Breve storia del teatro di corte e della musica a Napoli nei secoli xvii–xviii*, Naples, 1952.

—— 'La biografia di Nicola Piccinni alla luce di nuovi documenti', *Il Fuidoro*, 1954, i.

—— 'Giuseppe Porsile e la cappella di Barcellona', *GMN*, 1956, ii.

—— 'Francesco Provenzale', *Archivi d'Italia e rassegna internazionale degli archivi*, 1958, xxv.

—— *I teatri di Napoli nel'600, la commedia e le maschere*, Naples, 1962.

RADICIOTTI, G., *Giovanni Battista Pergolesi. Leben und Werk*, Enlarged German edn., ed. Cherbuliez, Zürich, 1954.

ROBERTI, G., 'La musica italiana nel secolo xviii secondo le impressioni di viaggiatori stranieri', *RMI*, 1900–1, vii–viii.

ROBINSON, M. F., 'The governors' minutes of the Conservatory S. Maria di Loreto, Naples', *RCRMA*, 1972, x.

SARTORI, C., 'Gli Scarlatti a Napoli', *RMI*, 1942, xlvi.

SOMERSET, H. V. F., 'Giovanni Paisiello, 1740–1816', *M & L*, 1937, xviii.

SONNECK, O. G., *Catalogue of opera librettos printed before 1800*, 2 vols., Library of Congress, 1914.

STALNAKER, W. P., *The beginnings of opera in Naples*, Dissertation, Princeton University, 1968.

TIBALDI-CHIESA, M., *Cimarosa e il suo tempo*, Milan, 1939.

TINTORI, G., *L'opera napoletana*, Milan, 1958.

VITALE, R., *Domenico Cimarosa*, Aversa, 1929.

VIVIANI, V., *Storia del teatro napoletano*, Naples, 1969.

WALKER, F., 'A chronology of the life and works of N. Porpora.' *Italian studies*, 1951, vi.

5. OTHER RELEVANT TWENTIETH-CENTURY SOURCES

ARNOLD, D., 'Orphans and ladies: the Venetian Conservatories (1680–1790)', *RMA*, 1962–3, lxxxix.

BARONI, J. M., 'La lirica musicale di Pietro Metastasio', *RMI*, 1905, xii.

BEZARD, Y., 'Le Président de Brosses et la Musique d'après une correspondance inédite', *Revue musicale*, 1922, iii.

BURT, N., 'Opera in Arcadia', *MQ*, 1955, xli.

CARSE, A., *The orchestra in the eighteeth century*, 2nd edn., Cambridge, 1950.

COLE, M. S., 'The vogue of the instrumental rondo in the late eighteenth century', *JAMS*, 1969, xxii.

DEAN, W., *Handel's dramatic oratorios and masques*, London, 1959.

DE DOMINICIS, G., *I teatri di Roma nell'età di Pio VI*, Rome, 1922.

DENT, E. J., 'A Jesuit at the opera in 1680', *Riemann-Festschrift, Gesammelte Schriften*, reprint, Tutzing, 1965.

DONINGTON, R., *The interpretation of early music*, London, 1963.

DOWNES, E. O. D., 'Secco recitative in early classical opera seria', *JAMS*, 1961, xiv.

FEDERHOFER, H., 'Vincenzo Righinis Oper Alcide al bivio', *Essays presented to Egon Wellesz*, Oxford, 1966.

FEHR, M., *Apostolo Zeno und seine Reform des Operntextes*, Zürich, 1912.

FREEMAN, R., 'Apostolo Zeno's reform of the libretto', *JAMS*, 1968, xxi.

GIAZOTTO, R., *Poesia melodrammatica e pensiero critico nel settecento*, Milan, 1952.

GOLDSCHMIDT, H., *Studien zur Geschichte der italienischen Oper im 17. Jahrhundert*, Leipzig, 1901.

—— *Die Musikästhetik des 18. Jahrhunderts und ihre Beziehung zu seinem Kunstschaffen*, Zürich, 1915.

HERIOT, A., *The castrati in opera*, London, 1956.

HESS, H., *Die Opern Alessandro Stradellas*, Leipzig, 1906.

KRETZSCHMAR, H., 'Allgemeines und Besonderes zur Affektenlehre', *JMP*, 1911, xviii.

LOEWENBERG, A., 'Gluck's *Orfeo* on the stage', *MQ*, 1940, xxvi.

NEWMAN, W. S., *The sonata in the baroque era*, Chapel Hill, 1959.

—— *The sonata in the classic era*, Chapel Hill, 1963.

OLIVER, A. R., *The Encyclopaedists as critics of music*, New York, 1949.

PIROTTA, N., 'Commedia dell'arte and opera', *MQ*, 1955, xli.

PREUSSNER, E., *Die musikalischen Reisen des Herrn von Uffenbach*, Kassel, 1949.

RATNER, L., 'Harmonic aspects of classic form', *JAMS*, 1949, ii.

ROBBINS LANDON, H. C., *The symphonies of Joseph Haydn*, London, 1955.

ROLANDI, U., *Il libretto per musica*, Rome, 1951.

RUSSO, L., *Metastasio*, 3rd edn., Bari, 1945.

SCHMITZ, H. P., *Die Kunst der Verzierung im 18. Jahrhundert*, Kassel, 1955.

STRUNK, O., *Source readings in music history*, New York, 1950.

TOWNELEY WORSTHORNE, S., *Venetian opera in the seventeenth century*, Oxford, 1954.

TUTENBERG, F., 'Die opera buffa-Sinfonie und ihre Beziehung zur klassischen Sinfonie', *AM*, 1926, viii.

WELLESZ, E., 'Giuseppe Bonno (1710–88). Sein Leben und seine dramatischen Werke', *SIM*, 1909–10, xi.

—— 'Die Opern und Oratorien in Wien von 1660–1708', *SM*, 1919, vi.

WESTRUP, J. A., 'The nature of recitative', *Henriette Hertz Trust lecture to the British Academy*, 1956.

WOLFF, H. C., *Die venezianische Oper in der zweiten Hälfte des 17. Jahrhunderts*, Berlin, 1937.

YORKE-LONG, A., *Music at court*, London, 1954.

Index

Abert, Anna Amalie, 67n71

Abert, Hermann, 82n24, 122, 147, 176n31, 190n29, 225n16, 235, 237n27

Abos, Girolamo, 17

Abreu, Giovanni, 3

Abridged sonata form, see: Sonata form

Académie royale de musique, Paris, 29

Accent, word, 106

Acciaccatura, 112

Act, shortened length of, 70

Act, third, 54–5; short, 67, 70–1, 200–2, 204; absence of, 71, 200, 202, 204; weak third act in comic opera, 198–9; end of third act in *Didone*, 79–82

Acting, stage, 60–2; comic, 42; in comic opera, 12

Actresses, at S. Bartolomeo theatre, 5

Adler, Guido, 85n29, 127n80

Afeltro, Michele, 19

Affections, 57, 87–8, 112, 122, 128

Agricola, Johann Friedrich, 73n7, 74n8, 104

Air, 64, 83, 157

Alessandri, Genaro, 28

Algarotti, Francesco, 33, 58, 65, 82n22, 128, 165–6, 177, 225

Allegorical figures, 180

Amenta, Nicolò, 189; *La Carlotta*, 210

Andreozzi, Gaetano, 18, 32, 165n16

Anfossi, Pasquale, 18

Appoggiatura, 108, 111–2, 126, 135

Aquilanti, Francesco, 189

Arabian Nights, 196

Arcadian Society, 42

Archbishop of Naples, 13

Argentina theatre, Rome, 8

Arlecchino, 191

Aria, 39, 41, 68–70, 72, 77–9, 83, 87ff, 102, 127, 151, 195, 203, 238; cadences in, 105–6, 108, 121, 126; cadenzas in, 104–5; categories of, 88–9, 135; criticisms of, 57–8, 128; *da capo* form of, 100–4, 143, 147, 149–51, 158, 228; distribution of, 52–5, 70, 203–4; embellishments in, 111–2, 122; embellishments in comic arias, 226; exit arias, 50–2, 55, 70, 195;

function of, 49–50, 55–9, 89, 158, 209; instrumentation of, 96–100, 109–10, 126; in intermezzos, 180, 182, 184–6; long texts of comic arias, 181–2, 206; musical styles of, 77, 82–3, 89–91, 95–6, 107ff, 120–2, 126–7, 132, 134–5, 143, 147; musical styles in comic arias, 205, 225–6; numbers of, 50, 52–4, 157, 204; parallels with instrumental music, 109–10, 113, 115, 120–1; poetic content of, 59–60, 182, 184–5; performance by singers of, 61–5

Aria cavata, 149

Aria del sorbetto, 203

Aria-finale, 235–6

Aria naturale, 149

Arietta, 52–4, 56, 58, 102, 150

Arioso, 76–7, 79–80, 82, 150

Aristotelean unities, 39

Arnold, Denis, 28n96

Arpeggio, 99, 110

Arteaga, Esteban de, 33, 42, 59–60, 71, 82n22, 112, 114n77, 128, 147

Astaritta, Gennaro, 128; *Tra i due litiganti il terzo gode*, 203

Astorga, Count, 4

Audiences, 86, 102, 104, 113, 168, 188n21; at the Fiorentini theatre, 11–2; at the S. Bartolomeo theatre, 11, 127; at the S. Carlo theatre, 9–10, 127, 149; like of ballets, 64–5, 165; like of duets, 64, 158; inattentiveness of, 10, 12, 64–5, 175; many attendances, 9, 102

Auditor of the Army, 10

Augustus II, Elector of Saxony, 7

Auletta, Pietro, 17, 228; *La locandiera*, 186, 208, 210–2Ex24

Austrians, 25, 189; see also: Court, Naples, Viceroy

Bach, Carl Philipp Emanuel, 75, 87, 121

Bach, Johann Christian, 67, 178

Ballet, 161, 186; audience love of, 64–5, 165; Charles III's love of, 162, 185; court ban at comic theatres, 163, 202; composers' attitude